Transgender Rights vs Women's Rights

Transgender Rights vs Women's Rights

From Conflicts to Co-existence

ROBERT WINTEMUTE

polity

Copyright © Robert Wintemute, 2025

The Author hereby asserts his moral right to be identified as author of the Work.

First published by Polity Press in 2025

Polity Press
65 Bridge Street
Cambridge CB2 1UR, UK

Polity Press
111 River Street
Hoboken, NJ 07030, USA

All rights reserved. Except for the quotation of short passages for the purpose of criticism and review, no part of this publication may be reproduced, stored in a retrieval system or transmitted, in any form or by any means, electronic, mechanical, photocopying, recording or otherwise, without the prior permission of the publisher.

ISBN-13: 978-1-5095-6075-2 – hardback
ISBN-13: 978-1-5095-6076-9 – paperback

A catalogue record for this book is available from the British Library.

Library of Congress Control Number: 2024948721

Typeset in 11 on 14 pt Warnock Pro
by Cheshire Typesetting Ltd, Cuddington, Cheshire
Printed and bound in Great Britain by CPI Group (UK) Ltd, Croydon

The publisher has used its best endeavours to ensure that the URLs for external websites referred to in this book are correct and active at the time of going to press. However, the publisher has no responsibility for the websites and can make no guarantee that a site will remain live or that the content is or will remain appropriate.

Every effort has been made to trace all copyright holders, but if any have been overlooked the publisher will be pleased to include any necessary credits in any subsequent reprint or edition.

For further information on Polity, visit our website:
politybooks.com

To my wonderful husband,
whom I would not have met,
had I been afraid to enter this debate

Contents

Acknowledgements	viii

1 How did we get here? From sympathy for transsexuals (1972) to a call to remove sex from birth certificates (2017)   1

2 Transgender rights vs women's rights: why the human rights of two groups often conflict   25

3 Transphobia: what is it, and what is instead protected political expression?   37

4 Common ground: transgender rights that are not questioned   54

5 Changing your legal sex: should it be possible and how easy should it be?   69

6 Protecting women-only spaces, categories and capacities   100

7 Protecting children from medical transition   121

8 Why transgender rights are not like LGB rights   145

9 From conflicts to co-existence between transgender rights and women's and children's rights   171

Notes   187

Acknowledgements

My greatest debt of gratitude is owed to Elise Heslinga, Associate Editor (Gender, Women's & Feminist Studies) at Polity, who asked me if I would be interested in writing a book on this topic. My response was an enthusiastic Yes! I would also like to thank all those involved in the production process at Polity, including Rachel Moore and Leigh Mueller.

Since I awoke from my "sex vs. gender identity" slumber in 2018 (see chapters 1 and 5), I have benefitted from conversations with many women, who have encouraged me to speak out about conflicts between some transgender demands and women's rights. I am grateful to all of you for educating me.

I would like to thank the organizers who allowed me to express my ideas, and to the audiences who listened and commented, at the first LGB Alliance Conference in London on 21 October 2021; at King's College London on 24 November 2021; at Université Paris-Panthéon-Assas (Paris 2) on 17 June 2022; at Universitat Pompeu Fabra in Barcelona on 10 October 2022; at Università di Bologna (Campus di Forlì) on 5 December 2022; at McGill University in Montréal on 10 January 2023; and at Université Lumière Lyon 2 on 15 January 2024. Thanks are owed in particular to Benjamin Moron-Puech (organizer of

Acknowledgements

ix

the Paris 2 and Lyon 2 events), who believes in the importance of public debate between people with different opinions.

Finally, I would like to thank Oonagh Gormley, Robert John and Sharon Stroick for reading and commenting on one or more draft chapters.

1

How did we get here? From sympathy for transsexuals (1972) to a call to remove sex from birth certificates (2017)

In December 2018, Maya Forstater lost her job in London because she posted tweets that some of her colleagues found offensive, such as: 'I think that male people are not women. I don't think being a woman/female is a matter of identity or womanly feelings. It is biology.'[1] In December 2019, when her claim of discrimination because of her gender-critical beliefs was dismissed (it was reinstated in June 2021), the author J. K. Rowling tweeted: '... force women out of their jobs for stating that sex is real? #IStandWithMaya.'[2] Ms Rowling has since been demonized as 'transphobic'.[3]

In December 2022, when two French authors attempted to discuss their concerns about medical treatment of children with gender dysphoria, protesters invaded the venue, a café in Brussels, and threw cat and dog excrement at the participants.[4] In January 2023, my own attempt (as a professor of human rights law and an expert on anti-discrimination law) to discuss conflicts between transgender rights and women's rights, at the McGill University Faculty of Law in Montréal, was shut down by a mob of over 100 protesters, convinced that I would be inciting the genocide of transgender persons around the world. One of them threw flour on me (a better material if one has to be assaulted!).[5]

Meanwhile, apart from the hostility (including accusations of 'transphobia') faced by anyone who publicly disagrees with any of the demands of the transgender-rights movement, we find governments, legislatures and courts reaching opposite conclusions regarding conflicts between transgender rights and women's rights. In February 2023, the United Kingdom government announced a new policy for England and Wales: male-to-female transgender persons[6] will no longer be held in women's prisons 'if they retain male genitalia or have been convicted of a violent or sexual offence'.[7] In California, a September 2020 amendment to the Penal Code provides that 'An individual . . . who is transgender . . ., *regardless of anatomy*, shall . . . [b]e housed at a correctional facility designated for men or women based on the individual's preference'.[8]

And in sports, Great Britain's Equality Act 2010 clearly permits the exclusion of 'a transsexual person as a competitor in a gender-affected [sport, game or other activity of a competitive nature] if it is necessary to do so to secure in relation to the activity – (a) fair competition, or (b) the safety of competitors'.[9] In the United States, a federal court reinstated the challenge of four female high school sprinters to the Connecticut policy that permitted two male-to-female transgender students to compete against and defeat them.[10] Another federal court upheld the challenge of a male-to-female transgender runner (aged around 14) to West Virginia's 'Save Women's Sports Act', stressing that the runner was taking puberty blockers and had not experienced elevated levels of testosterone. West Virginia has asked the US Supreme Court to review the decision.[11] And a Minnesota judge ruled that USA Powerlifting must allow a male-to-female transgender person to compete in the women's category, before the decision was reversed on appeal as premature.[12]

How did we get here: to a political climate (in many countries) in which it is controversial to state that there are physical differences between men and women,[13] and that these differences sometimes justify excluding male-bodied persons from women-only spaces and categories?

Abuse of sympathy and the escalation of demands from 2002 to 2017

The political tensions surrounding transgender rights today are the result of what I would call 'abuse of sympathy', which has led to an 'escalation of demands' by the transgender-rights movement, especially since 2002. Sympathy was the natural reaction of governments, legislatures and courts when first presented with the plight of transsexual persons, as they were known in the twentieth century. Such persons felt strongly that they were people of the opposite sex struggling to live in 'the wrong body'. Some had used hormones and surgery to make their bodies as similar as medically possible to those of the opposite sex. A male-to-female transsexual person might have undergone surgery to remove their penis and testes and construct a vagina. After such a difficult process, surely a humane society must allow the person to change their legal sex from male to female, so that their new identity documents will make their life easier?

In 1972, Sweden was the first European country to pass a law at the national level permitting a transsexual person to change their legal sex, provided that the person had been sterilized or was already infertile.[14] This was to prevent claims to be recognized as a 'male mother' or a 'female father', which I will discuss in chapter 6 on women-only spaces, categories and capacities. The rationale was probably that a person seeking legal recognition as a member of one sex must not retain the reproductive capacity of the opposite sex. Other European

4   Transgender Rights vs Women's Rights

countries gradually followed Sweden and generally required some form of surgery. From 1980 to 2002, a series of cases sought to convert developments at the national level into a human right under the European Convention on Human Rights.

The first, in 1980, was *D. van Oosterwijck* v. *Belgium* (female-to-male; breasts, uterus and ovaries removed, penis constructed), in which the European Court of Human Rights (ECtHR) declined to consider the merits of the complaint, because of a failure to exhaust all possible legal procedures in Belgium. But the Court later found no human right to change legal sex in 1986 in *Mark Rees* v. *United Kingdom* (female-to-male; breasts removed), in 1990 in *Caroline Cossey* v. *UK* (male-to-female; breast implants, male genitals removed, vagina constructed), and in 1998 in *Kristina Sheffield & Rachel Horsham* v. *UK* (male-to-female; 'gender reassignment surgery'). Each time, the Court upheld the British system (an individual could change their sex on their driver's licence and their passport but not on their birth certificate), while noting the distress that transsexual persons suffered and urging the UK Government to keep the need for legal reform 'under review'.

In 1992, in *B.* v. *France* (male-to-female; male genitals removed, vagina constructed), the stricter French system (changing an individual's first name was more difficult than in the UK and their birth sex was often revealed by their social security number) was found to violate the right to respect for private life in Article 8 of the European Convention.[15] (In countries outside Europe, human or constitutional rights equivalent to the rights in the European Convention can usually be found in a United Nations treaty, the Inter-American Convention, the African Charter or the national constitution.) France could have complied with the European Court's 1992 judgment by adopting the British system. Instead, French courts began to permit an individual to change their legal sex after surgery.[16]

In 2002, in *Christine Goodwin* v. *UK* (male-to-female; 'gender re-assignment surgery'), the ECtHR lost patience with the UK Government, concluding that 'post-operative transsexuals' have an Article 8 right to change their legal sex on their birth certificates, as well as an Article 12 right to marry a person of the sex opposite to their new legal sex (a person of the same sex as their birth sex).[17] The Court noted that 33 of the then 43 Council of Europe member states (the parties to the European Convention) allowed changes to birth certificates after 'gender re-assignment', and was 'struck by the fact that . . . the gender re-assignment which is lawfully provided [by the UK's National Health Service at public expense] is not met with full recognition in law, which might be regarded as the final and culminating step in the long and difficult process of transformation which the transsexual has undergone'. The Court also referred to 'the sexual identity chosen by [post-operative transsexuals] at great personal cost'.[18]

In 2002 in *Christine Goodwin*, the ECtHR accepted **the first transgender demand: change of legal sex after surgery resulting in sterilization**. However, it seems clear that the majority of transgender persons did not wish to have 'below-the-waist' surgery in 2002, and do not wish to do so today.[19] This gave rise to **the second transgender demand: change of legal sex with no medical treatment** (no hormones or surgery, no 'long and difficult process', no 'great personal cost'), **but with safeguards** (a diagnosis of gender dysphoria and a waiting period of two years) to ensure that this exceptional procedure could not be abused by persons born male who were not transgender. The UK Government agreed to this demand, which was incorporated into the Gender Recognition Act 2004 (GRA), even though it went well beyond what the ECtHR had required, and probably had no precedent at the national level anywhere in the world.

Acceptance of the second transgender demand means that, today in the UK, a person born male can obtain a Gender

Recognition Certificate and become legally female, even though they have a beard, a deep voice and male genitals. The law allows them to become legally female, even though most people seeing or hearing them would consider them male. In March 2007, when only the UK had a law of this kind, the second transgender demand (no medical treatment) became Principle 3 of the Yogyakarta (pronounced Jogjakarta) Principles (on the application of international human rights law in relation to sexual orientation and gender identity).[20] The Yogyakarta Principles is a civil-society document that aims to state the minimum requirements of *existing* international human rights law (but occasionally veers into advocacy for *new* obligations in international human rights law), and which is often cited in the UK as representing 'international best practice'.

In 2012, Argentina became the first country to accept at the national level **the third transgender demand: change of legal sex with no medical treatment and with no safeguards** (no diagnosis or waiting period), **based solely on self-identification**.[21] Since 2014 in Europe, the Argentine model has been adopted by 11 of 46 Council of Europe countries (Belgium, Denmark, Finland, Iceland, Ireland, Luxembourg, Malta, Norway, Portugal, Spain and Switzerland).[22] In April 2017, in *A.P., Garçon & Nicot* v. *France*, the ECtHR declined to make the third transgender demand (self-identification) a minimum European standard, because at that time only Denmark, Iceland, Malta and Norway had adopted the Argentine model (the Court did not mention Ireland).[23] The Court ruled that the European Convention permits 'the requirement to demonstrate the existence of a gender identity disorder' (the requirement to provide a diagnosis).[24] The Court did, however, make the second transgender demand (no surgery) a minimum European standard, even though it was the law in only 18 of 47 Council of Europe member states.[25] The no-surgery aspect of the GRA, which was optional in 2004, is thus now required by the case law of the ECtHR. It would appear that at least 17 of the 50 US states still require surgery, or do not permit a change of legal sex at all.[26]

In November 2017, the second version of the Yogyakarta Principles incorporated **the fourth transgender demand**. Principle 31 boldly claims that, under *existing* international human rights law, every country in the world has an obligation to '**end the registration of the sex . . . of the person in** identity documents such as **birth certificates**'. Until this is done, the third transgender demand (self-identification) must be accepted: 'no eligibility criteria, such as . . . a psycho-medical diagnosis . . . shall be a prerequisite to change one's . . . legal sex'.[27]

To summarize, transgender demands have escalated (at least in Europe) as follows:

- first demand (1972–2002) – change of legal sex on birth certificate after surgery resulting in sterilization;
- second demand (2002–12) – change of legal sex without medical treatment but with safeguards (a diagnosis and a waiting period);
- third demand (since 2012) – change of legal sex based solely on 'self-identification', without medical treatment or safeguards (no diagnosis or waiting period);
- fourth demand (since 2017) – removal of sex from birth certificates so that there is no legal sex to change.

The first demand sought a sympathetic response to the transgender person's surgery, a 'long and difficult process' involving 'great personal cost' (usually removal of the penis and testes in the case of a male-to-female transgender person). The second demand sought a much more generous response (no need for any medical treatment), but accepted the need for safeguards. The third demand's abandonment of safeguards, and the fourth demand's insistence on abolishing legal sex for everyone, demonstrate the transgender-rights movement's

8 Transgender Rights vs Women's Rights

failure to consider the impact of its demands on the 'rights of others', especially women, which will be the subject of chapter 2 on conflicts of rights.

How can we explain the rapid advances of the transgender-rights movement, especially since 2015? Two of the main causes (combined with others, such as the rise of social media) are: (i) the academic success of 'gender theory' and its attempt to make birth sex irrelevant; and (ii) the political and legal success of the lesbian, gay and bisexual (LGB) rights movement from 2000 to 2015.

The academic success of 'gender theory' and its attempt to make birth sex irrelevant

'Gender' is a word that I stopped using in 1996, because of its ambiguity. When an individual refers to their 'gender', you have no idea what they mean without further information or context. Since 1996, when I mean an individual's biological sex at birth, I have always used 'sex' and have always referred (in an academic context) to 'sexual activity', rather than 'having sex'. Today, for greater clarity and brevity, I use 'birth sex' when I mean biological sex.

The problem with 'gender' is that it has developed at least three meanings: (i) 'gender as synonym'; (ii) 'gender as behaviour'; and (iii) 'gender as feeling'. 'Gender as synonym' (or 'biological gender') applies when the speaker or writer uses 'gender' to mean birth sex: an objective, external, physical status of an individual that is observed and recorded at birth and never changes throughout the individual's life. Whatever physical changes a person makes to their body, their chromosomes will always reveal their birth sex (if they do not have a 'difference in sex development' or DSD). Historically, the motivation for using 'gender as synonym' has been to make it clear that the speaker or writer does not mean 'sex' in the

How did we get here? 9

sense of 'having sex' or 'engaging in sexual activity' (use of the reproductive organs associated with one's birth sex). Examples include 'gender equality' or 'gender pay gap'. Because 'gender as synonym' adds nothing to 'sex', it can easily be replaced and sufficiently clarified by 'birth sex' or 'sex equality' or 'female–male pay gap'. The Rome Statute of the International Criminal Court defines 'gender' as: 'the two sexes, male and female, within the context of society. The term "gender" does not indicate any meaning different from the above.'[28]

'Gender as behaviour' (or 'social gender') refers to 'social sex roles': the 'life script' that historically was handed to every baby, according to her or his birth sex.[29] (The 2011 Council of Europe 'Convention on preventing and combatting violence against women and domestic violence' refers to 'sex' on its own only once, refers to 'gender' 25 times, and defines 'gender' as 'the socially constructed roles, behaviours, activities and attributes that a given society considers appropriate for women and men'.)[30] Receiving the 'male life script' or the 'female life script' determined the individual's (or their parents') choices of, for example, clothing, hairstyle, make-up, first name, employment, sexual or romantic partner or spouse, and their involvement in childcare. Together, the life scripts read as follows. Men wear trousers; women wear dresses and skirts. Men have short hair; women have long hair. Men do not wear make-up; women may do so. Most first names (in English) are men-only or women-only. Men are doctors; women are nurses. Men are sexually attracted to and marry women. Women are sexually attracted to and marry men. Men earn money and fight wars. Women cook, clean and take care of children.

This meaning of gender is negative and restricts the choices of both sexes. It denotes something to be challenged and abolished wherever it is found in law and in society. An individual's birth sex determines the role that they might be able to play in human reproduction, but nothing more than that. If 'gender as behaviour' is abolished, any individual is free to make any

10 Transgender Rights vs Women's Rights

choice that is open to persons of the opposite sex. There is then no longer any such thing as 'gender-conforming' or 'gender-non-conforming' behaviour, because there are no expectations regarding 'social gender' to which one might conform or not conform. A man (or a person born male) wearing a dress is just a person who likes to wear dresses. Unlike birth sex, 'gender as behaviour' is entirely social, not a characteristic of an individual.

If we avoid 'gender as synonym' ('biological gender') and abolish 'gender as behaviour' ('social gender'), is there any need to use 'gender' at all? This brings us to the third meaning of 'gender', which is 'gender as feeling' (or 'gender identity'): an individual's subjective, internal, intangible feeling of being a person of one sex or the opposite sex or both or neither, regardless of the individual's actual birth sex. This meaning of 'gender' is considered positive and liberating: a characteristic of an individual to be explored, revealed and celebrated.

The most prominent exponent of 'gender theory' is Professor Judith Butler of the University of California, Berkeley. In her 1990 book, *Gender Trouble*, she 'question[s] "women" as the subject of feminism', after noting 'the political problem that feminism encounters in the assumption that the term *women* denotes a common identity'.[31] She asks: 'Is there some commonality among "women" that preexists their oppression ...?'[32] She is unable to find one, implicitly rejecting the fact that women have their bodies in common: they are persons born with female reproductive organs. She argues that 'When the [culturally] constructed status of gender is theorized as radically independent of sex, gender itself becomes a free-floating artifice, with the consequence that *man* ... might just as easily signify a female body as a male one, and *woman* ... a male body as easily as a female one.'[33] She cites the authors Monique Wittig and Michel Foucault as 'claiming that the category of sex would itself disappear ... through the disruption and displacement of heterosexual hegemony'.[34] Butler seems

How did we get here? 11

to use 'gender' in the sense of 'gender as behaviour', when she writes that 'gender . . . [is] an "act" . . . which is both intentional and performative . . . the action of gender requires a performance that is *repeated*.'[35] She seems not to support 'gender as feeling' when she refers to 'the illusion of gender identity as an . . . inner substance'.[36] She concludes by contemplating future 'configurations of sex and gender . . . confounding the very binarism of sex, and exposing its fundamental unnaturalness'.[37]

Butler's ideas have had a huge influence (some women would describe it as a negative one),[38] sweeping across universities and, through graduates, into the wider society. But, whatever she intended in *Gender Trouble* or subsequent writing, the dominant idea of 'gender' as distinct from birth sex has become 'gender as feeling' or 'gender identity'. Many people take it for granted today that every person has a true, inner 'gender', which might differ from their birth sex.

What is the purpose of 'gender identity'? It seems to be to universalize the possibility of 'gender as feeling', rather than to confine the phenomenon to transgender persons. The use of 'gender identity' in legal writing is relatively recent. In 1997, I wrote about 'transsexualism' and 'sexual orientation'.[39] In October 2000, I gave the Stonewall Lecture in London, with the title 'Lesbian and gay inequality 2000'.[40] By February 2002, my terminology had changed. I taught an intensive course at the University of Toronto on 'Comparative Sexual Orientation and Gender Identity Law' and began referring to LGBT persons. Uncritically following the trend in the LGB and transgender-rights movements, I thought for many years that I had both a male birth sex and a male 'gender identity': my body is male and, in my mind, I think and feel that I am a man. But in 2020, a gender-critical woman told me that she did not have a 'gender identity'. I thought about it and realized that I did not have one either. A quick glance at my genitals when using the toilet in the morning tells me my birth sex (male). Another glance before going to bed tells me that my birth sex is still the same. I do not 'feel' male. I do not 'identify' as male. I *am* male. It is a physical fact of my birth.

So is 'gender identity' a universal characteristic? I would argue that it is not and that 'transgender identity' is a more accurate and useful term. Some characteristics found in anti-discrimination legislation are universal. Everyone has a birth sex. Everyone has a set of racial or ethnic origins, meaning an ancestry or genetic heritage that might determine their physical appearance. Everyone has an age, determined by their date of birth. Everyone has a sexual orientation, if the possibilities are opposite-sex-attracted, same-sex-attracted, both-sex-attracted and neither-sex-attracted. Not everyone has a religion, so 'religion or belief' in Great Britain's Equality Act 2010 is defined as including 'lack of religion' and 'lack of belief'.[41] Similarly, not everyone currently has a disability, although they may develop one at some point in the future. This is why we do not say: 'Everyone has a disability.' Instead, we refer to 'non-disabled persons' (the majority, with regard to a particular disability).

I would argue that the same is true of 'gender identity'. We should not say: 'Everyone has a gender identity.' So how do we describe people who do not have a 'gender identity'? Because we are usually trying to distinguish the majority of people from the minority of transgender people, I would suggest that 'non-transgender persons' is sufficient. 'Cisgender' does not work. Apart from the facts that most people do not understand the term, and that in English 'cis' sounds like 'sissy' (a pejorative term for a feminine boy or man), 'cisgender' seeks to describe what for many people does not exist: an internal feeling that they are a person of the sex that corresponds with their birth sex. The same is not true of 'heterosexual'. Heterosexual people experience opposite-sex attraction, which is what the term 'heterosexual' describes.

The success of 'gender theory' has divided countries (in which women's, LGB and transgender rights are taken

How did we get here? 13

seriously) into two camps: those who believe that 'birth sex' trumps 'gender identity' in the event of a conflict (those who are 'gender-critical' or 'birth-sex-affirming'), and those who believe that 'birth sex' is an irrelevant detail (arbitrarily 'assigned at birth') and is always trumped by an individual's 'true gender' or 'gender identity' (those who are 'gender-affirming' or 'birth-sex-critical').[42]

The division can be illustrated by hypothetical reactions to a statement I heard an activist make at a conference: 'Sex is between your legs. Gender is between your ears.' One camp reacts by saying: 'Precisely! Sex is what matters. The law and society should be concerned with your body, not your mind.' The other camp reacts by saying: 'Precisely! Gender is what matters. The law and society should be concerned with your mind, not your body.'

The two camps disagree about how we should define a woman. Is it the person's body (reproductive organs and chromosomes), mind (thoughts and feelings) or behaviour (clothing and mannerisms) that provides the answer? For one camp, birth sex determines who is a woman. For the other camp, 'gender as feeling' or 'gender identity' determines who is a woman (possibly combined with 'gender as behaviour' or 'doing woman-like things'). Any person who feels that they are a woman is a woman (possibly combined, as Butler might prefer, with 'acting' or 'performing' 'like a woman').

These two conflicting viewpoints regarding who is a woman are very difficult to reconcile. One camp relies on biological science. The other camp relies on what can only be described as 'faith'. 'Gender as feeling' or 'gender identity' is similar to a religious belief, in that it cannot be objectively verified. As Helen Joyce (author of *Trans: When Ideology Meets Reality*) puts it, 'no one can determine a person's gender identity except that person, and no one else can challenge it. As with religious belief, it is entirely subjective. A simple declaration – 'gender self-identification' – is all it takes to override biology.'[43] Only

14   Transgender Rights vs Women's Rights

the sincerity of the subjective belief (of persons with a 'gender identity' that is different from their birth sex) can be examined. But, as we will see in chapter 3 on freedom of expression, there is currently a major difference between beliefs about religion and beliefs about 'gender'.

I can illustrate this difference by comparing the statement 'Jesus is the son of God' with the statement 'Trans women are women.' In a democratic society that respects freedom of religion, no one is obliged to believe that 'Jesus is the son of God.' Everyone is free to believe that this statement is true, to believe that it is false, or to have no opinion about it. But for many people who support the transgender-rights movement, the statement 'Trans women are women' is sacred, part of a credo ('I believe') or creed, which adds 'Trans men are men' and 'Non-binary people are valid.'[44] To disagree with this statement, by pointing out that 'trans women' are persons born male, is 'transphobic' and a form of blasphemy, for which the penalty is excommunication in the secular form of 'cancellation'. For example, on 27 July 2023, Labour Students (who support the UK's Labour Party) tweeted: 'Trans women are women and trans men are men – any statement to the contrary is transphobia and completely unacceptable.'[45]

Of course, an individual's same-sex sexual orientation cannot be proved objectively and is also a matter of faith. I have argued that, for the purposes of anti-discrimination law, sexual orientation is best compared with religion, not race.[46] But, as we will see in chapter 8 on why transgender rights are not like LGB rights, LGB persons do not ask others to believe anything that is contrary to biological science.

To conclude this discussion of 'gender', I would argue that the pendulum has swung too far. From a starting point (perhaps the 1950s) when birth sex dictated to a large extent what women and men could do in life, the pendulum has swung so far in the 2020s that many people consider it 'transphobic' to suggest that birth sex is ever relevant. The baby ('birth sex')

How did we get here? 15

has been thrown out with the bathwater ('social gender'). The growing gender-critical (birth-sex-affirming) movement is a sign that the pendulum is swinging back. One of the aims of this book is to contribute to that correction.

The political and legal success of the LGB-rights movement from 2000 to 2015

The second cause of the rapid advances of the transgender-rights movement, especially since 2015, is the political and legal success of the LGB-rights movement from 2000 to 2015. I have worked in this movement since 1985, including as a lawyer or expert witness in cases in national courts (in the US, the UK, Canada, Colombia and Argentina) and in international courts (the ECtHR, the Inter-American Court of Human Rights, and the Court of Justice of the European Union (CJEU)). This makes me very familiar with the movement's evolution. The three main stages in achieving equal rights for LGB people around the world tend to be: (i) criminal law reform, which includes repealing total prohibitions of same-sex sexual activity (including between consenting adults in private) and equalizing the age of consent to sexual activity; (ii) anti-discrimination legislation, which allows LGB people to be open about their sexual orientations without fearing discrimination in access to employment, housing, education and other goods and services; and (iii) family law reform, which includes equal access to marriage, second-parent adoption, joint adoption of unrelated children, and assisted reproduction techniques that are available to opposite-sex couples.

Sexual activity between men was decriminalized in France as early as 1791, as part of the French Revolution. The first reforms in the former British Empire took much longer: the French reform was adopted by Illinois in 1961, England and Wales in 1967, and Canada in 1969. In some US states,

16 Transgender Rights vs Women's Rights

such as Texas and Florida, sexual activity between men and between women remained criminalized until 2003, when the US Supreme Court struck down laws of this kind in *Lawrence & Garner* v. *Texas*.[47]

The first laws (at the national, state or provincial level) prohibiting discrimination based on sexual orientation were passed in Québec in 1977, Norway in 1981, and Wisconsin and New South Wales in 1982. Similar European Union legislation was adopted in 2000. Only in 2020 was protection against sexual orientation discrimination in employment extended across all 50 US states, by the US Supreme Court's decision in *Bostock* v. *Clayton County*, which applied 'sex' in Title VII of the Civil Rights Act of 1964 to cases of sexual orientation discrimination.[48]

As for family law reform, an important early step was taken in Denmark in 1989, which enacted the world's first 'separate and almost equal' registered partnership law for same-sex couples, as compensation for their exclusion from marriage. Similar laws followed in European countries and reached Vermont in April 2000. Then, in December 2000, the legislature of the Netherlands had the courage to pass the world's first law opening up civil (meaning legal, not religious) marriage to same-sex couples. The first same-sex marriages took place at Amsterdam City Hall on 1 April 2001. Other countries soon followed: Belgium (2003), Spain and Canada (2005) and South Africa (2006). In 2003, the first appellate courts ordered the issuance of marriage licences to same-sex couples in Ontario, British Columbia and Massachusetts. Litigation continued in US courts, culminating in the US Supreme Court's decision in *Obergefell* v. *Hodges* on 26 June 2015, which required equal access to marriage for same-sex couples in all 50 US states.[49]

This decision was perhaps the turning point. Same-sex marriage had been achieved across the US, after Canada (2005), Argentina (2010), New Zealand (2013), France (2013), England

and Wales (2013), Scotland (2014) and Ireland (May 2015). LGB-rights organizations (or the LGB-rights departments of general human rights organizations such as the American Civil Liberties Union (ACLU)) in the US, the UK and other countries seemed to fear that their work was done and that their funding might disappear.[50] This fear caused these organizations to prioritize transgender rights, or to take them on for the first time (as in the case of Stonewall in the UK in 2015).[51]

Meanwhile, male-to-female transgender persons had become increasingly prominent in the US. Laverne Cox appeared on the cover of *Time* magazine's 9 June 2014 issue, with the caption 'The transgender tipping point: America's next civil rights frontier'.[52] Caitlyn Jenner (winner as Bruce Jenner of the gold medal in the men's decathlon at the Montréal 1976 Olympics) came out as a male-to-female transgender person on the television programme *20/20* on 25 April 2015,[53] before appearing on the cover of *Vanity Fair* magazine's July 2015 issue.[54]

After LGB, time for T, the next great human rights issue?

For younger activists today, who have come of age after the success of the movements for equal legal rights for African Americans, the black majority in South Africa, women, disabled persons and LGB persons, transgender rights is the most important cause of their time. (Of course, it is also important for some older activists who participated in the prior movements.) Many activists passionately support the transgender-rights movement and see transgender persons as the most vulnerable minority in society. But when they hold their 'Trans Rights Now!' placards at demonstrations, many activists probably do not realize that most transgender rights are already legally

18 Transgender Rights vs Women's Rights

protected, and that protection was sometimes achieved before protection for LGB persons.

In European Union law, discrimination against transgender persons has been prohibited (as sex discrimination) in employment since 1996, and in access to goods and services since 2007. For LGB persons, the dates are 2003 and not yet (a Directive proposed in 2008 has yet to be adopted). The 2002 *Christine Goodwin* decision of the ECtHR gave transgender persons the right to marry a person of the sex opposite to their new legal sex (a person of the same sex as their birth sex). In 2025, same-sex couples in Europe still do not have an international law (European Convention) right to marry (as opposed to a right to marry under national law).

Many activists do not ask themselves whether current transgender-rights claims, such as change of legal sex based on 'self-identification', are about equal rights (the same rights as non-transgender persons) or exemptions from neutral general rules that apply to all (as we will see in chapters 4 and 5). Nor do they ask themselves whether some transgender-rights claims might conflict with the rights of women, because they tend to assume that transgender rights are absolute and that there can be no conflicts with the rights of women. Why? Because 'Trans women are women.'

It is unlikely that the transgender-rights movement would have made the rapid advances we have seen, since 2015, if the question of equal access to marriage for same-sex couples had not been resolved in so many countries. The transgender-rights movement has also benefitted greatly from its political coalition with the LGB-rights movement, which began in the late 1990s and early 2000s.

Judith Butler advocated an LGBT coalition in the 1999 Preface to *Gender Trouble*: 'I continue to hope for a coalition of sexual minorities that will transcend the simple categories of identity, that will refuse the erasure of bisexuality, that will counter and dissipate the violence imposed by restrictive

How did we get here? 19

bodily norms.'[55] Many people today are likely to think: 'I supported LGB rights. Transgender rights are like LGB rights. Therefore, I support all transgender demands.'

Today, however, lesbian women who say that 'women do not have penises' find themselves accused of 'transphobia' and of acting like racists in relation to their sexual relationships.[56] LGBT organizations are now dominated by the T and prohibit any disagreement with transgender demands. In chapter 8, I will ask whether (with the benefit of hindsight) the LGBT political coalition was a mistake from Day 1, because LGB and T did not have enough in common; and whether LGB now needs a 'divorce' from T.

My personal journey from transgender-rights supporter to women's-rights defender

In 1995, I began to meet transgender people at conferences. In September 1998, I attended the Transgender Agenda conference at Exeter College, University of Oxford, at which the majority of participants were transgender. In 2005, I published a book chapter on 'Sexual orientation and gender identity', in which I tried to be comprehensive with regard to both issues in the UK, and wrote: 'As by far the larger of the two minorities, LGB individuals have a moral duty to speak out on behalf of transsexual individuals.'[57] In 2006, I was one of the experts who met at Universitas Gajah Mada in Jogjakarta, Java, Indonesia to draft the first version of the Yogyakarta Principles. When transgender issues were discussed, I deferred to the transgender participants and did not raise any objections. For the next nine years, I did not question the reasonableness of any transgender demand.

In 2015, when I heard about Ireland's new law permitting change of legal sex based on 'self-identification',[58] I asked some questions for the first time. How would this affect women's sports? If, after retiring from the men's 100-metre event, the Jamaican Olympic-champion sprinter Usain Bolt were to 'self-identify' as female and enter the women's 100-metre event, what would happen? But I did not pursue the questions I had. I was mostly oblivious to the rapid legal, political and social changes taking place around me.

Then, at a summer school in 2018, I had a 'light-bulb moment'. A non-transgender student asked: when UK law began in 2014 to permit a married transgender person to change their legal sex without getting a divorce first (because same-sex marriage had become possible), why did this require the consent of the transgender person's spouse?[59] I explained that the spouse had consented to an opposite-sex marriage, not a same-sex marriage. The rule (called the 'spousal veto' by transgender-rights activists) sought to protect the non-transgender spouse against a unilateral conversion of the marriage by the transgender spouse into a same-sex marriage. If, for example, the non-transgender spouse had a strong religious objection to being in a same-sex marriage, the transgender spouse would first have to seek a divorce.

A transgender student rejected my explanation, arguing that I was comparing 'a fundamental human right' (the right of the transgender person to change their legal sex) with 'a contract' (the marriage). I pointed to the European Convention on Human Rights, which states several times that 'the protection of the rights and freedoms of others' is a reason why it might be 'necessary in a democratic society' to restrict a human right. When the transgender student continued to object, I said in frustration: 'Trans rights don't trump everything else!' The transgender student became angry and left the classroom. At this point, I realized that the student did not seem to have considered that non-transgender people have human rights too.

After this incident, my concerns about some transgender demands began to grow. In 2018, I was given a copy of the second version of the Yogyakarta Principles (I did not

How did we get here? 21

participate in its drafting). I put it on a bookshelf in my office without reading it. In 2020, a gender-critical woman asked me if I had read Principle 31 in the second version (obligation to remove sex from birth certificates). I had not done so and could not believe my eyes when I finally read Principle 31. It confirmed what I had learned at the summer school in 2018. Many people in the transgender-rights movement do not seem to have considered that non-transgender people, especially women, have human rights too, and that their rights must be taken into account in formulating transgender demands (see chapter 2).

On 1 April 2021, Julie Bendel and Melanie Newman published the article 'The trans rights that trump all' in the *Critic* magazine.[60] The interview included comments I made when Melanie interviewed me about the Yogyakarta Principles. The next day, I received an email from the executive director of the Brussels-based non-governmental organization ILGA-Europe (the European Region of the International Lesbian, Gay, Bisexual, Trans and Intersex Association) saying that the article had 'serious implications for us at ILGA-Europe'. On 16 April 2021, I was notified that 'the fact that we so profoundly disagree on trans rights and that you have made your own views very public makes it impossible for us to continue to work with you'. Even though I had done free legal work on LGB rights for the organization for over 20 years, including drafting many third-party interventions (amicus curiae briefs) for LGB cases in the ECtHR, ILGA-Europe summarily terminated its relationship with me. No debate. I was 'cancelled'.

The following month, in May 2021, I agreed to become a trustee of LGB Alliance, a new organization founded in 2019 as an alternative to Stonewall in the UK.[61] LGB Alliance seeks to prioritize LGB issues (as Stonewall did from 1989 to 2015). This means distancing itself from the transgender-rights movement and reserving the right to disagree with some transgender demands. In October 2021, I spoke at the first annual

22   Transgender Rights vs Women's Rights

conference of LGB Alliance at the Queen Elizabeth II Centre opposite Westminster Abbey in London. Transgender-rights activists demonstrated outside the building. At one point, they were chanting: 'Nazi scum off our streets!'[62]

This is not the first time that I have changed my mind. After learning about the centuries of persecution of Europe's Jewish minorities, culminating in the Holocaust, I supported Israel for many years. I visited Auschwitz in September 1987 and Israel in April 1988. But in 1998, I met a Palestinian-Israeli PhD student at my university. Later, I met a Palestinian-Canadian man whose parents were born in Haifa and Jerusalem but are not allowed to live in Israel. I gradually changed my mind about the situation in Israel–Palestine and became a defender of Palestinian human rights. In doing so, I was inspired by the legal maxim (and fundamental principle of procedural justice) inscribed above an entrance to the McGill University Faculty of Law, where I studied. It reads 'Audi Alteram Partem': 'Hear (or Listen to) the Other Side'. I listened to Palestinian people and changed my mind about the actions of the Government of Israel. And I have listened to women and changed my mind about some transgender demands.

All men (heterosexual, bisexual and gay) need to listen to women's concerns about transgender rights, because this issue is asymmetrical, as in the case of abortion. Men have no reason to fear the presence of female-to-male transgender persons. If such persons wish to use male communal showers or be housed in male prisons, or compete against men in sports competitions, there is no reason to exclude them. But most women (heterosexual, bisexual and lesbian) also need to empathize with women who are affected by some transgender demands. Because of the small number of male-to-female transgender persons, most women have probably not been directly affected by the entry of such persons into women-only spaces. Most women will never be sent to a women's prison, have probably not seen male genitals in a women's changing room, and do not participate in competitive sports, such as swimming or athletics (track and field). The number of women who are directly affected by conflicts between transgender rights and women's rights is thus quite small. But I will argue in chapter 6 that they are affected in unjustifiable and distressing ways.

From conflicts to co-existence

Having set the stage, I will develop my arguments in the chapters to come as follows. In chapter 2, I will consider conflicts of human rights, how common they are, and how we resolve them by drawing lines. In chapter 3, I will ask what 'transphobia' is and what is, instead, protected political expression. In chapter 4, I will point out the broad areas of agreement about transgender rights, which are rarely mentioned. In chapter 5, I will go back to our starting point (before Sweden's 1972 law) and ask whether it should be possible to change one's legal sex and, if so, how easy it should be. In chapters 6 and 7, I will examine the debates regarding the protection of women-only spaces and categories (including sports) and the protection of children (persons under 18) from medical transition. In chapter 8, I will explain why transgender rights are not like LGB rights and ask whether LGB needs a 'divorce' from T. Finally, in chapter 9, I will imagine how we might resolve the conflicts and achieve coexistence between transgender rights and women's and children's rights.

Finally, a few words explaining what this book is not. It is not a book about the history of debates within feminism about the meaning of 'gender', nor about the history of the struggle in the United Kingdom against some transgender demands and the women who have led that struggle. It is a book that deploys my expertise in human rights and anti-discrimination law to examine the legal arguments for transgender rights and for women's rights, and how to solve the problems that arise when the rights of the two groups conflict. For more historical or philosophical discussions of these issues, I would refer readers to Kathleen Stock's *Material Girls: Why Reality Matters for Feminism*,[63] Holly Lawford-Smith's *Gender-Critical Feminism*,[64] Alex Byrne's *Trouble with Gender: Sex Facts, Gender Fictions*,[65] Susan Dalgety & Lucy Hunter Blackburn (eds.), *The Women Who Wouldn't Wheesht: Voices from the Frontline of Scotland's Battle for Women's Rights*[66] and Jenny Lindsay's *Hounded: Women, Harms and the Gender Wars*.[67] I have tried to incorporate all developments of which I was aware as of 6 September 2024 (with occasional references to subsequent events).

2

Transgender rights vs women's rights: why the human rights of two groups often conflict

Imagine two groups shouting at each other in a public square: 'Trans rights are human rights!' 'Women's rights are human rights!' Both slogans are politically seductive, as was 'Lesbian and gay rights are human rights!' in the 1990s. But these slogans are legally empty as to the detailed content of the claimed human rights and the necessary limits on those rights. Neither transgender rights nor women's rights (nor LGB rights) are absolute. Human rights are not subjective and a matter of 'self-identification'. They are objective and require consideration of how the claimed human right of one group might conflict with the claimed human right of another group. The European Convention on Human Rights (1950) recognizes that it might be 'necessary in a democratic society' to restrict a claimed human right to protect 'the rights . . . of others'.[1] In United Nations human rights law, the same exception appears in the International Covenant on Civil and Political Rights (1966).[2]

At first, I thought that the only human right that is truly absolute is the right to be free from torture or inhuman or degrading treatment, which can never be justified, even in an emergency situation (such as combatting terrorist violence).[3] But there are debates even about this human right, because 'torture', 'inhuman treatment' and 'degrading treatment' must be defined. When is ill-treatment serious enough to come within one of these categories? In 2015, the ECtHR ruled, by 14 votes to 3, that a single slap in the face of a detained person by a police officer is 'degrading treatment' and a violation of this right.[4] Even with regard to this most fundamental human right, there sometimes has to be a debate.

Conflicts of human rights are surprisingly common, because the broad prima facie scopes of two human rights may overlap. The overlap and the resulting conflict force us to balance the interests of two groups and decide where lines can justifiably be drawn, because both human rights claims cannot succeed. A same-sex couple cannot have a right to be married by a religious organization if the religious organization has a right to refuse to marry the couple. The combination of lines that we draw in specific situations, which may take the form of exceptions to a general human freedom (such as freedom of religion) or to a general human right to be free from discrimination (such as discrimination based on sexual orientation), will often please neither group. When a line is drawn, one group's interest prevails over the other group's interest. But these lines are necessary to resolve conflicts of human rights and 'keep the peace' between the two groups.

Some examples of conflicts relate to human reproduction. Does the genetic father of a foetus have a right to veto an abortion sought by a pregnant woman, because he wishes to raise their child? Should his right to become a father (his right to respect for his family life), or his right to assert a 'right to life' of the foetus, prevail over her right not to continue a pregnancy and not to go through childbirth against her will? In 1980, the European Commission of Human Rights ruled against the potential father and in favour of the potential mother: any 'right to life' of the foetus, and the father's right to respect for his family life, may justifiably be limited to protect the life and health of another person, the pregnant woman.[5]

What if the woman is not yet pregnant, because her frozen embryo has yet to be implanted and the genetic father (her former partner) has withdrawn his consent to implantation? Does she have a right to become pregnant, give birth, and become a genetic mother, if this would force her former partner to become the genetic (and legal) father of a child against his will? In 2007, the ECtHR ruled against the potential mother and in favour of the potential father: the Court '[did] not consider that the [woman's] right to respect for the decision to become a parent in the genetic sense should be accorded greater weight than [the man's] right to respect for his decision not to have a genetically related child with her'.[6] Because the embryo had not yet been implanted, the man's human right not to become a genetic parent prevailed over the woman's human right to become a genetic parent.

In family law, when the relationship of the two legal parents of a child comes to an end, one parent might insist that the 'best interests of the child' require that the child reside full-time with that parent. Any other custody arrangement would violate that parent's right to respect for their family life (as well as the child's rights). But the other parent might insist the opposite: their right to respect for their family life (and the child's rights) require full-time residence with the other parent. Clearly, it is physically impossible for a child to sleep seven nights per week in two different homes. The conflict between the human rights of the two parents must be resolved, taking the best interests of the child into account. This will often mean a compromise, such as alternating stays of equal length in two residences, or staying mainly in one parent's home with regular visits to the other parent's home.

In media law, there can be a conflict under the European Convention between a publisher's Article 10 human right to freedom of expression (which includes freedom of the press) and the Article 8 human right of a celebrity to respect for her or his private life. In 2004, the ECtHR ruled in favour of

28   Transgender Rights vs Women's Rights

a celebrity and against a publisher, finding that articles and photographs published in German magazines violated the Article 8 right to respect for private life of Princess Caroline of Monaco: 'the public does not have a legitimate interest in knowing where [she] is and how she behaves generally in her private life even if she appears in places that cannot always be described as secluded [shopping, skiing, cycling or playing tennis in public] and despite the fact that she is well known to the public'.[7]

But in 2015, the ECtHR ruled in favour of a publisher and against a celebrity. The Court found that French courts had violated the Article 10 right to freedom of expression of *Paris Match* magazine, when the courts ordered the magazine to pay damages to the celebrity, Prince Albert of Monaco, for publishing an interview with a woman who claimed that he was the father of her son (when he was not married and was about to be enthroned as the hereditary ruler of Monaco): 'there is an undeniable public-interest value . . . in the existence of a child (particularly a son [and potential heir]) of the Prince, who was known at the relevant time as being single and childless'.[8] *Paris Match* had a clear Article 10 right to publish the interview.

Anti-discrimination laws (such as Great Britain's Equality Act 2010) contain many express exceptions that have been 'written in' to protect conflicting human rights, such as freedom of religion or the right of airline passengers to have their safety protected. If there is no express exception, an implied exception might have to be 'read in' to the anti-discrimination law to respect such rights. It is important to note that, despite the widespread 'equality, diversity and inclusion' policies of governments, businesses and universities, which appear to require 'inclusion' at all times, there is no absolute legal right to be 'included' in every situation. The express and implied exceptions in anti-discrimination laws are there to *permit exclusion*: less favourable treatment that is considered justified in particular circumstances and is therefore not discrimination.

These exceptions are rare with regard to discrimination based on racial or ethnic origin, but are more common with regard to discrimination based on other grounds.

Despite the prohibition of discrimination based on sex in employment, the Roman Catholic Church may refuse to hire female priests.[9] Despite the prohibition of discrimination based on religion in employment, a Muslim school may refuse to hire teachers who are not Muslim.[10] Despite the prohibition of discrimination based on disability in employment, an airline may refuse to hire a blind person as a pilot.[11] Despite the prohibition of discrimination based on age in employment, an airline might be able to require a pilot to retire at 65.[12] And despite the prohibition of discrimination based on sexual orientation in access to services, any religious organization may refuse to marry a same-sex couple.[13]

LGB human rights vs the human rights of religious individuals and organizations

I first began working on conflicts of human rights in 2002. I could see that prohibitions of discrimination based on sexual orientation in access to employment or to goods and services were becoming more common (a 2000 European Union Directive banning discrimination in employment had to be implemented in 15 countries by 2 December 2003 and in another 10 by 1 May 2004), just as more laws allowing same-sex couples to register their relationships were being passed (in 2001, the Netherlands had become the first country in the world to allow same-sex couples to marry). Clearly, there was potential for the relatively new right to freedom from discrimination based on sexual orientation to clash with the older right to freedom of religion. For example, would religious schools have to employ openly LGB teachers of subjects other than religion, such as mathematics? Would individual employees

30   Transgender Rights vs Women's Rights

with strong religious beliefs, or businesses whose owners held similar beliefs, be required to serve same-sex couples?

In February 2002, I gave a lecture at the University of Toronto entitled 'Religion v sexual orientation: a clash of human rights?'[14] I proposed that prohibitions of sexual orientation discrimination must apply to the public sphere (to public officials providing opportunities in the public sector) and to the secular private sphere (to commercial and other private-sector activities that are not inherently religious), but not to the religious private sphere (to a religious organization's decisions about who may be a religious leader or which couples it is willing to marry). I argued that 'religious individuals who accept employment in the public sector cannot insist on being exempted from serving ... same-sex couples, whether this involves selling them stamps ... or ... marrying them'. Similarly, 'Private sector ... service providers generally cannot cite their religious beliefs in denying ... [services] to ... same-sex couples' because they 'are engaged in business activities that are not inherently religious in nature'.[15]

Since 2002, judicial decisions of the ECtHR and the United Kingdom Supreme Court, and exemptions in the UK's marriage legislation, have generally followed the pattern that I proposed. In January 2013, the ECtHR ruled that a local government did not have to exempt a Christian employee from conducting civil partnership ceremonies for same-sex couples because of her religious beliefs, and could therefore dismiss her for refusing to do that part of her job.[16] In November 2013, the UK Supreme Court reached the same conclusion with regard to a private business, a Christian-owned hotel, which violated an anti-discrimination law by refusing a double-bedded room to two men who had registered a civil partnership.[17] The exception for services provided by religious organizations did not apply to the hotel, which was 'an organisation whose sole or main purpose is commercial'.[18] On the other hand, in 2013, when the UK Parliament introduced same-sex marriage in England and Wales, it made it legally impossible for the Church of England to marry a same-sex couple.[19] Other religious organizations may do so only if they choose to 'opt in'.[20] Similarly, when a Church of England priest married his same-sex partner in 2014 (in defiance of Church doctrine prohibiting priests from contracting same-sex marriages, as opposed to civil partnerships), and he was denied the licence he needed to be a hospital chaplain, the Church did not discriminate against him. The exception for 'employment . . . for the purposes of an organised religion' applied to the Church's decision.[21]

A more difficult case arose in 2014 when a Christian-owned bakery, which offered to put customers' designs on cakes (with no restrictions on the designs' content), refused the design submitted by a gay man, because it included the slogan 'Support Gay Marriage'. Like the Christian-owned hotel, the bakery did not have a right to discriminate in providing services, because its commercial purpose meant that it was not a religious organization. But would putting the slogan on the cake have been 'compelled speech'? The Northern Ireland Court of Appeal ruled that the bakery had discriminated on grounds of sexual orientation, and that the slogan would not require the bakery to promote or support gay marriage: 'The fact that a baker provides a cake for a particular [football or other] team or portrays witches on a Halloween cake does not indicate any support for either.'[22]

In October 2018, the United Kingdom Supreme Court disagreed about the presence of discrimination and the absence of 'compelled speech'. Because the bakery would have refused to put the slogan on a cake, whether the customer was heterosexual or LGB, there was no discrimination on grounds of sexual orientation.[23] (The Supreme Court did not consider whether discrimination could be based on the sexual orientation in the content of the customer's message, rather than the sexual orientation of the customer, as I argued in 2015.)[24] If there was discrimination because of the customer's political

32 Transgender Rights vs Women's Rights

opinion (which the Supreme Court doubted), it was overridden by the bakery owners' European Convention rights to freedom of religion and freedom of expression, which protect them against 'compelled speech'.[25]

In the United States, where there have been many cases about refusals to provide cakes, flowers or photographs for the marriages of same-sex couples, the Supreme Court decided an easier case in June 2018. A Christian-owned bakery refused to accept the order of two men because it did not 'make cakes for same-sex weddings'. The couple had not asked the bakery to put a slogan on their cake. Although the Court quashed the Colorado courts' conclusion that there had been sexual orientation discrimination, because the proceedings had been tainted by hostility towards religious persons, Justice Kennedy stated the general rule: '[religious] objections [to gay marriage] do not allow business owners ... to deny protected persons equal access to goods and services under a neutral and generally applicable [anti-discrimination] law'.[26] But in 2023, the Supreme Court held that a Christian-owned business has a First Amendment (freedom of expression) right to design websites for opposite-sex but not same-sex weddings. In doing so, the Supreme Court created what could become a very broad exception to Justice Kennedy's general rule: businesses may discriminate on the basis of sexual orientation if the goods and services that are refused involve 'expressive activity'.[27] The Court's commitment to this new exception will be tested if a future case involves racial discrimination, such as the refusal of a Christian-owned business to provide 'expressive services' for the wedding of a black–white couple.[28]

Jewish-Israeli human rights vs Palestinian human rights

After a visit to the Occupied West Bank in 2009, I began working on another conflict of human rights, one of the most tragic and longest running: the right of Jewish people to live in a homeland in peace and free of violence and discrimination vs the right of Palestinian people to live in a homeland in peace and free of violence and discrimination. When the British Empire conquered Palestine from the Ottoman Empire in 1918, it was not at all clear how these two rights could be reconciled in Palestine, where the population was 92 per cent Arab.[29] More than 100 years later, we are witnessing the consequences of a continuing failure by the British Empire, then the United Nations, and then the new State of Israel and its Western allies to consider 'the rights of others': those of the Arab majority in pre-1948 Palestine.[30]

Transgender human rights vs women's and children's human rights

Since 2018, I have become interested in a third conflict of human rights: the rights of transgender persons or their parents vs the rights of women or children (persons under 18). As we will see in chapter 4, in the vast majority of cases (when applying for most jobs or for university places, or when being served in a hotel or restaurant), the birth sex, the legal sex or the transgender identity of the applicant or customer is irrelevant. It does not matter whether the applicant or customer is female or male, as a matter of biology or law, or whether they identify as female or male. But in a relatively small number of situations (chapter 6), it does matter whether or not an individual can be considered a woman.

Returning to the opposing camps we saw in chapter 1, if one believes that a woman is a person whose 'true gender' or 'gender identity' is female, and that the person's birth sex is irrelevant, then there can be no conflicts between the rights of persons born male who identify as female and the rights of women. They are all women. If one believes that a woman is a

34 Transgender Rights vs Women's Rights

person whose body is female because her birth sex is female, then there is potential for conflicts when persons born male seek to enter spaces (toilets, changing rooms, hospital wards and prisons) or categories (in positive or affirmative action programmes or in sports) that are reserved for women.

The slogan 'Trans women are women' invites a misleading comparison with the hypothetical slogan 'Black women are women.' Black women are indisputably women, their skin colour being irrelevant to their inclusion in the category of 'women'. Is the same true of 'trans women', because possessing (or having possessed) male reproductive organs is irrelevant to inclusion in the category of 'women'? Spelling out the reality of the bodies of most 'trans women' makes it clear that there is a relevant physical difference (male genitals), unlike in the case of black women. If the slogan were 'male women are women', people would be more likely to spot the contradiction between 'male' and 'women' and say: 'Hold on!'

The legal question becomes whether segregation of women and men on the basis of birth sex can sometimes be justified. Or whether is it like segregation of different racial groups and should therefore be abolished in all circumstances. Sex is clearly not like race. In 1954, the US Supreme Court declared racial segregation unconstitutional, not only in schools, but in access to all public facilities, including toilets and drinking fountains.[31] Did similar challenges to sex-segregated spaces follow? No, not in the 1950s and not today, because these spaces are obviously different from racially segregated spaces: they are necessary to protect women and therefore justifiable. Anti-discrimination laws often have exceptions that clearly exclude them from the prohibition of sex discrimination.[32] In 1985, Thurgood Marshall, the first African American Justice of the US Supreme Court and a lawyer in the 1954 case on racially segregated schools, noted that a characteristic might be relevant in some circumstances but not in others: 'A sign that says "men only" looks very different on a bathroom [toilet] door than a courthouse door.'[33] By this, he meant that women may be excluded from men's toilets but not from the legal profession. Conversely, men may be excluded from women's toilets but not from the nursing profession.

Historically, the law and society have drawn a border between men and women in certain situations. Male-to-female transgender persons present a challenge to this border. Should they be able to cross it? Only if certain conditions are fulfilled? Or should the border be removed for all persons born male? Under the European Convention, this particular conflict of human rights could be described as 'the clash of the private lives'. Transgender persons have based their claims to a right to change their legal sexes on the right to 'respect for private life' in Article 8. But women can base their claims to the protection of women-only spaces on their own Article 8 right to 'respect for private life'. In chapter 5, I will consider the question of the legal border between men and women: should it be possible to cross it (by changing legal sex), what conditions should be imposed if crossing is possible, and what might be the consequences if the border were removed (if legal sex were abolished)? In chapter 6, I will ask whether, with or without a change of legal sex, male-to-female transgender persons should be permitted to enter spaces and categories that historically have been reserved for women.

In Chapter 7, I will consider a related conflict of human rights: medical treatment (puberty blockers, hormones and surgery) that seeks to change the bodies of children, who might change their minds when they turn 18. This conflict is different from those in chapters 5 and 6, in that it does not pit the rights of adult transgender persons against the rights of adult women. The conflict instead relates to the best interests of the child. On the one hand, if the child requests the medical treatment, the child's parents (supported by the 'gender-affirming' healthcare professionals proposing the treatment) will see themselves as promoting the best interests of their child by consenting to it, and will view any state interference as a violation of their right to respect for their family life (Article 8 of the European Convention). On the other hand, legislators, judges and other public officials may decide that the state has an obligation to prohibit the medical treatment, because the child cannot appreciate its long-term consequences and cannot therefore consent to it. In so doing, they can argue that they are protecting the rights of the child to bodily integrity and to a future private life (including sexual activity and potential procreation), which are protected by Articles 3 (prohibition of inhuman treatment) and 8 (private life) of the European Convention.

3

Transphobia: what is it, and what is instead protected political expression?

Before considering any specific conflicts between transgender rights and women's rights, we must establish the right to talk about these conflicts. Accusations of 'transphobia' are often used to shut down any kind of debate or discussion, by preventing defenders of women's rights from speaking at events held in public places, or by imposing employment-related and other sanctions on women who have spoken out. But does 'transphobia' include disagreement regarding how conflicts of human rights should be resolved?

The *Cambridge Dictionary* defines 'transphobia' as 'harmful or unfair things a person does based on a fear or dislike of transgender ... people'.[1] 'Transphobia' may manifest itself through anti-transgender hate crime (violence motivated by hatred of transgender persons) or hate speech (non-violent expression that incites hatred of transgender persons). The law of England and Wales on hate crimes treats 'hostility related to transgender identity' as an aggravating factor when sentencing a violent offender.[2] In Scotland (not yet England and Wales), the criminal offences of 'stirring up hatred' (hate speech) cover seven characteristics, including 'transgender identity'.[3] But most disagreement with specific transgender law-reform proposals (or with existing laws or policies) is not based on

38 Transgender Rights vs Women's Rights

any 'fear or dislike of transgender ... people' or any 'hostility related to transgender identity', and does not seek to 'stir up hatred' against transgender people. Disagreement is not hatred.

Just as there have been attempts to expand the definition of 'anti-Semitism' in ways that could include criticism of the Government of Israel's treatment of Palestinian people,[4] there have been attempts to expand the definition of 'transphobia' to include disagreement with specific law-reform proposals of the transgender-rights movement (or with existing laws or policies). The organization TransActual UK defines 'transphobia' as including 'Claiming there is a "conflict" between trans people's human rights and those of any other group', 'Using biological essentialism ['there are two immutable sexes'] to try and delegitimise trans people', 'the denial that trans women are women', 'claim[ing] that changing the law to allow trans people to change their birth certificate by signing a statutory declaration is an issue for women's rights' (see chapter 5), 'campaign[ing] to keep trans women out of women's toilets [or other single-sex spaces]' (see chapter 6) and 'claiming that trans children and young people are only "going through a phase" [and] attempting to deny [them] medical support' (see chapter 7).[5]

However offensive or hurtful some transgender-rights activists might find it, mere disagreement about these issues (including disagreement with the slogan 'Trans women are women') is entirely peaceful (there is no 'hate crime') and will generally come nowhere near the exceptional category of 'hate speech'. It will therefore constitute political expression protected by Article 10 of the European Convention on Human Rights, section 2(b) of the Canadian Charter of Rights and Freedoms, and the First Amendment to the United States Constitution (under which, unlike in Europe and Canada, there is no exceptional category of 'hate speech'). The argument that gender-critical views should be suppressed because of the sad reality that transphobic hate crimes occur[6] (just as LGB-phobic hate crimes occur) is a non sequitur: these views do not incite violence against transgender persons, so cannot be said to 'cause' transphobic hate crimes committed by third parties, most of whom are unlikely to have any knowledge of these views. Violence against transgender persons is illegal and the perpetrators should be charged, convicted and punished, but the existence of violence does not justify restrictions on political expression that does not incite violence.

An example of the problem: shutting down debate at McGill University

Until 10 January 2023, I had no personal experience of the 'no debate' position of many in the transgender-rights movement. I innocently proposed a talk at the Faculty of Law of McGill University in Montréal (where I had studied), with the title 'The sex vs. gender (identity) debate in the United Kingdom and the divorce of LGB from T'. In 2021 and 2022, I had given the same talk, focusing on the conflicts of human rights discussed in chapter 2, at universities in London, Barcelona and Bologna without incident (on each occasion there were no protesters). I assumed that a Canadian audience would be mildly interested in the current debate in the United Kingdom, but would see it as an anthropological curiosity with no relevance to Canada, a much more progressive country. I would have considered an audience of 30 to 50 people to be a huge success.

Three days before the seminar, a protest 'against McGill University's platforming of anti-trans voices' was announced on Facebook.[7] The next day, a friend drew my attention to the 'Open letter on McGill's platforming of TERFs ['trans-exclusionary radical feminists']'.[8] According to the letter's authors, by hosting my talk, 'McGill University [was] actively contributing to the genocide of trans people across the world.

40 Transgender Rights vs Women's Rights

... [E]very extra minute of airtime given to an anti-trans activist ... will contribute to the premature deaths of trans people worldwide.' By the morning of the seminar, newspapers were reporting that 'Trans activists plan protest against controversial speaker at McGill'[9] and that 'Demonstrators want to challenge the visit of a speaker judged transphobic'.[10]

When I arrived for the seminar, between 100 and 200 protesters, mainly students, had gathered outside the seminar room, blocking access for people who wanted to hear what I had to say. Videos captured the scene inside and outside the Faculty of Law building.[11] As I tried to enter the seminar room, protesters shouted: 'Shame on you!' Once I was inside, they chanted: 'Fuck your system! Fuck your hate! Trans rights aren't up for debate!' They were trying to drown me out from outside the room, so I had to speak as loudly as I could. After I had spoken for 15 or 20 minutes, protesters who had been pushing on the door succeeded in breaking into the room. One of them disconnected the video projector, so that my outline disappeared from the screen. They stood chanting. I was escorted to a side door. One of them threw flour on me. I sought refuge in the Dean's office until the mob dispersed.

The invasion of a university seminar room was an authoritarian and completely undemocratic breakdown of law and order that showed contempt for the Canadian Charter right to freedom of expression. But the protesters' attempt to silence me backfired spectacularly (as censorship often does). If they had ignored my seminar, or attended and participated in a civilized way during the question-and-answer period, my message would probably have reached no more than 50 people.

Instead, while seeking refuge in the Dean's office, I was interviewed by the CBC (public) and CTV (private) television networks. I said: 'I came to McGill with a controversial message: women have human rights too, but most women are afraid to speak up, because of the intimidation of the transgender-rights movement. The protesters gave me a first-hand experience of

Transphobia

this intimidation.' Five days later, after returning to London, I was interviewed by GB News ('Trans protestors SHUT DOWN university talk on women's rights'). As of 1 September 2024, the interview had been viewed more than 136,000 times on YouTube.[12] The protesters certainly strengthened my motivation to write this book. Six days after the seminar, I learned that my book proposal had been accepted.

Later, I was told that some of the opponents feared that I would 'indoctrinate' those who attended the seminar. It had not occurred to me, before the seminar, that my 'foreign' ideas might be seen as 'dangerous', because they might 'contaminate' the Canadian consensus on transgender issues. Indeed, some might have agreed with me that there are conflicts with women's rights that need to be discussed. I hope that the media attention[13] triggered by the protest made a small contribution to starting the same kind of debate in Canada that exists in the UK. I received messages of support, including these two:

> I am a [female] McGill student . . . the student body was incredibly hostile towards you, but there are many of us who are thankful for your bravery. . . . Thank you again for standing up for your beliefs; there are many of us who would like to agree with you but can't risk the backlash.

> I am writing to thank you and show my support regarding the debate around sex and gender that was to take place at McGill . . . As a black bisexual woman advocating for the protection of women's rights against gender ideology, I applaud you for organizing such an event and for all your work.

Why do many students today not understand the importance of freedom of expression?

In a democratic society, if there is disagreement about existing or proposed laws and policies, there must be debate, even if

42   Transgender Rights vs Women's Rights

that means hurting the feelings of people on one or both sides. The ECtHR made this clear in the *Handyside* v. *UK* case in 1976: 'Freedom of expression constitutes one of the essential foundations of [a democratic] society . . . it is applicable not only to "information" or "ideas" that are favourably received or regarded as inoffensive . . ., but also to those that offend, shock or disturb the State or any sector of the population.'[14] For over 50 years, the United States Supreme Court has also protected expression that many people consider 'offensive', including wearing a jacket with the slogan 'Fuck the Draft'[15] and burning the US flag.[16] In 2011, the Court upheld the right to protest near a soldier's funeral with signs that included 'Thank God for Dead Soldiers':

> speech cannot be restricted simply because it is upsetting or arouses contempt. 'If there is a bedrock principle underlying the First Amendment, it is that the government may not prohibit the expression of an idea simply because society finds the idea itself offensive or disagreeable.' . . . Indeed, 'the point of all speech protection . . . is to shield just those choices of content that in someone's eyes are misguided, or even hurtful'.[17]

In 2017, Justice Kennedy stated the principle in this way: 'A law that can be directed against speech found offensive to some portion of the public can be turned against minority and dissenting views to the detriment of all. The First Amendment does not entrust that power to the government's benevolence. Instead, our reliance must be on the substantial safeguards of free and open discussion in a democratic society.'[18]

In November 2021, as I prepared to give my talk for the first time, I asked myself: 'What has changed since *Handyside* in 1976? Why do many of today's students and activists not understand why it is important to respect the expression of their opponents, even if they consider it offensive?' I found a helpful explanation in Greg Lukianoff and Jonathan Haidt's

2018 book *The Coddling of the American Mind.*[19] In particular, they discuss 'the Great Untruth of Us Versus Them: Life is a battle between good people and evil people', which is prevalent among the generation that grew up with smartphones and social media. Seeing their opponents as 'evil' can make students and activists believe that their opponents must be silenced.

I found another helpful explanation in Helen Pluckrose and James Lindsay's 2020 book *Cynical Theories*, which examines the conflict between increasingly influential Postmodern Theory (rejecting the existence of objective truth or reality) and traditional Liberalism (which, like the *Handyside* judgment, defends freedom of expression and 'encourages disagreement and debate as means to getting at the truth').[20] The authors observe that 'we now have Social Justice texts . . . that express, with absolute certainty, that . . . sex is not biological and exists on a spectrum, language can be literal violence, [and] denial of gender identity is killing people'.[21] They also note:

> While universities in Western countries are supposed to be ardent defenders of liberal values such as freedom of debate, they are becoming increasingly bureaucratized, with power being taken away from professors and transferred to administrators – and increasingly being run like profit-oriented businesses. University administrators are as sensitive to public relations as corporate executives . . . the protection of academic freedom is frequently not the highest priority.[22]

In September 2021, *The Economist* warned of 'The threat from the illiberal left',[23] while in November 2022, the *Guardian* reported on the phenomenon of 'young illiberal progressives': 'Close to half of those surveyed [in the 13–24 age group] . . . think some people deserve to be "cancelled", . . . and more than a quarter say they have "very little tolerance for people with beliefs I disagree with"'.[24] Responding to the charge of

44 Transgender Rights vs Women's Rights

'intolerance', one younger journalist commented: 'While ... many [younger people] believe that cancellations go too far, I think there is some truth to the notion that we have less patience in the realm of debate. It might be that the way social media structures our social lives – where people can be "blocked" – has bled out into real-world attitudes.'[25]

In September 2022, in his book *The New Puritans: How the Religion of Social Justice Captured the Western World*, Andrew Doyle described 'the new puritans':

> '[A]ll ... [Trans Exclusionary Radical Feminists] are white supremacists' makes little sense. ... [But] outright bigotry and intolerance of dissent ... [are] characteristic of the new puritans. This is because the various branches of Critical Social Justice activism ... are all underpinned by a form of identitarianism. ... In these circles, there is no distinction between the racist, the sexist, the homophobe, the transphobe; each designation implies the other. One may as well use the term 'sinner' and leave it there.[26]

In 2023, there were several signs of growing resistance to 'cancel culture' and support for academic freedom at universities. In April, the Council on Academic Freedom was founded at Harvard University:

> The reason that a truth-seeking institution [like a university] must sanctify free expression is straightforward. No one is infallible or omniscient. ... The only way that our species has managed to learn and progress is by a process of conjecture and refutation: Some people venture ideas, others probe whether they are sound, and in the long run the better ideas prevail. Any community that disables this cycle by repressing disagreement is doomed to chain itself to error, as we are reminded by the many historical episodes in which authorities enforced dogmas that turned out to be flat wrong.[27]

In May, a younger writer spoke out against the 'Fear and self-censorship in higher education' that she had recently experienced:

> For a generation so keen on displaying individualism through gender identity, we are paradoxically terrified of being seen as different [in our opinions]. . . . Even if something is deemed unnerving or objectionable, isn't it more productive to debate – to seek and find common ground . . . – than to attack and punish others for differences of opinion and experience? If conversation is avoided or shut down, progress becomes hopeless. If, on the other hand, we are able to discuss and disagree, we can move past fear towards a healthier body politic.[28]

And in October, Greg Lukianoff and Rikki Schlott published *The Canceling of the American Mind*, a study of 'cancel culture', focusing on US universities. They unveil 'the Great Untruth of *Ad Hominem*: Bad people only have bad opinions'. One of their case studies examines the conduct of student protesters when a federal judge (seen as having conservative opinions) was invited to speak at Stanford Law School on 9 March 2023. The Dean of Stanford Law School sent a letter to the judge apologizing for the disruption of his speech by some students: 'Freedom of speech is a bedrock principle for the law school, the university, and a democratic society, and we can and must do better to ensure that it continues even in polarized times.'[29] She also announced that there would be 'a mandatory half-day session . . . for all students on the topic of freedom of speech and the norms of the legal profession'.[30]

The obligation to protect controversial expression

For the ECtHR, the fact that a speaker's views are considered 'offensive' by some, or are otherwise unpopular, does not

46 Transgender Rights vs Women's Rights

justify state interference with an event. On the contrary, the Court declared, in a 1988 case in which 'pro-choice' (of abortion) counter-demonstrators disrupted a march by 'pro-life' (anti-abortion) doctors in Austria, that public officials have a positive obligation (an obligation to take action) to protect events at which unpopular views are expressed:

> A demonstration may annoy or give offence to persons opposed to the ideas or claims that it is seeking to promote. The participants must, however, be able to hold the demonstration without having to fear that they will be subjected to physical violence by their opponents; such a fear would be liable to deter . . . groups . . . from openly expressing their opinions on highly controversial issues affecting the community. *In a democracy the right to counter-demonstrate cannot extend to inhibiting the exercise of the right to demonstrate.*[31]

Under the European Convention, there is clearly no right to shut down a meeting because one disagrees with the views being expressed at that meeting. The same is true in the US under the First Amendment, as Professor Erwin Chemerinsky explained in 2010 (and again in 2022):[32]

> Freedom of speech, on campuses and elsewhere, is rendered meaningless if speakers can be shouted down by those who disagree. The law is well established that the government can act to prevent a heckler's veto – to prevent the reaction of the audience from silencing the speaker. There is simply no 1st Amendment right to go into an auditorium and prevent a speaker from being heard, no matter who the speaker is or how strongly one disagrees with his or her message.[33]

Failure to provide adequate security for gender-critical events can affect those held indoors, such as the McGill seminar or a screening of the documentary film *Adult Human*

Female[34] at the University of Edinburgh, which was cancelled after transgender-rights activists occupied entrances to the venue and university security staff refused to intervene.[35] It can also affect events held outdoors in parks and other public spaces. These events are particularly vulnerable to physical attacks by protesters, as a video has documented.[36] For events held outdoors, it is often the police who fail to provide adequate security. On 22 May 2023, Reem Alsalem, the United Nations Special Rapporteur on violence against women and girls,[37] issued a statement on attempts to silence women with gender-critical views:

> Law enforcement agencies should ensure women's safety and rights to freedom of assembly and speech . . . Whereas counter-protesters also have [these rights] . . ., law enforcement must ensure that [they are] not exercised in a manner that prevents women from exercising their rights . . ., whether through threats, intimidation, or . . . violence, [or] where women's speech is . . . silenced by loud counter-protests. There is a positive legal obligation [on public authorities] to protect women . . ., including by keeping counter-protesters at a distance that is safe, and enabl[ing] women's speech to be audible. . . . Women and girls [and their male allies] who . . . engage in discussions around the definitions of sex[,] gender, and gender identity and the interaction of rights derived from these . . . should . . . be able to express themselves and their concerns . . . in safety and in dignity.[38]

In December 2021, the Law Commission recommended that the prohibitions of 'stirring up hatred' (hate speech) in England and Wales – which currently cover race, religion, disability and sexual orientation – be extended to include transgender identity, as well as 'sex or gender'.[39] The Commission's report also recommended that 'in extending the stirring up offences to cover hatred towards trans or gender diverse people, a new

48 Transgender Rights vs Women's Rights

protection should be introduced for [the] view that sex is binary and immutable, and the use of language which expresses this'.[40] In other words, hate speech should be prohibited, both against transgender people and against people holding gender-critical views.

Freedom of expression and employment

An employee expressing gender-critical views on social media will not generally be at risk of immediate physical attack, as opposed to a hostile response from other social media users who disagree with her or him. But she or he might find that her or his co-workers, feeling offended, have reported these views to their common employer who, agreeing with the co-workers, considers the views unacceptable and dismisses the employee. As mentioned at the start of chapter 1, this happened to Maya Forstater in London in December 2018. She lost her job for posting 'offensive' tweets such as: 'I think that male people are not women. I don't think being a woman/female is a matter of identity or womanly feelings. It is biology.'[41] An Italian friend compared her to Galileo, who was sentenced to house arrest by the Roman Inquisition in 1633 for saying that the earth revolves around the sun (rather than the other way around).

Because she worked for a private-sector employer, Ms Forstater could not invoke her right to freedom of expression under Article 10 of the European Convention and the UK's Human Rights Act 1998. That right can only be invoked against a public-sector employer (as is the case with the First Amendment in the US). So Ms Forstater challenged the non-renewal of her contract by relying on the prohibition of discrimination because of 'religion or belief' in the Equality Act 2010, which is defined broadly as including 'any ... philosophical belief'.[42] The Employment Tribunal dismissed her claim, finding that her belief that 'Being female is an immutable biological fact, not a feeling or an identity' was not protected by the Equality Act because it is 'not worthy of respect in a democratic society' (one of the requirements for the protection of a belief).[43]

When I read the Employment Tribunal's judgment, the errors in its legal reasoning were obvious to me. The judge had failed to distinguish between Ms Forstater's belief (expressed outside her workplace) and her action or conduct (in her workplace). Instead, the judge assumed that she would inevitably act on her belief in the workplace by harassing transgender co-workers and customers, even though there was no evidence that she had ever done so, or any reason to believe that she would do so in the future. The judge also put her belief 'at the same level as Holocaust denial or incitement to violence', as I wrote in a comment criticizing the Employment Tribunal's reasoning.[44] Echoing the Tribunal, on 18 May 2021, the head of Stonewall, the UK's largest LGBT-rights organization, compared anti-Semitic views with gender-critical views: 'With . . . controversial beliefs there is a right to express those beliefs publicly and where they're harmful or damaging – whether it's anti-Semitic beliefs, gender critical beliefs . . . – we have legal systems that are put in place for people who are harmed by that.'[45]

On 10 June 2021, the Employment Appeal Tribunal (EAT) found in favour of Ms Forstater: 'the gender-critical belief' is 'worthy of respect in a democratic society' and protected for all employees by the Equality Act 2010 (and for public-sector employees by the Human Rights Act 1998).[46] The EAT ruled, as I argued in my comment: (i) that the Equality Act 2010 'is concerned only with whether a person *has* the protected characteristic by being *of* the . . . belief in question, and not with whether a person *does* anything pursuant to that . . . belief'; and (ii) that 'it is only those beliefs that would be an affront to [European] Convention principles in a manner akin to . . . advocating Nazism, or espousing violence . . . that should be

50 Transgender Rights vs Women's Rights

capable of being not worthy of respect in a democratic society'.[47] Implicitly adopting the distinction between belief and action or conduct that I made in my comment, the EAT warned that its conclusion did not mean 'that those with gender-critical beliefs can indiscriminately and gratuitously refer to trans persons [in the workplace] in terms other than they would wish. Such conduct could, depending on the circumstances, amount to harassment of, or discrimination against, a trans person.'[48]

Ms Forstater's case returned to a different Employment Tribunal, which concluded that she had suffered direct discrimination (disparate treatment) because of her gender-critical belief when her contract was not renewed.[49] She was awarded compensation and interest in the amount of £106,000.[50] The EAT's *Forstater* judgment probably caused the University of Sussex belatedly to support its employee, the lesbian and gender-critical philosophy professor Kathleen Stock, when students called for her dismissal, but the campus environment was so hostile that she resigned in October 2021.[51] The judgment has been applied in several subsequent cases in which women expressed gender-critical beliefs.[52]

Disagreement is neither hatred nor an existential threat

After working on Palestinian human rights for several years, I became used to the fact that many supporters of Israel consider me 'anti-Semitic', because of the way I analyse the situation in Israel–Palestine. Since 2018, when I began to become aware of conflicts between transgender rights and women's rights, I have experienced a sense of 'déjà vu'. I have learned that many in the transgender-rights movement consider me 'transphobic' for even suggesting that there could be conflicts between transgender rights and women's rights. I have also noticed, in both contexts, references to 'rights to exist', which are threatened by disagreement.

What do these two contexts (Israel–Palestine, transgender persons – women) have in common? The pattern I have observed is: (i) 'victimhood' (one group focuses unduly on its own past or present suffering), which leads to (ii) 'unreasonable demands' (the group's demands fail to take into account the rights of others), which lead to (iii) 'accusations of hatred' (when third parties disagree with the group's unreasonable demands).

Returning to the conflicts of human rights discussed in chapter 2, was it 'LGB-phobic' to oppose same-sex marriage before it was introduced in a particular country? I would argue that it was not. Allowing same-sex couples to marry was a significant change to an important legal and social institution, about which many heterosexual people had legitimate concerns, for religious and non-religious reasons. Opposing same-sex marriage, and preferring an alternative registration system (such as civil partnership, civil union or registered partnership) did not imply any 'fear or dislike' of LGB individuals or same-sex couples. The concerns of many heterosexual people have been allayed as more and more countries in Europe and the Americas (along with South Africa, Taiwan, Thailand, Australia and New Zealand) have changed their marriage laws, with no negative effects on society.

Is it 'LGB-phobic' or 'Christian-phobic' to disagree about where lines should be drawn when Christian-owned businesses do not wish to serve same-sex couples? Once again, I would argue that it is neither. Reasonable people may differ about where these lines should be drawn. Indeed, in the Northern Ireland 'Support Gay Marriage' cake case, some LGB people supported the gay customer, while others supported the Christian-owned bakery. And the prominent LGB-rights advocate Professor Andrew Koppelman (author of *Gay Rights vs. Religious Liberty? The Unnecessary Conflict*) would grant more leeway to Christian-owned businesses than I would.

52   Transgender Rights vs Women's Rights

Is it 'anti-Semitic/anti-Jewish/Judeophobic' to defend Palestinian human rights? Bernie Steinberg, the former executive director of Harvard Hillel (an organization for Jewish students at Harvard University), recently put it this way:

> Let me speak plainly: It is not antisemitic to demand justice for all Palestinians living in their ancestral lands. The activists who employ this language, and the politics of liberation, are sincere people; their cause is a legitimate and important movement dissenting against the brutal treatment of Palestinians that has been ongoing for 75 years. ... If Israel's cause is just, let it speak eloquently in its own defense. It is very telling that some of Israel's own supporters instead go to extraordinary lengths to utterly silence the other side. Smearing one's opponents is rarely a tactic employed by those confident that justice is on their side. If Israel's case requires branding its critics antisemites, it is already conceding defeat.[53]

Mr Steinberg's comment applies with equal force to the transgender-rights movement. Those who have strong arguments, who are 'confident that justice is on their side', have no need to shut down debate or to smear their opponents as 'transphobic'.

Just as disagreement should not be equated with hatred of a group, it should not be seen as a threat to the group's existence. With regard to Israel–Palestine, one hears frequent references to Israel's 'right to exist'. No reasonable person is questioning the human right to life of every Jewish resident of the territories controlled by Israel. The question is *where* Israel has a 'right to exist' (within which borders) and *who* may be denied Israeli citizenship within those borders.

In the transgender context, the LGBT-rights organization Stonewall responded as follows to a 2018 petition calling on it to reconsider its approach to transgender rights: 'The petition ... asks us to acknowledge that there is a conflict between trans rights and "sex based women's rights". We do not and will not acknowledge this. ... We will always debate issues that enable us to further equality but what we will not do is debate *trans people's rights to exist*.'[54] It was claimed that my McGill seminar would contribute to 'the genocide of trans people across the world'. In a video of the protesters inside the Faculty of Law building, one of them can be heard exclaiming: 'You're erasing my existence!'[55]

The analogy I thought of (while in Montréal) is one person complaining to another: 'You're standing on my foot.' The reaction of the other person: 'You hate me and want to kill me! That's why you're complaining about my standing on your foot!' The first person replies: 'No, I do not hate you and I do not want to kill you. I just want to discuss how we can get your foot moved off my foot. The exercise of your rights is affecting my rights.' This reaction is experienced, in a very similar fashion, by defenders of Palestinian human rights (the reaction comes from supporters of Israel) and by defenders of women's rights (the reaction comes from the transgender-rights movement).

At this point, I hope that I have persuaded most, if not all, readers that one can, rationally and in good faith, with no 'fear or dislike' of transgender people (so without being 'transphobic'), raise potential conflicts between transgender rights and women's rights. After examining the rarely discussed 'common ground' in chapter 4, we can turn to the specific conflicts in chapters 5, 6 and 7.

4

Common ground: transgender rights that are not questioned

For some supporters of Israel, either you support all the poli-cies of the Government of Israel or you support the second genocide of the Jewish people. There is no middle position. For some transgender-rights activists (such as those who called on McGill University to cancel my seminar), either you sup-port all transgender demands or you support the genocide of transgender people around the world.

This is, of course, absurd. There are many middle posi-tions, both with regard to Israel–Palestine and with regard to transgender rights. What has struck me about conflicts between transgender rights and women's rights is that they concern a relatively small number of situations. In the vast majority of cases in which a transgender individual asserts a right, there is no conflict with the rights of women or any other group. These situations are what I call the large areas of 'common ground', in which transgender rights are not questioned (by most people in liberal democracies), and with regard to which there is agreement. These areas of agree-ment are rarely discussed, because the areas of disagreement monopolize our attention. But it is important to consider these areas of agreement before we examine the areas of

Common ground 55

conflict, so that we can put the areas of conflict into perspective.

Freedom from all forms of physical violence or harassment

Everyone has a human right to life (a right not to be killed by public officials or private individuals) and a right not to be subjected to physical violence. In the European Convention on Human Rights, these rights are found in Article 2 (right to life) and Article 3 (right to be free from 'torture or inhuman or degrading treatment or punishment'). They can also be found in other international human rights treaties and in national constitutions. They are generally given effect in every country through criminal laws against murder and assault or harassment. These human rights and these criminal laws apply, and have always applied, to transgender persons. Of course, the fact that violence against transgender persons is always illegal does not mean that it does not occur. As with other forms of violence, the questions are whether law enforcement officials take crimes against transgender persons seriously, and what action can be taken to prevent such crimes.

The 2011 case of *Halat* v. *Türkiye* in the ECtHR provides an example of a government's substantive obligation not to subject a transgender person to violence, and its procedural obligation to investigate a credible allegation of violence against a transgender person.[1] The applicant, a male-to-female transgender person, claimed that she[2] had been arrested and detained at a police station in Istanbul for eight hours. A police officer, who had accused her of engaging in prostitution at her home, insulted her and harassed her physically and verbally. He placed a baton on her genitals and her chest, forced her to show him her breasts, and ordered her to leave her home and the neighbourhood. He also threatened to kill her and

56   Transgender Rights vs Women's Rights

throw her body in a forest. He hit her on the hands, back and buttocks.[3] The Turkish Government argued that she had not in fact been arrested, that she had been unable to identify the police officer (who denied that the ill-treatment had occurred), and that the only evidence (apart from a hospital's medical reports) was the applicant's testimony.[4]

Faced with this factual dispute as to whether the detention and ill-treatment had occurred, a majority of five of seven judges of the European Court found the evidence insufficient and deferred to the Turkish courts, which had acquitted the police officer.[5] However, the majority ruled that the applicant's Article 3 procedural right to an 'effective investigation' of her complaint had been violated, because the entire process took over eight years, and because the initial investigation was not sufficiently independent of the local police.[6] The majority awarded her 15,000 euros in compensation.[7] The two dissenting judges held that the evidence of a friend waiting outside corroborated the applicant's claim that she had been detained at the police station. The burden of proof lay with the Turkish Government to explain why the applicant left the police station with physical injuries she did not have when she arrived there. It had failed to do so. Her substantive Article 3 right not to be subjected to 'inhuman or degrading treatment' had therefore also been violated.

The human right of transgender persons not to be subjected to violence (including more serious forms of physical harassment) is not in doubt. I am not aware of any gender-critical woman, man or organization that advocates any form of violence against transgender persons, let alone genocide.

Other unquestioned human rights of transgender persons

What are other unquestioned human rights of transgender persons? They include criminal-procedure rights and democratic

Common ground 57

rights. A transgender person has a right not to be arrested unless there is reasonable suspicion that they have committed a crime, a right to be brought promptly before a judge (who reviews the evidence justifying detention) and a right to a fair criminal trial. In searching for evidence to justify an arrest and a criminal charge, the police must respect the person's private life, home and correspondence, which will often require them to obtain a search warrant from a judge. In the European Convention, these rights are found in Articles 5, 6 and 8.

Like LGB and other persons, transgender persons have democratic rights to freedom of expression (including by electronic means), peaceful assembly (indoor and outdoor meetings of groups) and freedom of association (forming organizations). In the European Convention, these rights are found in Articles 10 and 11. In a democracy, these human rights allow transgender persons (and their allies) to organize political campaigns to change or defend existing laws and policies. In the 2010 *Alekseyev* v. *Russia* case, which concerned the City of Moscow's refusal to allow a Pride March, the ECtHR stressed how important these democratic rights are:

> the absence of a European consensus on [same-sex marriage and adoption] is of no relevance to the present case because *conferring substantive rights on homosexual persons is fundamentally different from recognising their right to campaign for such rights.* There is no ambiguity about the other member States' recognition of the right of individuals to openly identify themselves as gay, lesbian or any other sexual minority, and to promote their rights and freedoms, in particular by exercising their freedom of peaceful assembly.[8]

In the United States, the same rights of expression, assembly and association are guaranteed by the First Amendment.

58   Transgender Rights vs Women's Rights

Criminal law

Same-sex sexual activity cannot be criminalized, under the 1981 *Dudgeon* v. *UK* judgment of the ECtHR,[9] and the 2003 *Lawrence & Garner* v. *Texas* judgment of the US Supreme Court.[10] These judgments benefit transgender persons whose sexual activity would legally be considered same-sex.

Freedom from discrimination in employment and other areas (if birth sex is not relevant)

Like women and minorities (including LGB persons), transgender persons need legal protection against discrimination in employment, housing, education and access to goods and services, so that they can be open about their transgender identity and enjoy equal opportunities in society. Fortunately, most of the required legal protection already exists in most of Europe, the USA and Canada. It takes the form of anti-discrimination laws, applying to public and private organizations and individuals, that either prohibit discrimination because of 'gender identity' or 'gender reassignment', or prohibit discrimination because of 'sex', which has been interpreted as covering discrimination against transgender persons. In Canada – starting in 2002, but mainly from 2012 to 2017 – the federal government and all 13 provinces and territories amended their anti-discrimination laws by adding 'gender identity'.[11]

A 1996 case, known as *P.* v. *S. & Cornwall County Council*, caused the European Union and its (now 27) member states to take the sex-discrimination route. P. was a male-to-female transgender person who worked as a manager at an educational establishment run by a local government. Her birth sex (male) was not relevant to her job. Five months after informing her boss (S.) that she intended to undergo gender

Common ground

59

reassignment, P. was told that her employment would come to an end about three months later. She complained to an Industrial (now Employment) Tribunal, which referred her case to the highest court of the European Union, the Court of Justice in Luxembourg.

P. argued that her dismissal was sex discrimination in employment and therefore prohibited by a 1976 EU law.[12] The Tribunal asked the Court of Justice whether EU law on 'discrimination on grounds of sex prohibits treatment of an employee on the grounds of the employee's transsexual state'. The UK Government argued that it was not sex discrimination because the employer would also have dismissed a female-to-male transgender person, making the sex of the employee irrelevant. The dismissal was based on the fact of undergoing gender reassignment, not on sex. The Court of Justice rejected this argument, holding that 'discrimination arising... from... gender reassignment . . . is based, essentially if not exclusively, on the sex of the person concerned'. P. had been treated unfavourably compared with a non-transgender male who was not undergoing gender reassignment.[13]

The *P.* judgment had the dramatic effect of immediately prohibiting employment discrimination against transgender persons in 15 (now 27) EU countries. That effect was extended when a 2004 law prohibited sex discrimination in access to most goods and services (from late 2007).[14] For LGB persons, protection took longer and is not as broad. In 1998, the Court of Justice refused to apply the prohibition of sex discrimination in employment to a case of sexual orientation discrimination (no free travel benefits for the unmarried female partner of a female employee even though the unmarried female partner of a male employee was eligible).[15] Instead, a separate law had to be passed in 2000, which has prohibited sexual orientation discrimination in employment since late 2003.[16] As for access to goods and services (such as hotels and restaurants), a 2008 proposal for an EU law prohibiting discrimination based on

60   Transgender Rights vs Women's Rights

religion, disability, age and sexual orientation in this area has yet to be adopted.[17]

After the *P.* judgment, the UK did not need to amend its laws prohibiting sex discrimination. It would have been enough for UK courts to interpret 'sex' as covering 'gender reassignment'. But, in 1999, the UK Government decided to amend its laws by adding 'gender reassignment' as a separate prohibited ground (or protected characteristic).[18] 'Gender reassignment' now appears in the Equality Act 2010, which consolidated prior laws.

The question of whether 'sex' can cover 'gender identity/ reassignment' or 'sexual orientation' was addressed by the CJEU in 1996 and 1998, but did not reach the US Supreme Court until the case of *Bostock* v. *Clayton County*, decided on 15 June 2020.[19] The legal and political context of the case is important. At the time of the judgment, only 22 of 50 states had passed laws expressly prohibiting sexual orientation discrimination in public-sector and private-sector employment[20] (slightly fewer states had done so for gender identity). In states with no such laws, a patchwork of city and county laws provided some protection. In the federal Congress, beginning in 1974, attempts had been made to amend the federal Civil Rights Act of 1964 (which covers race, religion and sex) by adding sexual orientation (and later gender identity). As of June 2020, there was still no prospect of a bill being passed. Instead, LGB and transgender employees who had been dismissed (especially those with no protection under state, city or county law) turned to the prohibition of employment discrimination based on sex in Title VII of the Civil Rights Act of 1964. Could it be interpreted as applying to cases of discrimination based on sexual orientation and gender identity? Along with Professor Andrew Koppelman, I had argued since 1994 that cases of sexual orientation discrimination, correctly analysed, are also cases of sex discrimination.[21]

Common ground   61

By six votes to three, the US Supreme Court accepted the sex-discrimination argument in *Bostock*, which combined the cases of two gay men (Gerald Bostock and Donald Zarda) and one male-to-female transgender person (Aimee Stephens), all of whom had been dismissed from their jobs. In Ms Stephen's case, her birth sex (male) did not appear to be in any way relevant to her job as a funeral director at a funeral home. Like the *P.* judgment, *Bostock* had the dramatic effect of immediately prohibiting employment discrimination, not only against transgender persons, but also against LGB persons, in all 50 states.

Justice Gorsuch, writing for the majority, explained their conclusion:

> An employer who fires an individual for being homosexual or transgender fires that person for traits or actions it would not have questioned in members of a different sex. Sex plays a necessary and undisguisable role in the decision, exactly what Title VII forbids. . . . [I]t is impossible to discriminate against a person for being homosexual or transgender without discriminating against that individual based on sex.[22]

What are the 'traits or actions [an employer] would not have questioned in members of a different sex'? With regard to sexual orientation, this means that an employer may not dismiss men who are attracted to men (while retaining women who are attracted to men), and may not dismiss women who are attracted to women (while retaining men who are attracted to women). If attraction to men is permitted for women, it must be permitted for men. If attraction to women is permitted for men, it must be permitted for women. With regard to transgender persons, Justice Gorsuch implies that an employer may not dismiss a male-to-female transgender person for presenting as female at work (a person born male must be permitted the same 'traits or actions' as a person born female), and may not dismiss a female-to-male transgender person for presenting as male at work (a person born female must be permitted the same 'traits or actions' as a person born male).

But does *Bostock* make the birth sex of a transgender person irrelevant in all circumstances? Justice Gorsuch stressed the narrow scope of the Supreme Court's decision: 'The employers ... say sex-segregated bathrooms, locker rooms, and dress codes will prove unsustainable after our decision today. ... Under Title VII, ... we do not purport to address bathrooms, locker rooms, or anything else of the kind.'[23] He left these issues to be decided in future cases. In his dissent, Justice Alito criticized the majority for a judgment that looked like 'legislation' (amending Title VII rather than interpreting 'sex' as it was understood in 1964), and for refusing to consider the potential consequences of the transgender part of its decision for bathrooms, locker rooms, women's sports, and single-sex university housing.[24]

To summarize, transgender persons have more rights under EU law than LGB persons (discrimination in access to goods and services is prohibited if it is based on sex, including gender reassignment, but not yet if it is based on sexual orientation) or obtained them earlier (in 1996 rather than 2003 in the case of protection against employment discrimination). In the US, under Title VII of the federal Civil Rights Act of 1964, transgender persons and LGB persons obtained the same protection against employment discrimination in 2020. Neither group enjoys federal protection against discrimination in access to goods and services because the 1964 Act's Title II (on places of public accommodation) only applies to race and religion, not sex.

Less serious forms of physical or verbal harassment, which might not trigger a criminal prosecution, could be characterized as discrimination, both under EU law (which expressly states that harassment is a form of discrimination)[25] and under Title VII (judicial decisions have treated harassment as a form of discrimination).[26] If birth sex is relevant to a particular job

Common ground 63

(attendant in a women's locker room, guard in a women's prison), an employer might be able to justify refusing to hire a male-to-female transgender person (whose birth sex is male) because female birth sex is a 'genuine and determining occupational requirement' (EU law)[27] or a 'bona fide occupational qualification' (Title VII).[28] Situations in which birth sex is relevant will be considered in chapter 6.

Family law

Under both the European Convention on Human Rights and the United States Constitution, LGB and transgender persons are probably entitled to the same rights in family law. There are more judicial decisions with regard to LGB persons, but there is generally no reason to believe that these would not also apply to transgender persons. In the 2000s, transgender persons and their partners were arguably in a better position with regard to marriage. After the 2002 *Christine Goodwin* v. *UK* judgment of the ECtHR,[29] a couple in which one partner was transgender always had the right to marry. If they were a same-sex couple (based on birth sex), they had the right to become a legally opposite-sex couple (through a change of legal sex for the transgender partner). If they were an opposite-sex couple (based on birth sex), they could still marry (or remain married), by declining to exercise the right of the transgender partner to change their legal sex.[30] The same was true in any US state that permitted a change of legal sex. But, before 2010, LGB same-sex couples (in which neither partner is transgender) could not marry in most EU countries and US states.

Since 2010, the situation has improved greatly. LGB same-sex couples can marry in all 50 US states, as a result of the *Obergefell* v. *Hodges* judgment of the US Supreme Court in 2015,[31] and have a right to register their relationships (it does not yet have to be called a marriage) in all 46 Council

64   Transgender Rights vs Women's Rights

of Europe countries, as a result of the *Fedotova & Others* v. *Russia* judgment of the ECtHR in 2023.[32] (Of those countries, 22 call it a marriage.) While decisions allowing transgender persons to enter opposite-sex marriages did not benefit LGB same-sex couples, the converse is not true. Decisions allowing LGB same-sex couples to marry benefit transgender persons, because they make birth sex and legal sex irrelevant with regard to marriage. In countries that do not yet allow LGB same-sex couples to marry, a couple in which one partner is transgender has a choice: decline to exercise the transgender person's right to change their legal sex, so that the couple can marry (or remain married), or 'downgrade' to the alternative institution that is open to LGB same-sex couples ('civil partnership', 'civil union' or 'registered partnership').[33]

As for parental rights, judgments of the ECtHR have upheld the rights of LGB persons to be considered for custody of (or contact with) their own genetic children (without their sexual orientation being treated as a negative factor),[34] to adopt an unrelated child as an unmarried individual,[35] and to adopt their same-sex partner's genetic child.[36] The right to be considered for custody of (or contact with) one's genetic child has been extended to transgender persons.[37] There is no reason to believe that the rights relating to adoption would not also be extended to transgender persons in appropriate cases. The same is true in the US, where additional adoption rights are protected: the constitutional right of LGB same-sex couples to marry in all 50 states includes the right to adopt unrelated children jointly.

Freedom of 'gender expression' (choices of clothing, hairstyle, jewellery and make-up)

It seems implicit in the *P.* judgment in EU law, and the *Bostock* judgment in Title VII law, that a male-to-female transgender employee has the right to wear clothing, hairstyles, jewellery and make-up associated with women (and vice versa for a female-to-male transgender employee). This interpretation of what a prohibition of sex discrimination requires is narrow, because it creates an exemption from the general rule (compliance with sex-specific dress codes) for transgender employees. But should the general rule be abolished? Is it not long past time for appellate courts to declare that sex-specific dress codes are a form of direct sex discrimination? Any item of clothing or jewellery, any hairstyle, and any type of make-up that is considered acceptable for employees of one sex should be considered acceptable for employees of the opposite sex. A clear rule of this kind would benefit all employees and not require an exemption for transgender employees.

Since I published an article in 1997, part of which dealt with dress codes,[38] I have supported the right of any person, regardless of birth sex, to wear any form of clothing, jewellery or make-up, or choose any hairstyle, that is available to a person of the opposite sex. Because I support this right, I have never seen the need for a separate concept of 'gender expression' for transgender persons. Dress codes perpetuate 'social gender'. Abolishing dress codes is part of abolishing 'social gender'. If everyone has the same freedom to wear what they want, an individual's choice of clothing no longer expresses 'femaleness' or 'maleness'. It is simply the individual's preference.

Because challenges to sex-specific dress codes are infrequent, the argument that they are prohibited as direct sex discrimination has yet to be accepted by the ECtHR, the CJEU, the UK Supreme Court or the US Supreme Court. Indeed, Justice Gorsuch stressed in *Bostock* that the US Supreme Court was not ruling on the legality of dress codes under Title VII, which would have to be considered in a future case.[39] But one appellate court has accepted the argument, at least in one context, and cited my 1997 article in doing so.

66   Transgender Rights vs Women's Rights

In 2020, in the case of *Leung Kwok Hung*, the Hong Kong Court of Final Appeal found sex discrimination against a male prisoner who was obliged, unlike a female prisoner, to have his long hair cut short when he entered the prison.[40] A key factor was the failure of the Commissioner of Correctional Services to prove that, in Hong Kong society, 'the conventional hairstyle for men is a short one whereas for women, hair can be long or short'.[41] Would the Hong Kong Court of Appeal also find sex discrimination if a male employee of a bank was refused permission to wear a skirt to work? I would hope so, but the bank might argue that, in Hong Kong society, the convention is that skirts are only worn by women.

For the US Supreme Court, a ruling that sex-specific dress codes are sex discrimination violating Title VII would be consistent with its 1989 decision in *Price Waterhouse* v. *Hopkins*, in which Ms Hopkins had been advised that, to improve her chances of promotion to partner, she should 'walk more femininely, talk more femininely, dress more femininely, wear make-up, have her hair styled, and wear jewelry'.[42] The Court found that sex stereotyping played a part in the firm's decision not to promote Ms Hopkins, referring to 'the comments [quoted above] that were motivated by stereotypical notions about women's proper deportment'.[43]

In many countries, social changes in the twenty-first century would support appellate courts in finding that sex-specific dress codes are sex discrimination. As recently as 2018, British Airways dismissed a male check-in agent for wearing his hair in a 'man bun', even though the company considered this hairstyle acceptable for female check-in agents.[44] In September 2022, Virgin Atlantic Airways announced that its pilots, cabin crew and ground staff would be allowed to choose either the 'female' or 'male' uniform, 'no matter their gender, gender identity, or gender expression'.[45] In November 2022, British Airways relaxed some of its rules by allowing women and men to wear make-up and carry handbags, and men to wear

Common ground

their hair in a 'man bun', but maintained 'female' and 'male' uniforms.[46]

Which transgender rights might conflict with women's rights?

None of the wide range of transgender rights discussed above conflicts with women's rights. Claims to these rights are about 'equal rights' and freedom from direct discrimination (disparate treatment in the US) based on sex, gender identity or gender reassignment. This means that they are essentially claims to be treated in the same way as non-transgender persons. Controversial transgender rights involve demands to be exempted from neutral rules: the neutral rule that everyone's birth sex is their legal sex, and that entry into single-sex spaces and categories (sports and other positive or affirmative action) depends on birth sex.

The first three transgender demands (see chapter 1) are for the right to change one's legal sex (even though birth sex cannot be changed), and to do so subject to a gradually shrinking list of conditions (medical treatment or a diagnosis and a waiting period), which ideally should shrink to no conditions ('self-identification'). The fourth transgender demand is to have sex removed from birth certificates, so that there is no formal recognition of legal sex that needs to be changed. This would go beyond an exemption from a general rule and would involve abolishing the general (neutral) rule, whether or not abolition would be good for women. The question of whether it should be possible to change your legal sex from your birth sex, and how easy it should be, will be discussed in chapter 5. The question of whether a change of legal sex should make a difference with regard to access to single-sex spaces and categories will be discussed in chapter 6. The potential conflict between the right of parents to decide how to treat their child's gender dysphoria, and the right of the child to be protected from medical treatment with permanent consequences, will be discussed in chapter 7.

5

Changing your legal sex: should it be possible and how easy should it be?

From the time I started my doctoral thesis on LGB human rights (at the University of Oxford in 1987) until now, I have rarely written about transgender issues. Most of the time, I have maintained a position of polite silence. As a non-transgender person, I could not claim to understand what it is like to have a transgender identity, to suffer distress because of one's birth sex, and to consider it necessary to make physical changes to one's body. I left it to transgender people to say what legal reforms they needed. I assumed that whatever they proposed must be reasonable and would not affect the rights of others. I did not ask myself whether women would consider particular transgender-related proposals reasonable.

An exception to my position of polite silence was a 2005 book chapter entitled 'Sexual orientation and gender identity', in which I tried to discuss both LGB and transgender issues in UK law. In this chapter, I wrote:

> What sexual orientation discrimination and gender identity discrimination have in common is that they are both 'minority' forms of sex discrimination, which are often not recognised as sex discrimination because they involve what the majority sees as disturbing departures from traditional social sex roles

70   Transgender Rights vs Women's Rights

(eg, in the case of a gay man, wishing to marry another man, or in the case of a transsexual woman who was born male, wishing to have her penis surgically removed). LGB individuals and transsexual individuals are therefore both members of 'sex discrimination minorities'. As by far the larger of the two minorities, LGB individuals have a moral duty to speak out on behalf of transsexual individuals.[1]

I wrote this chapter in December 2003 and updated it in March 2004, as the Gender Recognition Act 2004 was about to become law (on 1 July), along with the Civil Partnership Act 2004 (on 18 November). The Gender Recognition Act permitted individuals with gender dysphoria to change their legal sex, while the Civil Partnership Act allowed same-sex couples to register their relationships and acquire almost all the rights and duties associated with marriage (but not the right to marry). I can see that my attempt to embrace the relatively new 'LGBT political coalition' meant changing my terminology from 'male-to-female transsexual person' in a 1997 article[2] to 'transsexual woman who was born male' in the book chapter.

What changed between 2004 (book chapter updated) and 2018, when I first became aware of conflicts between transgender rights and women's rights? It would be fair to say that I awoke from my slumber, during which I did not pay attention to the escalation of transgender demands that I described in chapter 1. The 'light-bulb moment' in 2018 that ended my slumber (described in greater detail in chapter 1) was the hostile reaction of a transgender student to my explaining why a limit had been placed on the right of a married transgender person to change their legal sex: to protect 'the rights of others', i.e., the right of a spouse in an opposite-sex marriage not to be forced into a same-sex marriage against her or his will. This limit meant that a married transgender person could only change their legal sex with the consent of their spouse or after obtaining a divorce.

Changing your legal sex 71

At the time, I said to the student that I did not necessarily agree with this limit. Now, I consider it a reasonable limit. In 2016, the Women and Equalities Committee of the House of Commons of the UK Parliament agreed: 'marriage ... is ... a legal contract between two consenting parties, the terms of which cannot be changed without the consent of both parties. ... [W]here one party transitions, the non-trans spouse does have a legal right to be consulted ... [T]his right must also be given due weight.'[3] Stephanie Hayton, the wife of Debbie Hayton (a male-to-female transgender person), has written: '

> When the government looked at the so-called 'spousal veto', Debbie initially repeated the trans-activist mantra that no cis person could stop a trans person from living as their true self. I questioned why the partner should have no say: a marriage is an agreement between two people, so why should the trans person have all the power? Surely there was a way forward which respected the rights of both in a difficult situation? Debbie started to see another perspective which recognised both parties.[4]

My awakening caused me to pay attention to the public debate about amending the Gender Recognition Act 2004 to permit 'self-identification', which was triggered by the publication of a UK Government consultation document in July 2018.[5] In 2020, I became aware of Principle 31 of the 2017 Yogyakarta Principles, which calls for the removal of sex from birth certificates (I had participated in the drafting of the 2007 version of the Principles). As I gradually realised how far the demands of the transgender-rights movement had gone, I began to think about how we got here: the 'abuse of sympathy' and 'escalation of demands' that I described in chapter 1. This caused me to go back to the beginning (in Europe, Sweden in 1972) and ask a hard question: was the first demand (change of legal sex after surgery) a reasonable one? Or should governments have said

72 Transgender Rights vs Women's Rights

no and offered alternative legal protection? In the remainder of this chapter, I will adopt a 'blank-slate perspective' and consider five options for governments with regard to change of legal sex (options A to E). In doing so, I will ask myself what advice I would give to a country that has taken no action to date.

The database of the LGBTI-rights organization ILGA World indicated (as of January 2024) that 'gender marker change' (change of legal sex) is 'possible' or 'nominally possible' in a minority of 78 of 193 United Nations member states (40.4%).[6] The majority of UN member states are classified as 'not possible' (75 member states, 38.9%)[7] or 'varies' (1 member state, the USA, 0.5%) or 'no data' or 'unclear' (39 member states, 20.2%).[8] Combining the latter three totals, change of legal sex is 'not possible' or 'varies' or there are 'no data' or the situation is 'unclear' in 115 of 193 UN member states (59.6%). The Argentine 'self-identification' model has been adopted across the country in 16 member states (8.3%),[9] and can also be found in parts of Australia, Canada, Mexico and the USA.

Whether change of legal sex should be possible appears to be an issue in 59.6% of UN member states. Whether to remove existing conditions attached to change of legal sex, and move to 'self-identification' in all or parts of the country, is an issue in a further 32.1% of member states (40.4% where change of legal sex is possible, minus 8.3% where 'self-identification' exists). Change of legal sex (and the conditions attached to it) therefore appears to remain an issue in 91.7% of member states. Removing sex from birth certificates is an issue in 100% of member states, given that no UN member state appears to have done it. (The Australian state of Tasmania is not an exception.)[10]

Option A: no change of legal sex but legal protections against hostility (reject first demand)

The first option for governments is not to allow a transgender person to change their legal sex (the situation in 59.6 per cent of UN member states), but to provide strong legal protections against the hostility that the person might face because of the difference between their birth (and legal) sex and their appearance (these legal protections are probably not present in many of these member states). Is it cruel, harsh or intolerant even to mention this option?

I am among those who believe, based on biological science, that each human being has one of two sexes, female or male, and that no human being can change her or his sex. My belief is not affected by the fact that a small percentage of people have differences of sex development (DSDs) which, in some cases, can make their birth sex ambiguous. Helen Joyce puts it this way:[11]

> Like all mammals, humans come in two sexes. (The existence of intersex conditions [DSDs] in no way changes this fact. It is a highly misleading umbrella term for rare developmental disorders of the genitals and gonads, some of which are so minor their 'sufferers' do not even know about them, and hardly any of which raise any doubt as to whether an individual is male or female or where they place on any sort of putative 'sex spectrum'.)[12]

The evolutionary biologist Colin Wright agrees:

> males are the sex that produce small gametes (sperm) and females produce large gametes (ova). There are no intermediate gametes, which is why there is no spectrum of sex. Biological sex in humans is a binary system. . . . In humans, and transgender . . . people are no exception, . . . reproductive

74   Transgender Rights vs Women's Rights

anatomy [testes or ovaries] is unambiguously male or female over 99.98 percent of the time.[13]

Birth sex is a lottery. The presence of an X or Y chromosome in the sperm cell that fertilizes the egg determines (in the vast majority of cases) whether the eventual foetus develops as female or male. No one chooses her or his birth sex ('conception sex' might be more accurate). Checking the genitals of a newborn is like opening a fortune cookie. If babies could talk to each other, they might ask: 'What did you get? Girl or boy?' Our only options are to accept our birth sex or to reject it. We cannot change it. I will return to this biological truth in chapter 9.

In the *Christine Goodwin* v. *UK* case in 2002, the ECtHR was influenced by medical advances in surgery and hormones and the existence of DSDs:

> While it . . . remains the case that a transsexual cannot acquire all the biological characteristics of the assigned sex . . ., the Court notes that with increasingly sophisticated surgery and types of hormonal treatments, the principal unchanging biological aspect of gender identity [sex] is the chromosomal element. It is known however that chromosomal anomalies may arise naturally (for example, in cases of intersex conditions . . .) and in those cases, some persons have to be assigned to one sex or the other . . . It is not apparent to the Court that the chromosomal element . . . must inevitably take on decisive significance for the purposes of legal attribution of gender identity [sex] for transsexuals.[14]

But 'increasingly sophisticated surgery' is not enough. A true 'change of sex' would require (at least) the removal of a set of male reproductive organs (penis, prostate and testes) and its replacement with a set of female reproductive organs (vulva, vagina, uterus and ovaries), or vice versa. This is and always has been medically impossible. No amount of surgery or hormones can give a person born male a uterus, ovaries and the potential to menstruate or become pregnant. Nor can surgery or hormones give a person born female testes that produce sperm and a penis that ejaculates semen.

As Lord Nicholls put it in 2003 in the *Bellinger* case in the House of Lords (now the UK Supreme Court), 'a normal body of one sex can be altered . . . to give the appearance of a normal body of the other sex. But there are still limits to what can be done. Gonads cannot be constructed. . . . Chromosomal patterns remain unchanged. The change of body can never be complete.'[15] He referred to surgery that creates 'a false vagina' or 'a false penis'.[16] I used to tell my students that these terms were 'transphobic'. Now, I would say that these terms are blunt but biologically accurate.

In the 1990s, we referred to 'male-to-female transsexuals' but did not describe them as women. At some point after 2010 or 2015, the slogan 'Trans women are women' became commonly used as a shorthand for the political claim that a 'trans woman' *is* a woman, even 'a real woman', and should therefore be treated as a woman in all circumstances. Is it true that a 'trans woman' is a woman? Although it might offend many transgender persons and their allies, the answer must be no. A 'trans woman' – or, as I would put it a 'male-to-female transgender person'[17] – is a person who was born male (the 'male' in 'male-to-female' makes the person's birth sex clear) and whose body is, always has been, and always will be fundamentally male, regardless of any use of hormones or surgery to change its appearance, and regardless of the person's transgender identity (the 'female' in 'male-to-female' makes the person's transgender identity clear). A subjective belief, feeling or identity cannot change the objective fact of birth sex.

In 2015, when the prominent feminist Germaine Greer was interviewed by Kirsty Wark for the BBC television programme *Newsnight*, Ms Wark suggested that some people might

76 Transgender Rights vs Women's Rights

consider Ms Greer's views 'hurtful' or 'insulting'. Ms Greer said: 'I don't think that post-operative transgender men, i.e., M-to-F transgender people, are women' and 'I think that a great many women don't think that … M-to-F transsexual people look like, sound like, or behave like women, but they daren't say so.'[18] I think it is likely that the majority of women around the world agree with Germaine Greer and do not believe that 'trans women' are women, although they might be afraid to say so. Politicians in the UK and other countries are becoming increasingly aware of this mainly silent group of women. A 2018 poll asked 'about a person who was born male and has male genitalia but who identifies as a woman. … [W]ould you consider this person to be a woman or a man?' The response 'man' or 'not … a man or a woman' was chosen by 53% of women and 64% of men (59% of all respondents, with 23% choosing 'don't know' or 'prefer not to say').[19]

Given that no one can change their birth sex, should anyone be allowed to change their legal sex? I would argue that the law has an interest, in limited circumstances (which have shrunk over time), in treating a person's objective birth sex as relevant (see chapter 6) and in providing a convenient means for the person to prove her or his birth sex, but no reason to attach any legal significance to a person's subjective gender identity, which can vary over time and take an infinite number of forms (at least 58 according to Facebook in 2014).[20] Lack of formal legal recognition of a person's gender identity would be the same as the lack of formal legal recognition of a person's political or religious identity.

When I read the first judgment of the ECtHR in favour of a transgender applicant, *B. v. France* in 1992, I struggled to understand the Court's very brief reasoning about 'private life': the applicant, a post-operative male-to-female transgender person, 'finds herself daily in a situation which, taken as a whole, is not compatible with the respect due to her private life' under Article 8 of the European Convention on Human

Rights.[21] There was no interference with her private life and no direct discrimination against her (compared with non-transgender persons). She was complaining about neutral rules regarding birth registration, identity documents and social security numbers that were applied to everyone. The injustice found to violate Article 8 (by a vote of 15 to 6) was better explained by the applicant and the former European Commission of Human Rights, the lower tribunal which had ruled in her favour.

The applicant argued that 'by failing to allow the indication of her sex [male] to be corrected in the civil status register and on her official identity documents, the French authorities forced her to *disclose* intimate personal information to third parties'. She referred to 'the reality of the psycho-social sex of transsexuals' and stressed that 'Transsexuals could . . . not . . . carry out one of the many transactions of daily life where proof of identity is necessary, without *disclosing* the discrepancy between their legal sex and their apparent sex'. Because social security numbers started with 1 for men and 2 for women, 'A transsexual was . . . *unable to hide* his or her situation from a potential employer and the employer's administrative staff.'[22] According to the Commission, 'the applicant, as a result of the frequent necessity of *disclosing* information concerning her private life to third parties, suffered distress which was too serious to be justified on the ground of respect for the rights of others'.[23]

The French Government acknowledged that 'The applicant might . . . in the course of her daily life experience a number of embarrassing situations, but they were not serious enough to constitute a breach of Article 8'. It argued that 'Miss B. had succeeded in passing as a woman despite her male civil status. . . . [A] transsexual who did not want third parties to know his or her biological sex was in a similar situation to that of a person wishing to keep other personal information secret (age . . .).'[24] In the French Government's view, 'Transsexuals

78 Transgender Rights vs Women's Rights

... kept their original chromosomal sex; only their appearance could be changed. But the law should fasten on the reality.'[25]

In *B.* v. *France* in 1992, the ECtHR faced the challenge of reconciling the biological fact that birth sex does not change and the social fact that disclosing a true birth sex, seen as inconsistent with a transgender person's appearance, can cause negative reactions in daily life. Today, the non-governmental organization Transgender Europe describes this tension between birth sex and appearance in a similar way:

> Every time you fly, get a new job, or even pick up a parcel from the post office, you're asked for official identification. An ID that does not reflect your gender ... can cause dysphoria. However, if how you present is different than your ID, it can also lead to much greater issues. This can impact your access to essential services. At worst, it can actually lead to discrimination or harassment.[26]

What is the solution to this problem? Should we treat the legal sex of a transgender person (based on their birth sex) as a 'shameful secret' and the problem to be fixed? 'Change of legal sex' allows birth sex to be hidden and disclosure avoided. Or should we treat the negative reaction to the transgender person's true birth sex as the problem to be fixed through 'protection against discrimination'? The ECtHR chose 'change of legal sex' in *B.* v. *France* in 1992, and later in *Christine Goodwin* v. *UK* in 2002. The CJEU provided a different solution ('protection against employment discrimination') in the *P.* case in 1996 (see chapter 4).[27] It did so because, unlike the ECtHR, it had no power to review national legislation on the registration of birth sex (and whether or not legal sex could be changed), but it could provide protection against employment discrimination. Did the CJEU choose the better solution?

Travelling back in time to 1972, and with the benefit of hindsight, I would argue that Sweden (the first European country to

Changing your legal sex 79

pass a law at the national level permitting change of legal sex) took the wrong fork in the road. Sweden's reform caused other European countries to follow. Cumulative reforms in multiple European countries eventually caused the ECtHR to require change of legal sex in its *B.* v. *France* (1992) and *Christine Goodwin* v. *UK* (2002) judgments.

What were the two forks? The first fork was allowing change of legal sex. The second fork was refusing change of legal sex (because it is biologically false and there is no human right to have false documents created), but protecting transgender persons against any form of violence, harassment or discrimination they might experience, because their appearance does not match social expectations about the birth sex disclosed by their legal documents.

Why was the second fork not taken? My explanation is that it was because, in 1972, anti-discrimination law in Europe was in its infancy. In the UK, the Race Relations Act 1968 prohibited discrimination based on 'the ground of colour, race or ethnic or national origins', but discrimination based on sex (or religion, disability, age or sexual orientation) was legal. The Equal Pay Act 1970 and the Sex Discrimination Act 1975 (covering sex discrimination in areas other than pay) did not come into force until 29 December 1975. European Union law required 'equal pay without discrimination based on sex',[28] but did not protect women against refusals to hire or promote them or dismissals until 1976.[29] It was silent with regard to race, religion, disability, age and sexual orientation until 1997.[30] The concept of harassment as a form of discrimination barely existed in Europe or North America before the publication in 1979 of Professor Catharine MacKinnon's book *Sexual Harassment of Working Women: A Case of Sex Discrimination.*[31] And in Sweden, there was very little anti-discrimination law before 1974. Although equal pay for women and men was required from 1948, this was only in state employment, not in the private sector. Other forms of

80 Transgender Rights vs Women's Rights

sex discrimination were not prohibited until 1973, and again only in state employment.[32]

If the Swedish legislature had known how far the demands of the transgender-rights movement would go – from change of legal sex after surgery to 'self-identification' and even the removal of sex from birth certificates – would it have said no? Perhaps it would have considered the second fork? In the case of Sweden, these questions about the past are purely hypothetical. But in the 113 countries (and in parts of the USA)[33] that do not yet permit change of legal sex, members of the government and the legislature will be aware of developments in the 16 countries with 'self-identification' everywhere, as well as the 'self-identification' that exists in parts of Australia, Canada, Mexico and the USA. They might be persuaded to take the second fork: to refuse change of legal sex and provide protection against discrimination instead.

What about the 63 countries (including the UK) that allow change of legal sex but do not allow 'self-identification', even in parts of the country? What should they do? Move 'forward' to 'self-identification' across the country? Maintain the status quo? Or recognise that the second fork is the better solution, repeal their legislation allowing change of legal sex, and ensure that there is strong protection for transgender persons against violence, harassment and discrimination? Should the ECtHR, in appropriate future cases, reconsider its judgments in *B.* v. *France* and *Christine Goodwin* v. *UK*, perhaps for countries that provide sufficient protection? It is important to note here that Hungary and Russia, which have recently repealed their laws allowing change of legal sex, have reached the outcome I have proposed but for the wrong reasons, because their motivation was clearly both anti-transgender and anti-LGB. It is unlikely that, in the absence of change of legal sex, either country is committed to protecting transgender persons. Indeed, in 2023, Russia banned 'medical interventions aimed at changing the sex of a person' (presumably hormones and surgery).[34] This unusual ban applies to adults of any age, not just minors (see chapter 7).

However politically unlikely it might be in 2025, let's imagine a proposal to repeal the Gender Recognition Act 2004. What would the consequences be? As Professors Rosa Freedman and Rosemary Auchmuty pointed out in 2018, 'All the areas of discrimination identified by the [ECtHR] in [*Christine Goodwin*] and in the parliamentary debates leading up to the Gender Recognition Act 2004 have been removed'.[35] Christine Goodwin complained that she had 'to pay the higher motor insurance premiums applicable to men', that 'she and her [male] partner could not marry because the law treated her as a man' and that she was 'ineligible for a State pension at the age of 60, the age of entitlement for women' (vs 65 for men).[36]

Today, birth sex in the UK matters much less than it did in 2002, but it still matters in limited circumstances (see chapter 6). All three of Christine Goodwin's complaints about UK law have been resolved: since 2012, higher motor insurance premiums for men have been prohibited by EU law;[37] since 2014 (except in Northern Ireland), all couples have been able to marry whether they are legally opposite-sex or same-sex;[38] and since 2018 the state pension age has been equalized at 65 or higher.[39] These three complaints all involved direct sex discrimination affecting all men or all legally same-sex couples. The solution was to remove the sex discrimination for all, rather than introduce special exceptions (through change of legal sex) for transgender people.

From 6 April 2005 to 5 April 2021 (a total of 16 financial years), 6,010 full Gender Recognition Certificates (GRCs) were issued.[40] This represents around 0.01 per cent of the UK's population, or around 1 in every 10,000 people. Why have so few GRCs been issued? In 2020, Professor Stephen Whittle explained that most transgender people find that they do not need a GRC (which allows the sex on their birth certificate to be changed), because they rarely need to show their birth

82 Transgender Rights vs Women's Rights

certificate. He mentioned retirement and marriage. Since the reforms mentioned above, a GRC has no effect on your state pension age or your right to marry the spouse of your choice.[41]

Long before the 2004 Act, while refusing to amend birth certificates, the UK adopted the (very British) pragmatic compromise of issuing passports and driving licences to transgender persons in a way that did not disclose their birth sex. Indeed, the ECtHR noted in *Cossey* v. *UK* that 'In 1976 the applicant [born male] was issued with a United Kingdom passport as a female'.[42] In the UK, passports and driving licences are used to prove an individual's identity in daily life far more often than birth certificates. For a passport, it is sufficient to send 'a letter from your doctor or medical consultant confirming your change of gender is likely to be permanent'.[43] A GRC is not required. A passport indicates the holder's sex as M or F. An X is not an option.[44] For a driving licence, 'If you've changed your gender identity, you need to provide . . . a deed poll [or] a statutory declaration.'[45] Again, a GRC is not required. A driving licence indicates the holder's sex in the second digit of the driver number (0 or 1 for men, 5 or 6 for women), which would not be obvious to most people.[46]

If GRCs are abolished, should this pragmatic compromise be maintained? One could argue that it has worked well for a long time and should be left alone. On the other hand, one could argue that identity documents should be consistent and that protection against disclosure of birth sex is no longer needed in the UK. Indeed, a passport or driving licence stating the transgender person's gender identity rather than their birth sex could be used to support a claim to enter the women-only spaces and categories to be discussed in chapter 6. Given the strong protection against discrimination because of gender reassignment in the Equality Act 2010, and the treatment by the criminal law of England and Wales of 'hostility related to transgender identity' as an aggravating factor when sentencing a violent offender,[47] perhaps it is enough to include a current photograph (showing the holder's post-transition appearance) in identity documents that mention birth sex.

Option B: change of legal sex after surgery (accept the first demand)

Prior to 2004, all European countries that permitted change of legal sex required some form of surgery. One reason why governments insisted on surgery was to ensure sterilization, so that a person born male could not retain a male reproductive capacity while being legally recognized as female, and a person born female could not retain a female reproductive capacity while being legally recognized as male. The transgender person had to choose between changing their legal sex and retaining their fertility. Apart from sterilization, surgical requirements vary from country to country. In the Chinese region of Hong Kong, very strict conditions (going beyond sterilization) had to be satisfied before a transgender person's sex on their identity card could be changed:

> (i) for sex change from female to male • removal of the uterus and ovaries; and • construction of a penis or some form of a penis;
> (ii) for sex change from male to female • removal of the penis and testes; and • construction of a vagina.

In 2023 in the case of *Q. and Tse*, the Hong Kong Court of Final Appeal declared that 'the ... Policy requiring ... full Sex Reassignment Surgery ... as a necessary condition for altering gender markers on Hong Kong Identity Cards, violate[s] the appellants' rights under Article 14 of the Bill of Rights and [is] unconstitutional'.[48]

In doing so, the Hong Kong court cited and followed the judgment of the ECtHR in the 2017 case of *A.P., Garçon & Nicot*

84   Transgender Rights vs Women's Rights

v. *France*, in which the ECtHR ruled that France could not require sterilization (through surgery or hormonal treatment) as a condition of a change of legal sex, but could require the applicants 'to demonstrate the existence of a gender identity disorder'.[49] The ECtHR prohibited sterilization even though the majority of Council of Europe member states (29 of 47) either did not allow change of legal sex (7) or made sterilization a condition of change of legal sex (22). Only 18 member states did not require sterilization, including France which, while the case was pending, passed new legislation stating that a change of legal sex could not be refused because 'an applicant has not undergone medical treatment, surgery or sterilisation'. The ECtHR upheld the requirement that 'the existence of a gender identity disorder' must be demonstrated because 36 member states required a psychiatric diagnosis.[50]

Sterilization requirements have always been vulnerable to the charge that sterilization is 'forced' or 'coerced', even though sterilization can be avoided simply by not requesting a change of legal sex. The ECtHR ruled in *A.P., Garçon & Nicot* that a transgender person's exercise of their Article 8 right to change legal sex could not be made contingent on consenting to sterilization:

> Making the recognition of transgender persons' gender identity conditional on sterilisation surgery or treatment . . . which they do not wish to undergo . . . amounts to making the full exercise of their right to respect for their private life under Article 8 . . . conditional on their relinquishing full exercise of their right to respect for their physical integrity . . . [under Article 8 and] Article 3 [prohibition of inhuman and degrading treatment].[51]

Option B is thus no longer permitted in Europe. This means that a government must turn to Option A (which makes surgery or other medical treatment voluntary and unco-erced, because it is never 'rewarded' with a change of legal sex) and hope to persuade the ECtHR to reconsider its case law and permit this option. Or the government must turn to Option C, which does not require surgery or other medical treatment.

Option C: change of legal sex without medical treatment but with safeguards (accept the second demand)

Option C represents the status quo in the UK under the Gender Recognition Act 2004. As explained above, it has become the minimum standard for all 46 Council of Europe countries, since the ECtHR's 2017 judgment in *A.P., Garçon & Nicot* v. *France*. But the UK had a choice after the ECtHR's 2002 judgment in *Christine Goodwin* v. *UK*, which only required change of legal sex for 'post-operative transsexuals', who had undergone a 'long and difficult process of transformation' and had chosen their 'sexual identity . . . at great personal cost'. Indeed, the ECtHR added that 'any "spectral difficulties" [caused by change of legal sex], particularly in the field of family law, are both manageable and acceptable if confined to the case of fully achieved and post-operative transsexuals'.[52] Why did the Gender Recognition Act 2004 not require surgery?

A surgery requirement was discussed in the debates in the House of Lords and in the House of Commons. Lord Chan (non-affiliated) tabled an 'amendment that requires applicants to have undergone sex reassignment surgery', because it 'is a sign that the applicant is convinced that it will be a permanent change. . . . [S]ome transsexuals . . . on medical grounds of serious life-threatening diseases are unable to undergo sex reassignment surgery. Those cases can be judged on individual merit by the gender recognition panel.'[53] Lord Turnberg (Labour) replied: 'operations . . . are not without risk. Most individuals are likely to be fearful and others may simply not be

86   Transgender Rights vs Women's Rights

fit. The fact that most do go through with all this is a testament to their determination, but to insist that they all do so seems quite unnecessarily cruel.'[54] Lord Filkin (Labour) also opposed the amendment:

> Most people who have gender dysphoria undoubtedly wish to have surgery. The individual wishes to bring his or her bodily state into alignment with that person's profound belief. Most will have done so. To require those persons to do so is wrong ... Some people may be too old to be able to cope with the rigours of surgery. ... [W]here a person has not had surgery I would expect the [gender recognition] panel to be more alert in inquiring whether there were sufficient evidence of commitment to a permanent change.[55]

But Baroness O'Cathain (Conservative) was not convinced: 'One of my great concerns about the Bill is that an individual can have a [GRC] without having surgery. It depends [only] on how determined that person is in his or her own mind about the belief that he or she is of the opposite sex. I find that very distressing.'[56] Lord Filkin did not share her concern:

> Such people who do not have surgery are few. There are usually good reasons ... If the panel is not convinced that [they] are committed to living in a permanent state it will not grant them a gender certificate. However, to turn it the other way, for the state almost to say that unless people go through a process of bodily mutilation they will not have a legal recognition is wrong.[57]

The following week, Lord Filkin said: 'Sex and gender are not determined purely by chromosomes. Recognition, therefore, cannot depend purely on chromosomes. Similarly, having or lacking the right genitalia is not the nub of the Bill, and surgery should not be a precondition either. ... We do not intend to compel transsexual people to undergo surgery, even though most wish to do so.'[58]

When the Bill reached the House of Commons, Sir Patrick Cormack (Conservative) questioned the assumption that 'most wish to do so': 'will [Lynne Jones] accept . . . that a very large percentage of these people undergo no physical changes or surgery, and remain physically exactly what they are, male or female?'[59] Lynne Jones (Labour) denied this: 'The majority of transsexual people want to undergo a medical process that will leave them physically as congruent as possible with their gender identity. . . . It may not always be medically possible . . ., but in my experience, the majority of transsexual people want to undergo the full transition.'[60]

The UK Government does not seem to have presented any data about the percentage of transgender people who were having genital surgery in 2002 or 2003. According to a 2023 survey by the *Washington Post* newspaper, 'Less than a third [of transgender adults in the USA] have used hormone treatments or puberty blockers, and about 1 in 6 have undergone gender-affirming surgery or other surgical treatment to change their physical appearance'. The transgender-rights organization Press for Change (which urged the UK Government not to include a surgery requirement) provided the following advice to applicants: 'There is no requirement that you undergo genital reconstruction surgery, but unless for reasons of health, . . . it is not a good idea to simply say you do not want it. Better to state that you intend to have it in the future when the surgical waiting list has spaces.'[61]

Instead of including a surgery requirement in the Gender Recognition Act 2004, the UK Government inserted safeguards. The November 2003 report of the Joint Committee on Human Rights described the Bill as 'a sensitive and sensible compromise . . . allowing pre-operative transsexual people to have their acquired gender recognised, with the Gender Recognition Panel providing a safeguard against premature or

88 Transgender Rights vs Women's Rights

frivolous applications'.[62] In fact, the Panel provides three safeguards: it checks that the applicant has a diagnosis of gender dysphoria (a good reason to apply for an exemption from the general rule that one's birth sex is one's legal sex for life); has 'lived in the acquired gender' for two years before applying for a change of legal sex; and 'intends to continue to live in the acquired gender until death'.[63] These triple safeguards prevent misuse of the procedure, especially by persons born male who are not transgender.

The UK Government agreed to what I called in chapter 1 'the second transgender demand' (change of legal sex with no medical treatment but with safeguards), even though the Gender Recognition Act 2004 went well beyond what the ECtHR had required in 2002 in *Christine Goodwin* v. *UK*, and probably had no precedent at the national level anywhere in the world. Acceptance of the second demand means that, today in the UK, a person born male can obtain a GRC and become legally female, even though they have a beard, a deep voice and male genitals. The law allows them to become legally female, even though most people seeing or hearing them would consider them male. One example of a person who is theoretically eligible for a GRC is the bearded 'transgender woman' Alex Drummond.[64] (It is not clear whether having a beard would be considered inconsistent with 'living in the acquired [female] gender'.) The possibility of change of legal sex without medical treatment struck me as very generous when I first heard about it.

Through the 2004 Act, the UK 'leapfrogged' the 2002 *Christine Goodwin* v. *UK* judgment of the ECtHR. This move was followed by other countries, such as Spain in 2007, and eventually led to the *A.P., Garçon & Nicot* v. *France* judgment in 2017, making legislation like the 2004 Act compulsory for all 46 Council of Europe countries. It now represents a compromise between Option A (no change of legal sex but protection against discrimination) and Option D (change of legal sex with

Changing your legal sex 89

no safeguards, or 'self-identification'), which pleases neither side. In 2018, Professors Freedman and Auchmuty recommended leaving this compromise alone:

> the law as it currently stands works well enough as a compromise measure, setting up a reasonably high bar for people who want to transition. The goal should not be to lower that bar, by allowing anyone at any time to self-declare that their gender identity does not match their biological sex, but rather to create societies where men can do or be anything they like without needing to be viewed a 'woman' in order to do so.[65]

In 2022, I made the same recommendation in a newspaper comment entitled 'The Scottish Parliament should leave the Gender Recognition Act as it is', noting that the 2004 Act complies with the ECtHR's 2017 judgment in *A.P., Garçon & Nicot v. France*.[66]

Option D: change of legal sex without medical treatment or safeguards ('self-identification') (accept the third demand)

In this section, I will start by explaining the path from the first legislative discussion of 'self-identification' in the UK in 2015 to the rejection of the proposal by the UK Government (for England and Wales) in September 2020, and the blocking of the Gender Recognition Reform (Scotland) Bill (passed by the Scottish Parliament in December 2022) by the UK Government in January 2023. The order that blocked the Bill was upheld by a Scottish court in December 2023. I will then consider whether 'self-identification' (currently off the political agenda in the UK) is a good idea.

In 2012, Argentina 'leapfrogged' the UK's Gender Recognition Act 2004 with a law permitting 'self-identification', probably

90   Transgender Rights vs Women's Rights

the first in the world at the national level. The law provides that: 'Any person may request the rectification of the registration of their sex ... when [it does] not coincide with their self-perceived gender identity.'[67] No medical treatment is required and there are no safeguards. It is not necessary to provide a diagnosis of gender dysphoria (or to give any reason why the individual needs to change their legal sex) and there is no waiting period. Any person born male has a right to change his legal sex to female simply by completing the appropriate form. In the Province of Buenos Aires, it takes about 20 working days.[68]

One of the first countries to adopt the Argentine model was Ireland in July 2015. The Gender Recognition Act 2015 only requires the applicant to submit 'a statutory declaration declaring that he or she – ... (ii) has a settled and solemn intention of living in the preferred gender for the rest of his or her life'.[69] In January 2023, it was reported that a female-to-male transgender person in Ireland had received a Gender Recognition Certificate eight days after applying for it.[70]

In February 2015, the LGB-rights organization Stonewall, founded in 1989, announced that 'it would now be campaigning for all of the LGBT community and was beginning a path to trans inclusion'.[71] After the 7 May 2015 UK election, the Women and Equalities Committee of the House of Commons decided to conduct an inquiry into transgender equality and 'consulted informally with representatives of two key stakeholder organisations, Press for Change and Stonewall', before starting the inquiry.[72] The Committee's report, published on 14 January 2016, recommended that the UK Government 'update the Gender Recognition Act, in line with the principles of gender self-declaration that have been developed in other jurisdictions'.[73] In July 2018, the UK Government (under Prime Minister Theresa May) published a consultation document on 'Reform of the Gender Recognition Act'.[74] Following a turbulent public debate and a change of prime minister (to Boris Johnson), the UK Government announced on 22 September

2020 that it would not be proposing 'self-identification' (for England and Wales): 'We have looked carefully at the issues raised in the consultation . . . It is the Government's view that the balance struck in [the 2004 Act] is correct, in that there are proper checks and balances . . . and . . . support for people who want to change their legal sex.'[75]

Meanwhile, the Scottish Government pushed ahead with 'self-identification'. On 22 December 2022, the Scottish Parliament (which has the power to legislate on this matter for Scotland only) approved the Gender Recognition Reform (Scotland) Bill.[76] It permits change of legal sex without a diagnosis of gender dysphoria and reduces the waiting period for adults from two years to six months (three months of living in 'the acquired gender' plus a three-month 'reflection period').[77] The six-month waiting period is a safeguard that does not exist in Argentina or Ireland. Some transgender-rights activists would not consider this procedure to be 'self-identification', but it would have made change of legal sex easier than under the Gender Recognition Act 2004.

On 17 January 2023, the UK Government's cabinet minister for Scotland made an order preventing the Bill from receiving Royal Assent (the approval of the UK's head of state, King Charles III, which is normally automatic) and therefore from becoming law (an Act of the Scottish Parliament). The cabinet minister's reasons for exercising (for the first time) his power to block a bill passed by the Scottish Parliament included the Bill's impact on the powers of the UK Parliament with regard to 'Equal opportunities' and 'Social security schemes', and 'the creation of two parallel and very different regimes for issuing . . . gender recognition certificates within the United Kingdom'. In particular, he said that the Bill did not have 'sufficient safeguards to mitigate the risk of fraudulent . . . applications . . . [T]here is a risk of people self-excluding from sex-segregated settings [see chapter 6] as a result of concern about the possibility of someone with malicious intent being able to obtain

92 Transgender Rights vs Women's Rights

a gender recognition certificate.'[78] On 15 February 2023, Scotland's first minister resigned, with one commentator writing about 'How self-ID helped bring down Nicola Sturgeon'.[79]

As of election day (4 July 2024), the former (Conservative) UK Government had rejected 'self-identification' for England and Wales and blocked an attempt to introduce it in Scotland. What might the new (Labour) UK Government do? Perhaps sensing that supporting 'self-identification' might cost it votes (Labour's leader Keir Starmer had been asked whether a woman can have a penis or whether only women have cervixes),[80] on 24 July 2023, almost a year before the election, the Labour Party clarified its policy: 'The requirement to obtain a medical diagnosis of gender dysphoria remains an important part of accessing a [GRC]. . . . [G]ender dysphoria is no longer classified – and stigmatised – as a psychiatric disorder. It can help refer trans people into the [National Health Service] for support services.' The main change that the Labour Party would make to the Gender Recognition Act 2004 would be to convert the multi-person Gender Recognition Panel into a one-person Registrar, and reduce the number of required reports from medical doctors and psychologists from two to one.[81] An opinion poll in October 2023 found that this clarification of Labour's policy (rejected by Stonewall)[82] was supported by 67 per cent of respondents.[83]

The Scottish Government sought judicial review of the UK Government's decision to block the Gender Recognition Reform (Scotland) Bill. On 8 December 2023, a Scottish court dismissed the petition.[84] On 20 December 2023, the Scottish Government announced that it would not appeal.[85] It seems clear that 'self-identification' is no longer on the political agenda in England and Wales or in Scotland. The UK is resisting 'self-identification' as strongly as it did change of legal sex from 1986 to 2002 (when it defended four cases in the ECtHR).

If 'self-identification' ever returns to the political agenda in the UK, is it a good idea? I would argue that the Gender

Recognition Act 2004 is very generous and that the UK Parliament should not amend it for England and Wales (or the Scottish Parliament for Scotland), especially because the ECtHR does not require the UK to amend it. Proponents of change consider the requirement of a diagnosis of gender dysphoria to be humiliating or stigmatizing. But we must remember that a transgender person seeking a change of legal sex is asking for an exemption from the general rule that a person's birth sex is their legal sex for life, because their birth sex never changes. Exemptions have conditions. We can justifiably attach conditions to crossing the legal border from male to female, or female to male, just as we attach conditions to crossing an international border, acquiring a new citizenship, being granted refugee status, being approved as an adoptive parent, obtaining disability benefits or being granted the status of conscientious objector to military service. In none of these situations is it sufficient to 'self-identify' as a visitor, citizen, refugee, adoptive parent, disabled person or conscientious objector, without an assessment process in which questions are asked.

The procedure under the 2004 Act has been described as 'difficult, humiliating, and inaccessible for many trans people, requiring a large amount of time, money, and evidence to apply'.[86] Is it? Not if the two-year waiting period and the £5 application fee[87] are compared with naturalization as a British citizen, which has a six-year waiting period (for those not married to a British citizen), a demanding 'Life in the UK Test', a complicated application form and a fee of £1,630.[88] By shortening the waiting period to six months, and removing the diagnosis requirement, the Scottish Bill assigned a low value to the status of being legally female, compared with the status of being legally a British citizen.

With 'self-identification', no questions are asked, such as: 'Why do you need to change your legal sex?' 'Self-identification' assumes that the answer 'because I want to change it' is

94 Transgender Rights vs Women's Rights

sufficient. When Amnesty International encouraged people to respond to the UK Government's 2018 consultation, its recommendations included: 'There is no need for a period of reflection. *Trans people know who they are* and retaining a period of reflection would contribute to stigma against trans people as it would imply their ability to self-determine is not adequate.'[89] This is consistent with Amnesty's 'I AM WHO I SAY I AM' T-shirt, in the colours of the transgender Pride flag.[90]

Similarly, in expressing disappointment with the Labour Party's rejection of 'self-identification', transgender barrister Robin Moira White asked: 'Why ... can [trans people] still not be trusted when they say who they are?' She stressed the importance of distinguishing 'predatory men' from 'trans people'.[91] Yes, this is important. But how is it possible with 'self-identification' and 'no questions asked'? The safeguards in the 2004 Act are there to make it unlikely that a predatory man will obtain a GRC. The safeguards are precautions, like locking the door of your apartment or house, or security checks at airports. These precautions are not meant to insult transgender people, your neighbours, or air passengers with good intentions.

If it is possible to abuse 'self-identification', it will be abused. In May 2018, it was reported that a man, intending to demonstrate the possibility of abuse, stood for the position of women's officer of the local Labour Party in Basingstoke (England), saying 'I self-identify as a woman on Wednesdays.'[92] Also in 2018, it was reported that a man in the Canadian province of Alberta had changed his legal sex from male to female to obtain cheaper car insurance: 'Under the rules in place at the time, Albertans needed to produce a doctor's note to switch the gender marker on their personal documents. In June [2018], the government scrapped the doctor's note requirement for adults, allowing them to declare their marker as M, F or X.'[93] And in June 2023, it was reported that a man in Switzerland, which has 'self-identification', changed his legal sex from male to female to avoid compulsory military service.[94]

Perhaps the most exaggerated case for 'self-identification' was made by the former United Nations Independent Expert 'on protection against violence and discrimination based on sexual orientation and gender identity', Victor Madrigal-Borloz, in June 2021: 'legal recognition on the basis of self-determination is the key to protecting trans and gender-diverse persons from the ... extrajudicial execution, forced disappearance, torture and ill-treatment, beatings and harrowing emotional pain being inflicted on them'.[95] The causal connection between the ease with which legal sex can be changed and 'extrajudicial execution' and 'torture' is not obvious. Violence will often be triggered by the combination of a male-to-female transgender person's clothing associated with women and their male physical appearance, whether the legal sex in the person's identity documents is male or female.

Option E: removal of sex from birth certificates so that there is no legal sex to change (accept the fourth demand)

Option E is the most radical one of all: sex would be removed from birth certificates so that there would be no legal sex to change. Women and girls would be deprived of a convenient way of proving their birth sex (without an examination of their genitals or chromosomes), if it became necessary to do so in one of the situations in which birth sex still matters (chapter 6). In 2013, the year after Argentina's 'self-identification' law, the Third International Intersex Forum in Malta declared: 'In the future, *as with race or religion*, sex or gender should not be a category on birth certificates or identification documents for anybody.'[96]

96 Transgender Rights vs Women's Rights

In 2017, the second version of the Yogyakarta Principles (introduced in chapter 1) claimed in Principle 31 that, as a matter of existing international human rights law, all 193 United Nations member states have an obligation to 'end the registration of the sex and gender of the person in identity documents such as birth certificates'.[97] When I first read Principle 31, this demand struck me as outrageous, given that, to my knowledge, not a single country in the world has done this. It is certainly not a neutral statement of international human rights law, but an example of the second version of the Yogyakarta Principles veering into advocacy. In a 2020 report to the UN General Assembly, the UN Special Rapporteur on the right to privacy, after citing the Yogyakarta Principles, repeated the demand in Principle 31.[98]

In 2021, the American Medical Association (AMA) announced that it:

> will advocate for the removal of sex as a legal designation on the public portion of the birth certificate. . . . [I]nformation on an individual's sex designation at birth would still be collected . . . for medical, public health, and statistical use only. . . . Designating sex on birth certificates as male or female . . . perpetuates a view that sex designation is permanent and fails to recognize the medical spectrum of gender identity.[99]

And in 2022, 'Future of Legal Gender', a research project funded by the UK's Economic and Social Research Council,[100] published its final report, entitled 'Abolishing legal sex status'.[101] The authors propose, like the AMA, that 'Sex . . . would no longer be legally . . . assigned (. . . by registering sex on birth certificates). . . . [T]he Gender Recognition Act 2004 . . . would become redundant. Sex . . . could continue to be recorded . . . for . . . statistical purposes, but would no longer form part of an individual's legal status.'[102]

Who benefits from what the authors call 'decertification of . . . sex'? The authors see it as offering 'benefits to people who do not fit the current binary framework of women and men, and who are placed, or feel obliged, to squeeze into one category or another'.[103] The beneficiaries are a small minority of people who identify as transgender or 'non-binary', or have DSDs. And what about a much larger group, women, who represent 51 per cent of the population in England and Wales?[104] How do they benefit? It is not obvious how ceasing to consider sex an important fact about an individual's birth, which is worth 'certifying' because it still matters in some circumstances (chapter 6), will help to improve the status of women in society. The term 'decertification' strikes me as resembling 'decriminalization' (of same-sex sexual activity, a good thing) and 'certified insane', which implies that being born female, like insanity, is something undesirable and stigmatized. Women should welcome their 'decertification' as female!

What lies behind these proposals to abolish legal sex is a false analogy between sex and race (which, unlike sex, is very rarely of legal relevance). The race analogy can be found in the 1995 book *The Apartheid of Sex: A Manifesto on the Freedom of Gender*, by the transgender author Martine Rothblatt.[105] The book opens with a prediction: 'In the future, labelling people as "male" or "female" will be considered just as unfair as South Africa's now-abolished practice of stamping "black" or "white" on people's ID cards.'[106] Every prison will house both men and women (no more women's prisons) and there will be 'mandatory, injected contraceptives for all inmates'.[107] There will be 'no sex-segregated athletic competition'. Instead, men and women will compete against each other in 'objective weight- or height-based categories'.[108] We will see 'the elimination of sex on . . . birth certificates, and . . . the elimination of sexually segregated public facilities, such as washrooms [toilets]', which will have only 'closed-door stalls'.[109] 'Sexual orientation will evolve towards a unisexual model' and 'gay, straight, and even bisexual labels will lose all meaning'.[110] '[T]he best way to end the oppression of women is to end the apartheid of sex.'[111]

98   Transgender Rights vs Women's Rights

When I first read Ms Rothblatt's book in 1996, I appreciated her support for same-sex marriage, but did not think about the implications of her other proposals. When I re-read her book in 2023, I was both shocked by her other proposals and grateful that she had so clearly stated the full 'transgender agenda' so early. We were definitely warned! Option E is a very bad idea, especially if it would result in Ms Rothblatt's world of men and women in the same prison and no women's category in sports. We have a system that has served us well: to protect women, it records birth sex and attaches legal significance to birth sex in certain circumstances, which I will discuss in chapter 6. If we look back to the demands of the LGB-rights movement, it did not seek to 'liberate' heterosexual women from marriage by abolishing marriage. Instead, it sought equal rights and ended up with the same choices for same-sex couples as for opposite-sex couples (in the UK): to marry, form a civil partnership, or live together without registering. Option E goes far beyond seeking equal rights for transgender people. It seeks to 'liberate' women, without their consent, from the recording of birth sex and the legal protections associated with birth sex. Better protection of the human rights of a small minority must not come at the expense of the human rights of the majority of the population.

Conclusion

With regard to change of legal sex, my 'blank-slate' preference is Option A: refusing change of legal sex (because it is biologically false and there is no human right to have false documents created), but protecting transgender persons against any form of violence, harassment or discrimination they might experience, because their appearance does not match social expectations about the birth sex disclosed by their legal documents. Option C (change of legal sex with no medical treatment but with safeguards) is an alternative, especially if it already exists (as in the UK), and if it would be politically impossible to abolish it and move to Option A. Options D ('self-identification') and E (removing sex from birth certificates) are both bad for the rights of women and should be resisted.

6

Protecting women-only spaces, categories and capacities

Chapter 5 was about the principle: should it be possible to change your legal sex and how easy should it be? This chapter is about the exceptions: situations in which the birth sex of a person born male justifies their exclusion from a particular women-only space (such as a changing room or a prison), a particular women-only category (in a positive or affirmative action programme or in competitive sports) or a legal status linked to a women-only capacity (such as pregnancy and the legal status of 'mother'), even if the legal sex of the person born male has been changed to female, and regardless of the person's transgender identity.

The exceptions discussed in this chapter raise political and legal issues in every country, state or province in the world, even those with 'self-identification'. In countries, states or provinces where change of legal sex is not possible, the exceptions are simpler. A person born male may be excluded from women-only spaces and categories because they are legally male. In countries, states or provinces where change of legal sex is possible – after a process with safeguards like those in the UK's Gender Recognition Act 2004, or through 'self-identification' – a person born male who has changed their legal sex to female may be excluded from women-only spaces and categories because their birth sex is male (they are biologically male). We will see that Great Britain's Equality Act 2010 has two sets of exceptions. One is for transgender persons born male who remain legally male, because they do not hold Gender Recognition Certificates (GRCs): they may be excluded because of their birth (and legal) 'sex'. The other is for persons born male who hold GRCs and are legally female: despite their legal sex, they may be excluded because of their 'gender reassignment'. Germany's 2024 law on change of legal sex contains exceptions for 'gender-specific toilets, changing rooms, saunas, or sports clubs'.[1]

A lawyer hearing about a new principle immediately wonders what exceptions might be justifiable. This was the case in July 2015 when a colleague told me about Ireland's new 'self-identification' law (I had not heard of such a law before). I thought about when birth sex matters and asked him:

> If gender recognition only requires a statutory declaration, how can bad faith declarations be detected? Hypothetically, a non-trans man could make a statutory declaration that his preferred gender is female, to benefit from a positive [affirmative] action programme, or to participate in a sex-segregated sport in the women's division. Would he be asked to prove that he is a trans woman? If so, how?

I mentioned 'bad faith' because my initial concern was persons seeking to abuse the new procedure. But, as we will see, the same questions about access to women's categories, in positive (affirmative) action programmes and in sports, arise in the case of good-faith transgender persons who were born male but are legally female. After briefly noticing some potential problems with change of legal sex in 2015, I resumed my slumber until 2018.

It is important to note that almost all the examples discussed in this chapter involve male-to-female transgender persons.

102   Transgender Rights vs Women's Rights

This is because the presence of a female-to-male transgender person is unlikely to have a negative effect on a men-only space or a men-only category in sports, and because men-only categories for positive (affirmative) action addressing under-representation of men are not as common as women-only categories. Female-to-male transgender persons will, however, be discussed, along with male-to-female transgender persons, in the context of the legal statuses of 'mother' and 'father', which are linked to the women-only capacity of pregnancy and the men-only capacity of insemination.

Spaces: toilets, changing rooms, hospital wards and prisons

I will start with women-only physical spaces in which privacy may be limited, and in which it might be possible to be seen partly or fully naked, or to see another person partly or fully naked. Toilets, changing rooms, hospital wards and prisons are physical spaces in which two rights to 'respect for private life' (under Article 8 of the European Convention on Human Rights) collide. A male-to-female transgender person claims a right to have their private life respected through a change of legal sex, which will prevent disclosure of their birth sex. They then claim a right, consistent with their new legal sex, to enter women-only spaces. However, the women in the women-only spaces also have a right to respect for their private lives, which in this context means not having to be seen naked by persons born male, and not having to see male genitals.

The male-to-female transgender person can rely on the *B.* v. *France* (1992) and *Christine Goodwin* v. *UK* (2002) judgments of the ECtHR. The women can rely on several judgments of the ECtHR, including *Valašinas* v. *Lithuania* (2001), in which the facts were:

Protecting women-only spaces, categories and capacities 103

The chief [prison] guard, P., conducted the [security] search [after a visitor had left] ... P. told the applicant to take off his clothes. When the applicant was only in his underwear, a female prison officer, J., came into the room. P. then told the applicant to strip naked. ... [He] submitted to the order, taking off his underwear, in the presence of Ms J. She was watching ... with the rest of the officers ... The applicant's body, including his testicles, was examined by the male officers. The officers wore no gloves, touching the applicant's sexual organs and then the food given to him by his relatives, without washing their hands.[2]

The ECtHR concluded that: '*Obliging the applicant to strip naked in the presence of a woman*, and then touching his sexual organs and food with bare hands showed a clear lack of respect for him, and diminished ... his human dignity ... [T]he search ... amounted to degrading treatment within the meaning of Article 3.'[3] This reasoning would also apply if a woman were obliged to strip naked in the presence of a man or a person born male.

In *Wainwright* v. *UK* (2003), as a condition of visiting her son, a woman was required by female prison officers (who did not touch her) to undress completely, in a room with lights on and the window blinds up, in which others might have been able to see her from outside. The distress this caused her was not severe enough to make the treatment 'degrading treatment' violating Article 3. But the treatment did violate her Article 8 right to respect for her private life, because it was disproportionate to the aim of fighting the drugs problem in the prison.[4]

Finally, in *Yunusova & Yunusov* v. *Azerbaijan* (2020), the ECtHR found that 'a male [police] officer intruded in [a] toilet while [a woman, Yunusova] was using its facilities and observed her in a state of undress'. This was 'an interference with [her] right to respect for her private life', which could not be justified and therefore violated Article 8.[5]

104 Transgender Rights vs Women's Rights

To date, no case in the ECtHR has involved a direct conflict between a transgender person's human right and a woman's human right. Let's imagine a hypothetical case. A woman is showering in the communal shower room of a public swimming pool. She notices that a person with male genitals is showering next to her. Which 'right to respect for private life' prevails? I would argue that it is clearly the woman's right. The original (1992) rationale for the transgender person's right (preventing disclosure of birth sex) does not apply, given that displaying male genitals amounts to voluntary disclosure of birth sex. The transgender person could be said to have waived their right to respect for their private life in this situation. Unless she consented in advance to the presence of the transgender person, the woman has not waived her Article 8 right. As the author Helen Joyce puts it:

> When men who identify as women are granted access to space and services set aside for us, that destroys women's rights. We are physically weaker than men, who perpetrate nearly all physical and sexual violence against us. Our capacity to play a full part in public life therefore requires us to be able to exclude men – all men, however they identify – from places where we are naked or otherwise vulnerable.[6]

Incidents like my hypothetical do occur, even though most do not go to court. The US Department of Education (Office for Civil Rights) is investigating an alleged incident in March 2023 at a high school in Wisconsin: 'four freshman girls [aged 14 to 15] were showering in the locker room with their swimsuits on when an 18-year-old student entered the shower area, told them "I'm trans by the way" and then fully undressed, revealing male genitalia'.[7] In June 2021, a woman complained that a person was displaying a penis in the women's section at a Korean spa in Los Angeles. A video records her saying, as staff try to explain the person's presence: 'What sexual orientation?

I see a dick. It lets me know he's a man. . . . He is not a female.'[8] After five people filed reports with the police, a registered sex offender was charged with indecent exposure.[9] In March 2024, a woman complained about a male-to-female transgender person who was shaving in the female locker room of her gym in Fairbanks, Alaska. Her membership was terminated because she took a photograph of the person who was shaving and posted it online.[10]

Some cases do go to court. In June 2023, a Korean spa near Seattle, which provides body scrub and other services to naked women (and where male genitals had been seen several times), lost a challenge to Washington State's Law Against Discrimination, which had been enforced against the spa's 'female-only policy' excluding transgender persons who retain male genitalia (on its website: 'biological women are welcome'). The only exception in the Washington law prohibiting exclusion from 'a place of public resort' because of sex or sexual orientation (defined as including 'gender expression or identity') appears to be 'behavior or actions constituting a risk to property or other persons'.[11] After receiving a complaint, the Washington State Human Rights Commission found discrimination based on gender identity: 'the "biological women" policy focuses on the genitals of patrons rather than allowing transgender women to access your facilities based on their gender identity'.[12]

Unlike the Washington State Law Against Discrimination, the Equality Act 2010 (which applies in Great Britain – i.e., England, Wales and Scotland) contains pairs of detailed exceptions that protect women-only spaces. One pair of exceptions relates to 'single-sex services'. The main exception permits 'providing a service only to persons of one sex' if it is 'a proportionate means of achieving a legitimate aim' (which requires a case-by-case assessment of alternatives to single-sex provision) and if certain conditions are satisfied. These conditions include the fact that the service is provided in a hospital (single-sex wards), or that 'a person of one sex might reasonably object to the presence of a person of the opposite sex' (separate male and female changing rooms), or that 'there is likely to be physical contact between a person . . . to whom the service is provided and another person . . ., and [that person] might reasonably object if [the recipient] were not of the same sex' (any service involving intimate personal health or hygiene).[13]

The second exception permits what would otherwise be discrimination because of 'gender reassignment' in 'the provision of a service only to persons of one sex', if it would be 'a proportionate means of achieving a legitimate aim'. If the two Korean spas in Los Angeles and near Seattle were in Great Britain, they could probably rely on the main exception to exclude a male-to-female transgender person who does not hold a GRC and is therefore legally male (exclusion because of the person's 'sex' is permitted), and on the second exception to exclude such a person who holds a GRC and is legally female (exclusion because of the person's 'gender reassignment' is permitted).[14] The same would be true of the women providing genital-waxing services in Vancouver, who were subjected to complaints of discrimination based on gender identity filed by a male-to-female transgender person. The complaints were rejected in 2019, not because of an exception, but because the service offered by the women to the public was removing genital hair from vulvas, not from scrotums.[15]

As part of their 2015 proposals to amend the Gender Recognition Act 2004 to allow 'self-identification', several transgender-rights organizations urged the UK Government to amend the exceptions protecting single-sex services, so as to prohibit the exclusion of transgender persons.[16] In its 2023 announcement about retaining the 2004 Act's requirement of a diagnosis of gender dysphoria, the Labour Party stressed that 'nothing in our modernised gender recognition process would override the single-sex exemptions in the Equality Act . . . [T]here will always be places where it is reasonable for

Protecting women-only spaces, categories and capacities 107

biological women only to have access. Labour will defend those spaces.'[17]

Labour's position is supported by public-opinion polls. For example, as of 31 January 2024, YouGov's tracker showed 56% in favour of separate toilets for men and women, with a further 34% supporting separate toilets combined with sex-neutral toilets.[18] And in October 2023, when members of the Labour Party were asked whether 'it should be legal to provide services and spaces that are only for women who were female at birth, even if that means excluding transgender women', 62% said yes.[19] This result is similar to one obtained in 2018 when the question was: 'Do you think someone who identifies as a woman but was born male and still has male genitalia should or should not be free to use female changing rooms where women and girls are undressing/showering?' 59% of respondents said that they should not, while only 14% said that they should.[20]

When the legal right to exclude a transgender person from a particular space exists, how should it be enforced, and should the use of surgery to remove the person's male genitals make a difference? When she commented on the Labour Party's clarification of its policy on single-sex spaces, transgender barrister Robin Moira White wrote: 'When were you last asked for a birth certificate at a toilet or changing-room door?'[21] It is true that practical enforcement of the exceptions can be difficult. But there is a difference between being able to do something, such as using a woman-only space, and having a legal right to do it, if you are challenged and there is a dispute. Use of the space might cause no problems if there is no display of male genitals, because privacy is maintained in a single-user (toilet or changing) cubicle. If male genitals have been removed, some service-providers might make an exception, as in the case of the Korean spa near Seattle. In other contexts, such as prisons or sports (to be discussed below), the main concern might be the average strength advantage of persons who have gone

108   Transgender Rights vs Women's Rights

through male puberty. In these contexts, the removal of male genitals would not make a difference.

In prisons, where the transfer of prisoners is closely monitored (no one can stroll into or out of a prison), the exclusion of male-to-female transgender persons does not present the practical difficulties that can arise with toilets and changing rooms. But, as with toilets, changing rooms and hospital wards,[22] officials must be willing to exercise their legal right to exclude persons born male, in order to protect women. Over time, they have done the opposite, placing post-surgery male-to-female transgender prisoners in women's prisons, and later extending this policy to those (with or without a GRC) who have not had surgery.[23] A 2021 judicial review of this policy relying on the single-sex exceptions in the Equality Act 2010 was unsuccessful. The High Court ruled that: 'The key point about those [exceptions] ... is ... that the minister was under no obligation to apply them, either generally or in any particular case.'[24]

It is true that the exceptions permit, but do not require, exclusion. But failure to use the exceptions could violate the human rights of women. Prison officials are public authorities with positive obligations under the European Convention on Human Rights (made enforceable in the UK by the Human Rights Act 1998) to protect women against 'inhuman or degrading treatment' (including any sexual or other assault) under Article 3, and to respect their private lives under Article 8. In *Edwards* v. *UK* (2002), prison officials put Christopher Edwards in the same cell as a mentally ill man, who stamped and kicked Mr Edwards to death. The ECtHR found that the UK had breached its positive obligation under Article 2 to protect the life of Mr Edwards.[25] The same reasoning could apply to the victims of Karen White, a male-to-female transgender person with male genitals and no GRC who, while held in a women's prison in 2017, sexually assaulted two female prisoners.[26]

Protecting women-only spaces, categories and capacities 109

It was not until the scandal in Scotland in January 2023, involving the actual or planned placement in women's prisons of two violent male-to-female transgender prisoners (Isla Bryson and Tiffany Scott),[27] that politicians finally took their positive human rights obligations towards women seriously. The previous policies in Scotland[28] and England and Wales were quickly modified. For England and Wales, the new policy is that 'transgender women who are sentenced to custody . . . will not be held in the general women's [prison] estate if they retain male genitalia or have been convicted of a violent or sexual offence – unless in the most exceptional cases . . . Transgender women prisoners who cannot be safely housed in a men's prison can be imprisoned in a specialist unit.'[29]

Although the human-rights organization Sex Matters would like the UK Government to go further, by excluding all persons born male from women's prisons (regardless of the offence they committed or their genitalia),[30] the new policy is a step forward. It vindicates the analysis of Professor Jo Phoenix:

> the rights of women offenders to single sex provision in prisons, to safety and well-being, and to privacy and dignity are in tension with transgender rights in prisons. To ask an already marginalized demographic [women offenders] to bear the burden of risk, the possibility of retraumatization, and the loss of dignity and privacy in order to validate the sense of identity . . . of a relatively small number of [transgender] individuals is, perhaps, the wrong balance of competing rights, especially given that there is so little evidence that such risks are worth bearing.[31]

In addition to the new policy on prisons, the former Conservative government announced plans to require 'New restaurants, offices and hospitals in England . . . to have separate male and female toilets . . . [to] combat growing concerns about "privacy and dignity" in gender-neutral facilities'.[32]

110   Transgender Rights vs Women's Rights

Spaces: refuges

To the extent that there is limited privacy in refuges for women who have been raped, or who have suffered other forms of violence committed by men, the arguments for (and legal exceptions permitting) the exclusion of male-to-female transgender persons are the same as those seen above for toilets, changing rooms, hospital wards and prisons. But in the case of refuges, regardless of how much physical privacy can be provided, the question of the potential negative effect of the presence of a person born male on the recovery of female survivors of male violence must also be considered.

In her book *Defending Women's Spaces*,[33] Karen Ingala Smith begins with discussion of women-only refuges (of which she has decades of experience), before considering most of the other women-only spaces, categories and capacities discussed in this chapter. She argues that: 'Refuges are single-sex ... [because] ... males ... pose a threat to women's safety and one of the most effective means by which we can keep women and children in refuges safe is by keeping males out of them ... Risk assessment is about identifying risks posed by violent men' to women and children, not deciding 'whether a male is a suitable person to live in a women's refuge'.[34] 'Women who have been subjected to men's violence and ... are living with ... a trauma response deserve somewhere to feel safe and relax ... where they don't feel on-guard all the time ... because of the presence of men.'[35]

In its April 2022 guidance on 'Separate and single-sex service providers', Great Britain's Equality and Human Rights Commission gives this example of a case in which an exception could be applied: 'A domestic abuse refuge offers emergency accommodation to female survivors. Feedback from survivors indicates that they would feel uncomfortable sharing accommodation with trans women for reasons of trauma and safety. The provider decides to exclude trans women from the refuge. It compiles a list of alternative sources of support.'[36]

Spaces: occupational requirements

If it is legal to exclude a male-to-female transgender person, as a client or customer, from one of the women-only spaces discussed above, it should also be possible to exclude such a person from employment in one of these spaces. The Equality Act 2010 contains an exception for occupational requirements – i.e., situations in which only a person of a particular sex, race, religion or sexual orientation can do the job. As applied to 'gender reassignment', the Act permits a requirement 'not to be a transsexual person' if it would be 'a proportionate means of achieving a legitimate aim'.[37]

A case of this kind arose in Canada. In *Vancouver Rape Relief Society* v. *Nixon*, the Society refused to offer Ms Nixon, a male-to-female transgender person, a volunteer position as a 'peer counsellor[] for female victims of male violence'. It took the view that 'a woman had to be oppressed since birth to be a volunteer at [the Society] and that because she had lived as a man she could not participate'. In 2015, the British Columbia Court of Appeal allowed the Society to exclude Ms Nixon, not because of an occupational requirement (the volunteer position was treated as a service offered to the public rather than a form of employment), but because of an exception allowing a non-profit organization to grant a preference to its members.[38] From 2021 to 2024, the Edinburgh Rape Crisis Centre took the opposite view regarding an occupational requirement to be a non-transgender woman, when it employed a male-to-female transgender person as its chief executive officer.[39]

112 Transgender Rights vs Women's Rights

Spaces: associations

The Equality Act 2010 permits associations of 25 or more members to limit their membership to persons who 'share a protected characteristic' (other than colour).[40] This means that an association of women, including one of lesbian women, is permitted. But, in a February 2023 report entitled 'Lesbians without liberty',[41] the human-rights organization Sex Matters asks whether an association of lesbian women may exclude a male-to-female transgender person who is attracted to women and holds a GRC. They note the UK Government's view that:

> Where an individual has changed their sex [to female] for the purposes of the 2010 Act by obtaining a full GRC, the association is therefore not able to refuse membership on the grounds of their previous sex [male]. They also cannot restrict membership to people who are not covered by the gender reassignment characteristic [who are not transgender] because an association's membership can only be based on a shared protected characteristic and not the absence of it.[42]

Unlike in the case of the pair of exceptions for single-sex services (discussed above), and the pair of exceptions for sports (to be discussed below), the 2010 Act permits a women-only association to exclude prospective male members because of their 'sex', but not prospective (legally) female members because of their 'gender reassignment'. It is possible that the drafters did not contemplate this possibility, or that they did not see it as raising the same concerns about privacy (members of associations are usually fully clothed when they meet).

On the other hand, a women-only chat or dating app (an electronic space) might qualify as a single-sex service under the Equality Act 2010, to which the 'gender reassignment' exception could be applied. In August 2024, an Australian court ruled that there had been indirect discrimination based on gender identity when the female-only social-media platform 'Giggle for Girls' blocked a male-to-female transgender person (who is legally female), based on the male-looking photograph the person had submitted.[43] The outcome might have been different if Giggle had argued that its policy of requiring a female-looking photograph was not indirect discrimination because it was 'reasonable in the circumstances' ('a proportionate means of achieving a legitimate aim' in the UK) to create an 'online women's refuge'. Australia's federal Sex Discrimination Act 1984 has an exception (section 32) for 'the provision of services the nature of which is such that they can only be provided to members of one sex',[44] which allows Giggle to exclude persons who are legally male. But, unlike the Equality Act 2010 in Great Britain, the Australian law has no 'gender identity' ('gender reassignment') exception that would permit the exclusion from a women-only service of a male-to-female transgender person who is legally female.

Categories: positive (affirmative) action

There is a similar problem with regard to positive (affirmative) action programmes that seek to address the under-representation of women in various parts of society. Subject to certain conditions, the Equality Act 2010 permits an employer to prefer 'persons who share a protected characteristic' – for example, women.[45] May the employer exclude male-to-female transgender persons holding GRCs from the category of 'women' because of their 'gender reassignment'? May a political party do the same when drawing up a women-only shortlist of candidates to represent the party in a particular electoral constituency?[46] The Scottish Government has issued guidance regarding the Gender Representation on Public Boards (Scotland) Act 2018 ('50% of non-executive members [should be] women'),[47] which states that 'woman'

114   Transgender Rights vs Women's Rights

in the Act includes a person born male who holds a GRC. In December 2023, the highest court of Scotland upheld the guidance,[48] but the UK Supreme Court heard an appeal on 26–27 November 2024.

The Senedd Cymru (Electoral Candidate Lists) Bill (which deals with elections to the legislature of Wales) appears to go beyond the Scottish Act. The Equality and Human Rights Commission warned the Senedd that the Bill could violate the Equality Act 2010 because it 'appears to base eligibility[,] for inclusion on the [50% women] list, on candidates' declarations of whether or not they are a woman . . . as opposed to their legal sex'.[49] An alternative to inclusion in the category of 'women' would be a separate category of 'transgender persons'. However, any such 'quota' might be filled very quickly, if it is based on the percentage of the population who are transgender.

The problem of the omission of exceptions based on 'gender reassignment', with regard to associations and positive (affirmative) action (as well as with regard to charities),[50] could be solved by adding more exceptions, or by amending the Equality Act 2010 to make it clear that 'sex' means 'birth sex' (biological sex). Sex Matters is urging the UK Government to use its power under the Gender Recognition Act 2004 to make an order that would amend the 2010 Act.[51] (An Act of the UK Parliament would not be required.) Before losing the election, the Conservative Party agreed to do so.[52] The private member's Health and Equality Acts (Amendment) Bill, introduced on 11 March 2024, would do so.[53] It remains to be seen whether the UK's new Labour government will be willing to clarify the 2010 Act, especially if the UK Supreme Court declines to do so.

Categories: competitive sports

Women's categories in competitive sports can be seen as an example of positive (affirmative) action in favour of women.

Without separate categories, men would take every place in the final of every event in, for example, athletics (track and field) and swimming, at every level of competition everywhere in the world. Rarely, if ever, would any woman qualify. A 2020 study noted that 'approximately 10,000 males have personal best times that are faster than the current Olympic 100 m female champion'.[54] It is for this reason (because of their physical advantages, the fastest men are faster than the fastest women) that an exception for sport was included in the Gender Recognition Act 2004, allowing organizers to 'prohibit or restrict the participation as competitors' of transgender persons with GRCs.[55] The concern was and remains that a male-to-female transgender person with a GRC would have an unfair advantage when competing against women.

As in the case of single-sex services, a pair of exceptions now appears in section 195 of the Equality Act 2010, which defines a 'gender-affected activity' as 'a sport, game or other activity of a competitive nature in circumstances in which the physical strength, stamina or physique of average persons of one sex would put them at a disadvantage compared to average persons of the other sex'.[56] The main exception permits the exclusion of any person born male, who does not hold a GRC, because of their birth (and legal) 'sex' (male).[57] The second exception permits the exclusion 'of a transsexual person as a competitor in a gender-affected activity if it is necessary to do so to secure in relation to the activity – (a) fair competition, or (b) the safety of competitors'. A male-to-female transgender person may be excluded because of their 'gender reassignment', even if they hold a GRC that has made their legal sex female.

It is important to note that 'fair competition' does not mean the Olympic Games or other international or national competitions for 'elite' athletes. Every person who participates in a competitive sport at any level (from school to university to masters) wants a fair competition, whatever their age or ability.

116   Transgender Rights vs Women's Rights

I have participated in masters athletics (track and field) for many years. The age groups start with 35–39 and go up to 95–99 and then 100 and over. In September 2018, while attending the World Masters Athletics Championships in Málaga (Spain), I watched a male-to-female transgender person win the bronze medal in the 80-metre hurdles final for one of the age groups for women. I wondered whether this was fair and how the woman who finished fourth might feel.

'Inclusion' in sport does not mean inclusion in the category of your choice, whether that category is defined by sex, age, weight or type of disability (as in Paralympic sports). As Helen Joyce puts it: 'Allowing males to identify as women for the purposes of entry to women's competitions makes no more sense than allowing heavyweights to box as flyweights, or able-bodied athletes to enter the Paralympics, or adults to compete as under-eighteens.'[58] Two recent books by successful female swimmers make the case for fairness requiring the exclusion of male-to-female transgender persons from women's sports. Olympic silver medallist Sharron Davies published *Unfair Play: The Battle for Women's Sports*.[59] Riley Gaines, who tied with Lia Thomas for fifth place in the 200-yard freestyle at the 2022 NCAA (US universities) swimming championships, published *Swimming against the Current: Fighting for Common Sense in a World That's Lost Its Mind*.[60]

The two exceptions in section 195 of the Equality Act 2010 permit the exclusion of male-to-female transgender persons, but do not require it. If organizers do not rely on these exceptions, or if no comparable exceptions exist in rules at the international or national level, the result is unfairness so obvious that any member of the public can see it. Two prominent examples have occurred in university sports in the US. CeCé Telfer (400-metre hurdles on the track) ranked 200th as a man in 2016 (NCAA Division II) but, as a woman, won the NCAA Division II national championship in 2019.[61] Lia Thomas (500-yard freestyle swimming) ranked 65th as a man in 2018–19

Protecting women-only spaces, categories and capacities 117

(NCAA Division I) but, as a woman, won the NCAA Division I national championship in March 2022.[62] The spectacular rises in their rankings, when they switched from competing against men to competing against women, demonstrate the continuing advantages of male puberty, regardless of any hormonal treatment. A 2018 poll asked respondents: 'Do you think someone who identifies as a woman but was born male should . . . be allowed to compete in female-only sporting events?' – 60 per cent said no, while only 13 per cent said yes.[63]

International sports federations have begun to recognize the unfairness of allowing male-to-female transgender persons to compete in the women's category. Three months after Lia Thomas's victory, FINA (now World Aquatics) announced a new policy: 'Male-to-female transgender athletes (transgender women) . . . are eligible to compete in the women's category in FINA [swimming] competitions and to set FINA World Records in the women's category . . . if they can establish to FINA's comfortable satisfaction that they have not experienced any part of male puberty beyond Tanner Stage 2 or before age 12, whichever is later.'[64] Thomas's attempt to challenge the policy in the Court of Arbitration for Sport was unsuccessful.[65] In March 2023, World Athletics adopted a similar policy.[66] But the different rules of World Para Athletics allowed a male-to-female transgender person, Valentina Petrillo, to compete in the women's category at the Paris 2024 Paralympics.[67]

In 2021, the human-rights organization Sex Matters argued that 'Retaining dedicated female categories and replacing "male" with "open" categories may be the fairest way to balance inclusion claims.'[68] In a 2023 comment welcoming the new policy of World Athletics, tennis champion Martina Navratilova (who is lesbian) agreed: 'I think the best idea would be to have "biological female" and "biological girls" categories and then an "open" category.'[69]

In the United States, the 50 states are divided, with 24 appearing to allow under-18 male-to-female transgender

118   Transgender Rights vs Women's Rights

students to participate in girls' sports at school and 26 not allowing it.[70] Some of the laws disallowing participation are being challenged in the courts (West Virginia's law is now before the US Supreme Court), as is a Connecticut policy that allowed participation (see chapter 1). In Canada, male-to-female transgender athletes have been permitted to participate in, for example, women's powerlifting[71] and cricket.[72]

Women-only capacities

Only women menstruate, become pregnant, give birth and are at risk of cervical cancer. Only men ejaculate semen and are at risk of prostate cancer. Only a woman can be a genetic mother. Only a man can be a genetic father. Equality for women requires acknowledging biological reality. Allowing people born male to claim that they are not fathers but instead 'mothers', and people born female to claim that they are not mothers but instead 'fathers', is not good for women. There is a denial of biological reality from both sides: an intrusion by persons born male into the category 'mother', and an escape by persons born female from the category 'mother'.

Unreasonable transgender demands do not affect most women. Few are likely to see male genitals in a swimming-pool changing room or a hospital ward or a prison, or find themselves competing with a male-to-female transgender person for a political party's nomination (in a constituency reserved for a woman), or in a sports competition. That is probably why many women are happy to signal their virtue by proclaiming that 'Trans women are women', and to ignore the harms to the relatively small number of women who are concretely affected by unreasonable transgender demands (small because the number of transgender persons is small).

But linguistic changes affect and are noticed by all women. You cannot say 'women who menstruate' because

Protecting women-only spaces, categories and capacities 119

male-to-female transgender persons do not menstruate, and some female-to-male transgender persons do menstruate (see J. K. Rowling's June 2020 tweet).[73] You cannot say 'pregnant women' because male-to-female transgender persons do not get pregnant, and female-to-male transgender persons who get pregnant do not identify as women. Nor can you say that 'only women have a cervix' (see the August 2021 comment of Rosie Duffield MP).[74] In October 2021, the author Margaret Atwood got in trouble for tweeting a link to a newspaper comment: 'Why can't we say "woman" anymore?'[75] And in July 2022, the actress Bette Midler faced an online backlash after tweeting: 'They don't call us "women" anymore; they call us "birthing people" or "menstruators", and even "people with vaginas"! Don't let them erase you! Every human on earth owes you!'[76] In March 2024, a female Justice of the Supreme Court of Canada, in a case in which a man was accused of penetrating a woman's vagina without her consent, referred to 'a person with a vagina'.[77]

The Gender Recognition Act 2004 has a clear exception for parenthood: a GRC 'does not affect the status of the person as the father or mother of a child'.[78] In 2020, the England and Wales Court of Appeal extended this exception, by making it clear that a GRC does not affect parenthood after the GRC is issued. This meant that a female-to-male transgender person who gave birth to a child, after receiving a GRC, still had to be registered as the child's mother.[79] In 2023, the ECtHR reached the same conclusion in symmetrical cases from Germany. The European Convention on Human Rights does not require the registration of a female-to-male transgender person who gave birth as the 'father' of a child,[80] or a male-to-female transgender person who provided sperm as the 'mother' of a child.[81] Although there are legitimate concerns about a birth certificate 'outing' a transgender parent,[82] these can be addressed by reforms to birth certificates. Reforms could distinguish accurate information about the woman who gave birth and the

120   Transgender Rights vs Women's Rights

child's genetic father (if known), held in the official record but treated as confidential, and a short-form certificate that could say 'parent' and be presented at a school.

Conclusion

In 2022, while I was following the debate about the Gender Recognition Reform (Scotland) Bill, in which it was frequently said that the exceptions in the Equality Act 2010 (discussed above) would solve all the problems that 'self-identification' might cause, I wondered: 'What is the point of a change of legal sex?' In most situations in life, both your birth sex and your legal sex do not matter (are irrelevant), so changing your legal sex makes no difference. In the relatively small number of situations in which your birth sex matters (is relevant), it trumps your legal sex (if it is different from your birth sex), so changing your legal sex makes no difference. Do the exceptions in the Equality Act 2010 make the benefit of a GRC purely symbolic, bringing psychological satisfaction to its holder (who can say that their gender identity has been legally recognized), but no additional legal rights?

7

Protecting children from medical transition

Should all children (persons under 18) be allowed to receive medical treatment (puberty blockers, opposite-sex hormones, surgery) to relieve their gender dysphoria (mental distress related to their birth sex), facilitate their 'passing' as members of the opposite sex as adults, and prevent suicide, because some of them might be 'truly transgender'? Or should all children be protected from medical treatment with potentially permanent consequences before they turn 18, because most might eventually decide that they can accept their bodies and do not need medical treatment to change them? In choosing between these two options, the most important question is: how do we know whether a particular child is 'truly transgender' or not?

The best interests of the child

As mentioned at the end of chapter 2, this chapter examines a conflict that is different from those in chapters 5 and 6. It does not pit the rights of adult transgender persons against the rights of adult women. The conflict instead involves two competing visions of 'the best interests of the child'. The United

122   Transgender Rights vs Women's Rights

Nations Convention on the Rights of the Child states that: 'In all actions concerning children, whether undertaken by public or private social welfare institutions, courts of law, administrative authorities or legislative bodies, the best interests of the child shall be a primary consideration.'[1]

On the one hand, if the child says that she or he wants medical treatment, the child's parents (supported by the 'gender-affirming' healthcare professionals offering the treatment) will see themselves as promoting the best interests of their child by consenting to it, and will view any state interference with their decision as a violation of their right to respect for their family life (Article 8 of the European Convention). On the other hand, legislators, judges and other public officials may decide that the state has a positive obligation to prohibit the treatment, because the child cannot understand its long-term consequences and cannot therefore consent to it. In so doing, public officials can argue that they are protecting the rights of the child to bodily integrity and to a future private life (including potential sexual activity and procreation), under Articles 3 (prohibition of inhuman treatment) and 8 (private life) of the European Convention. One vision of the child's best interests focuses on relieving the child's current distress (the child's short-term best interest). The other vision focuses on preserving the child's right to change her or his mind as an adult and accept her or his body (the child's long-term best interest).

Two judgments of the ECtHR can be cited as examples of a government's positive obligation, in some circumstances, to interfere with family life by taking action to protect children from their parents. In *A. v. UK*, a stepfather was acquitted by a jury of assault, despite beating his stepson (aged nine) with a garden cane with sufficient force to cause bruising. The ECtHR concluded that the UK had failed to provide 'adequate protection' to the boy and violated Article 3, because the 'reasonable punishment' defence in the criminal law of England and Wales was too wide.[2] In *Z & Others* v. *UK*, social services took over

Protecting children from medical transition 123

four years to move four children to foster care, after the first report of problems in their mother's home. A child psychiatrist, who saw the children after their removal, described it as 'the worst case of neglect and emotional abuse that she had seen in her professional career'. The UK's failure to protect the children violated Article 3.[3]

The benefit to 'truly transgender' children

Supporters of medical transition of children argue that it will benefit children who are 'truly transgender'. In 2008, the psychiatrist and lawyer Richard Green wrote: 'Having spent a decade heading the adult gender identity clinic at Charing Cross hospital, the world's largest treatment programme for transsexuals, I have interviewed many patients who regretted not having treatment during their early teens.' He described 'the anguish of the young teenage transsexual as the body changes in the direction of the wrong sex' and criticized the UK for allowing 'the "wrong puberty" ... to progress for years before treatment', resulting in 'unwanted body changes [that are] traumatic'. He cited the case of a male-to-female transgender person denied hormone treatment 'until the age of 16, by which point she already had an Adam's apple, a deep voice and facial hair'.[4]

A similar view was expressed in ITV's 2023 documentary 'The Clinic' (about the Tavistock Gender Identity Development Service, or GIDS, in London) by Susie Green, the former chief executive officer of Mermaids, an organization supporting 'trans, non-binary and gender-diverse children'. She described forcing a boy who says that he is a girl to go through male puberty, to make sure that it is not what he wants, as 'barbaric' and 'torture'.[5]

The benefits to the 'truly transgender' child of prescribing puberty blockers (often to be followed by opposite-sex

124   Transgender Rights vs Women's Rights

hormones at 16 and surgery at 18) have been described as: (i) giving the child 'time to think' about whether to progress to hormones and surgery, by 'pausing' her or his puberty; and (ii) preventing unwanted and distressing physical changes associated with puberty (periods and breast development for girls, facial hair and voice deepening for boys), especially changes that could later make it harder to 'pass' as a member of the opposite sex. In the case of GIDS, Hannah Barnes explains in her book, *Time to Think: The Inside Story of the Collapse of the Tavistock's Gender Service for Children*, that little or no psychotherapy was offered to children after they went on puberty blockers, which meant that there was little or no exploration with professionals of what their next step should be.[6]

As for the benefits of preventing physical changes, they are arguably greater in the case of male-to-female transition than female-to-male (although stopping the development of breast tissue might avoid a future mastectomy). These benefits must be weighed against the potential negative effects of puberty blockers on bone health, growth in height, fertility and sexual pleasure (ability to achieve orgasm).[7] In the male-to-female case, suppressing growth of the penis makes constructing a vagina more difficult.[8] Indeed Marci Bowers, who performs male-to-female genital surgery, has said that she is 'not a fan' of puberty blockers, both because of how they complicate surgery and because of the negative effect on sexual pleasure: 'If you've never had an orgasm pre-surgery, and then your puberty's blocked, it's very difficult to achieve that afterwards.'[9]

The harm to children who will eventually change their minds

Before the 'affirmative' model ('if a boy says that he is a girl, or a girl says that she is a boy, that is the child's true gender identity, which must be affirmed') superseded the model of 'watchful

Protecting children from medical transition   125

waiting' (psychological support but no medical transition of children),[10] most studies showed that a substantial majority of children who thought they were transgender before puberty changed their minds ('desisted') and accepted their bodies after going through puberty.[11] Indeed, in his 1987 book *The Sissy Boy Syndrome: The Development of Homosexuality*, in chapter 4 ('Cross-gender boyhood; homosexual manhood'), Richard Green (who called for puberty blockers in the UK in 2008) reported that, of the males in the 'feminine boy' group who were interviewed in adolescence or young adulthood, 'Three-fourths of them were homosexual or bisexual.'[12] A 2016 review article concluded that 'desistence of [gender dysphoria] still seems to be the case in the majority of children with [gender dysphoria]'.[13] 'A follow-up study of [139] boys with Gender Identity Disorder', published in 2021, found that 88 per cent had 'desisted' (changed their minds about being transgender), while 12 per cent had 'persisted' (continued to identify as female).[14]

If a child, who thought that she or he was a person of the opposite sex, was put on puberty blockers and a pathway to opposite-sex hormones (98 per cent of GIDS patients who started puberty blockers chose hormones)[15] and surgery, but was not 'truly transgender' and would have desisted if she or he had received no medical treatment, all of the treatment was unnecessary and clearly harmed that child. Some of these children have had the courage as young adults to admit that they made a mistake by consenting to medical treatment, and that they need to 'detransition'. One such child is Keira Bell, whose judicial review case will be discussed below.

In her book, *Irreversible Damage: Teenage Girls and the Transgender Craze*,[16] Abigail Shrier explains how social-media contagion seems to have caused sudden growth in the number of teenage girls who identify as male and seek medical treatment. Some of them might not have started treatment (such as taking testosterone, which can cause them to grow facial hair

126   Transgender Rights vs Women's Rights

and permanently lower their voices), or might not have had post-18 surgery, if they had been required to wait until they turned 18 before starting treatment. Psychiatrist Az Hakeem, who has supported 'detransitioners' in his clinical practice,[17] discusses this phenomenon in his book *DETRANS: When Transition Is Not the Solution*, and concludes: 'It is my firmly held clinical opinion that no child can have the mental capacity to give informed consent for any hormonal or surgical "sex changing" procedures.'[18] In *Time to Think*, Hannah Barnes tells the stories of seven children: Ellie and Alex (who desisted), Phoebe and Hannah (who are happy with their medical treatment), Jacob (who regrets taking puberty blockers), and Jack and Harriet (whose medical treatment started after they turned 18; Jack is happy with it, while Harriet has detransitioned). In 'The Clinic', viewers hear from Libby (male-to-female, who is happy with her puberty blockers) and Jasmine (female-to-male, who has detransitioned after puberty blockers, testosterone and a double mastectomy).[19]

Every child who is not 'truly transgender', but receives medical treatment before turning 18, has been harmed. It seems that the majority of these children are same-sex-attracted and might have grown up to be happy lesbian, gay or bisexual adults, with unchanged bodies, but for medical intervention. Hannah Barnes points out that, among patients referred to GIDS in 2012 who were asked about their sexual orientation, 90% of natal females were lesbian or bisexual and 80.8% of natal males were gay or bisexual. In the early Dutch study of puberty blockers, which led to their being offered by GIDS, the figures were 100% for natal females and 94% for natal males.[20] This is why many lesbian, gay or bisexual adults are so determined to protect children from medical transition. They recall their childhoods as feminine boys or masculine girls and realize that, if they were children today, they might find themselves referred to a clinic like GIDS, prescribed puberty blockers, and put on a pathway to opposite-sex hormones and surgery.

Protecting children from medical transition

Debra Soh, Andrew Doyle and others have described this as the new 'conversion therapy': a boy who might have grown up to be a gay man is 'converted' into a heterosexual woman; a girl who might have grown up to be a lesbian woman is 'converted' into a heterosexual man.[21]

The risk of suicide

The 'trump card' of those who support medical transition of children is that, regardless of the potential harms, both to children who are 'truly transgender' and to those who are not, it is necessary because children denied medical transition are likely to commit suicide. Is this true? Fortunately, suicide is rare, and youth suicide is even rarer. In 2022 in England and Wales, the suicide rate for persons aged 10 to 14 was 0.5 per 100,000. For persons aged 15 to 19, the rate was 5.1 per 100,000. Among all age groups, these were the lowest rates. The highest rate (15.2 per 100,000) was for persons aged 50 to 54.[22] Among the patients of GIDS, suicide was more common than in the general population, but still rare: 'From 2010 to 2020, four patients were known or suspected to have died by suicide, out of about 15,000 patients (including those on the waiting list).'[23] A Finnish study published in 2024 concluded that: 'Clinical gender dysphoria does not appear to be predictive of . . . suicide mortality when psychiatric treatment history [for other mental health problems] is accounted for.'[24]

The risk of suicide is clearly not a 'trump card' if one examines the data. Leor Sapir has called for an end to 'the suicide narrative' in the USA (the practice of asking parents 'would you rather have a live daughter or a dead son?') to encourage consent to puberty blockers as 'life-saving treatment':

> If activists wanted to get serious about addressing the supposed 'epidemic' of suicide among transgender youth, they would do

128   Transgender Rights vs Women's Rights

three things. First, they would read the studies on suicide more carefully. Second, . . . they would take the therapeutic focus off . . . gender and, without completely excluding gender . . ., place it on the more plausible causes of teen distress. And third, they would resist the temptation for suicide fearmongering and lay off the simplistic narrative that suicide results from not being 'affirmed' in one's 'gender identity'.[25]

Balancing the potential benefits of medical treatment against the potential harms

In balancing the potential benefits of medical treatment for 'truly transgender' children against the potential harms to children who would later change their minds (in the absence of medical treatment), we must ask the question mentioned in the first paragraph of this chapter: how do we know whether a particular child is 'truly transgender' or not? The answer seems clear. It is impossible for a child, a parent, a healthcare professional or a judge to know what a child will want when she or he turns 18 (as opposed to what the child says that she or he wants now). No such crystal ball exists.

In *Time to Think*, Hannah Barnes frequently raises this dilemma: 'Almost every GIDS clinician I have spoken with is honest and open about the fact that they simply could not predict which young people would grow up to be happy trans adults, and which would not; who would always identify as trans, and who would not. . . . Clinicians say it was impossible to differentiate those who would benefit from those who would not.'[26] Marcus Evans, who resigned from the board of governors of the Tavistock Trust (which runs GIDS) in 2019, put it this way:

With minors, informed consent for medical treatment generally may be expressed by parents. But these decisions usually

Protecting children from medical transition 129

are taken when a child has a life-threatening physical illness or requires surgery. Relying on informed consent ... to gender-based medical interventions with life-long consequences, when *no one can be certain what the child will think in 10 years' time*, is more questionable. The whole idea of treating gender dysphoria medically is to shift the focus of the problem from the mind into the body. But while beliefs may change, the effects of such medical interventions may be irreversible.[27]

In the end, what we have to balance is: (i) delaying treatment for the minority of 'truly transgender' children, who will want treatment as adults, against (ii) causing permanent harm to the majority of children with gender dysphoria, who will later change their minds and accept their bodies. Former GIDS psychologist Anna Hutchinson explained to Hannah Barnes how the 'affirmative' model prioritized perceived benefit to the minority over prevention of harm to the majority: 'the "non-trans-for-life group" are just not given a second thought.' They are treated as *'collateral damage'*: 'Because everybody is so [focused on] the needs of those who identify as trans for life, the second group got totally, totally ignored ... [T]hat's where the harm was coming in.'[28]

To me, it is clear how the balance should be struck. Medical treatment of children with gender dysphoria should be delayed until they turn 18, to protect the majority of these children, who will change their minds and accept their bodies. (My conclusion might be the same even if studies showed that fewer than 50 per cent of children change their minds. But that is a hypothetical question that I will consider if and when those studies are published.) A child cannot decide whether she or he can accept her or his post-puberty body, unless she or he goes through the only puberty she or he can have and experiences her or his post-puberty body, with the only set of mature reproductive organs she or he will ever have. Although some children may strongly believe that they are a person of the

130 Transgender Rights vs Women's Rights

opposite sex 'born in the wrong body',[29] their right to change their minds should be protected until they turn 18.

A friend asked me whether, as in the case of an abortion for a pregnant teenage girl, the decision to have medical treatment for gender dysphoria should be left to the child, her or his parents, and the family's doctor. My response was that an abortion does not usually change the body of a woman or teenage girl permanently. Future pregnancies remain possible. A better comparison is voluntary sterilization for the purpose of contraception. One of the effects of puberty blockers and opposite-sex hormones can be permanent infertility. The Royal College of Obstetricians & Gynaecologists describes 'regret' as a significant risk of female sterilization: 'Regret is . . . more common if sterilisation is undertaken below 30 years of age, if the woman is childless.'[30] In Europe, sterilization for contraceptive purposes is permitted at the age of 18 in the UK, France, Germany, Spain and Italy, but only at 25 in Iceland, Norway, Sweden, Denmark, Portugal and Austria,[31] and only at 30 in Finland (unless the woman has already had three children).[32]

If we decide that it is better to postpone medical treatment for gender dysphoria until the age of 18, to allow the majority of children to change their minds and accept their bodies, does that mean that a transgender identity for life is a bad outcome? Anna Hutchison put it this way when she spoke to Hannah Barnes:

> some of those kids would not have ended up identifying as trans had they not been put on the medical pathway. . . . [T]hat doesn't mean . . . that identifying as trans is a bad outcome. But what is a bad outcome is creating a cohort of people who are medically dependent who'd never needed to be.[33]

The bad outcome is the potential physical health problems that a non-transgender woman or man might experience because

Protecting children from medical transition 131

of unnecessary use of synthetic hormones for life or unnecessary surgery.

Society does not have to be neutral in this regard. A life without hormones and surgery *is* an easier life, and is therefore one to be preferred, if it can be achieved for the majority of children with gender dysphoria. Saying this implies no disrespect for transgender adults who decide that they need to change their bodies. One commentator correctly noted the 'value judgment' implicit in the Final Report of the Cass Review (to be discussed below): 'Cass's report . . . seems to have a clear, paramount goal: making living life in the sex you are assigned at birth as attractive and likely as possible. . . . [T]hat is a value judgment: It is better to learn to live with your assigned sex than try to change it.'[34] With regard to persons under 18, I agree with this value judgment.

Well-meaning clinicians in the Netherlands were the first in the world to prescribe puberty blockers to children with gender dysphoria.[35] The 2006 Dutch Protocol, as it became known,[36] was exported to other countries, including the UK and the USA, despite its thin evidence base and the absence of replication of its findings.[37] The idea of medical treatment of children with gender dysphoria has been taken to its logical conclusion by transgender writer Andrea Long Chu, author of the 2018 comment 'My new vagina won't make me happy'.[38] In a 2024 comment, 'Freedom of sex: the moral case for letting trans kids change their bodies', she argues:

> We will never be able to defend the rights of transgender kids until we understand them . . . as full members of society who would like to change their sex. It does not matter where this desire comes from. . . . We must be prepared to defend the idea that . . . everyone should have access to sex-changing medical care, regardless of age, gender identity, . . . or psychiatric history. . . . The freedom of sex does not promise happiness. . . . [W]here there is freedom, there will always be regret. . . . If

we are to recognize the rights of trans kids, we will also have to accept that, like us, they have a right to the hazards of their own free will.[39]

If children exercise their 'freedom of sex' and make a mistake, it is tough luck for them. This is, of course, the polar opposite of the protection of children from medical transition that I have proposed, and is unlikely to gain the support of a majority of voters. A 2023 *Washington Post* – KFF poll found that '68 percent of adults oppose access to puberty-blocking medication for transgender children ages 10–14 and 58 percent oppose access to hormonal treatments for transgender kids ages 15 to 17.'[40]

Like change of legal sex (discussed in chapter 5), I would argue that the Dutch Protocol, and all subsequent medical treatment of children with gender dysphoria, has been a mistake. Although the goal of relieving distress caused by puberty was understandable, the fact that transgender adults say that they wished they had received puberty blockers as children (see Richard Green's 2008 statement above) is irrelevant. This amounts to projecting the wishes of transgender adults onto children with gender dysphoria, even though we have no way of knowing which children will want to be transgender adults when they turn 18.[41]

If we rule out medical treatment for children with gender dysphoria, we must of course provide psychological support to help children to manage their feelings (including suicidal thoughts). Children suffer mental distress (including suicidal thoughts) for many different reasons. The same interventions can be deployed to support children with gender dysphoria. As Hannah Barnes puts it, 'it is not easy to say no to a child in distress, desperate for something they believe will help them feel better. But sometimes, adults must.'[42]

How can we stop the medical treatment of children with gender dysphoria? It is very difficult for the healthcare

Protecting children from medical transition   133

professionals and pharmaceutical companies who are offering it, and for the children and parents who have consented to it, to admit that a mistake has been made. A third party must intervene. I will now consider three options: judicial decisions on the ability of children or parents to consent to medical treatment; self-restraint by public-sector healthcare providers; and legislation to prohibit medical treatment of children with gender dysphoria.

Judicial decisions on the ability of children or parents to consent to medical treatment

It is often easier for individuals, supported by non-governmental organizations, to challenge existing practices in court, than to mount a political campaign for new legislation. In January 2020, Keira Bell, a young lesbian woman who detransitioned after being prescribed puberty blockers and testosterone by GIDS (before she turned 18), and after having a double mastectomy at 20, became the lead claimant in a judicial review of GIDS's practices.[43] Bell argued in the England and Wales High Court (EWHC) that 'children ... under 18 are not competent to give consent to the administration of puberty blocking drugs. Further, ... the information given ... by [GIDS] is misleading and insufficient to ensure such children ... are able to give informed consent.'[44] With regard to informed consent, the GIDS Service Specification concedes that 'there is limited scientific evidence for the long-term benefits [of opposite-sex hormones] versus the potential harms of the intervention. There are also concerns that it is uncertain whether or not a young person will continue to identify as transgender in the future.'[45] The EWHC found it unnecessary 'to consider whether parents could consent to the treatment if the child cannot lawfully do so because this is not the policy or practice of [GIDS]'.[46]

134   Transgender Rights vs Women's Rights

In reviewing the evidence, the EWHC noted that 'the lack of a firm evidence base for [the use of puberty blockers] is evident from the very limited published material as to the effectiveness of the treatment', and that 'the treatment may be supporting the persistence of [gender dysphoria] in circumstances in which it is at least possible that without that treatment, the [gender dysphoria] would resolve itself'.[47] The EWHC quoted from Bell's witness statement:

> I started to realise that the vision I had as a teenager of becoming male was strictly a fantasy and that it was not possible. My biological make-up was still female and it showed, no matter how much testosterone was in my system or how much I would go to the gym. . . . I started to just see a woman with a beard, which is what I was. I felt like a fraud and I began to feel more lost, isolated and confused than I did when I was pretransition.[48]

The legal question for the EWHC was whether, under the 1986 *Gillick* decision,[49] a person under the age of 16 is competent to consent to taking puberty blockers (PBs), taking into account her or his individual characteristics. To be *Gillick* competent, the EWHC ruled that

> a child would have to understand . . . (ii) the fact that the vast majority of patients taking PBs go on to CSH [cross-sex hormones] . . .; (iii) the relationship between taking CSH and subsequent surgery . . .; (iv) the fact that CSH may well lead to a loss of fertility; (v) the impact of CSH on sexual function; [and] (vi) the impact that . . . this treatment pathway may have on future . . . relationships.[50]

Although GIDS argued that 'the consequences of taking PBs on [the children's] fertility . . ., or on their sexual life, may be viewed as a relatively small price to pay for what may be

Protecting children from medical transition 135

perceived as a solution to their immediate and real psychological distress', the EWHC observed that 'their weighing of risks and benefits when they . . . start taking PBs [might not] prevail in the longer-term'.[51]

The EWHC concluded that 'It is highly unlikely that a child aged 13 or under would be competent to give consent', that 'It is doubtful that a child aged 14 or 15 could understand and weigh the long-term risks', and that, in the cases of children aged 16 or 17 (who are legally able to consent), 'clinicians may well regard these as cases where the authorisation of the court should be sought'.[52]

The *Bell* judgment of the EWHC was quickly followed by a second judgment of the EWHC in a different case, *AB*, in which a mother sought a declaration that she and her child's father could consent to the prescribing of puberty blockers to their 15-year-old child (XY), who was born male but had identified as female from the age of ten.[53] The judge ruled, stressing that she did not intend to depart from *Bell* (she was one of three judges in that case), that 'whether or not XY is *Gillick* competent to make the decision about PBs, her parents retain the parental right to consent to that treatment'.[54]

On 17 September 2021, the England and Wales Court of Appeal (EWCA) reversed the decision in *Bell* as inappropriate for a court:

> The present proceedings do not require the courts to determine whether the treatment . . . is a wise or unwise course or whether it should be available . . . Such policy decisions are for the National Health Service, the medical profession and its regulators and [the UK] Government and Parliament. The treatment of children for gender dysphoria is lawful in [England and Wales]. . . . Nothing about . . . puberty blockers allows for a real distinction to be made between . . . contraception [for a girl under 16] in *Gillick* and . . . puberty blockers in this case.[55]

136 Transgender Rights vs Women's Rights

The EWCA did not consider whether the potentially permanent effects of puberty blockers might be more serious than the temporary effects of contraception.

In England and Wales, it is now clear that children or their parents may legally consent to treatment with puberty blockers. But parents may also refuse to 'affirm' their child's gender identity and refuse to support the child's request for medical treatment. It is not clear how the courts would respond to a case in which a 12-year-old sought puberty blockers despite the opposition of one or both of her or his parents. A California bill (AB 957) would have provided that, in child custody disputes, the court must consider 'the health, safety and welfare of the child [which] includes *a parent's affirmation of the child's gender identity*'.[56] The intention seems to have been to authorize courts to favour an affirming parent over a non-affirming parent, in the event of disagreement. Governor Newsom refused to sign the bill into law.[57] As for whether courts or legislatures should get involved in decisions about medical treatment of children with gender dysphoria, transgender actress Laverne Cox has expressed her opposition: 'If you are a parent with a trans child, it is your business. If you're not, it's none of your business.'[58]

Self-restraint by public-sector healthcare providers

The concerns about GIDS discussed in *Time to Think*, which led to Keira Bell's judicial review, also prompted NHS England to commission the Independent Review of Gender Identity Services for Children and Young People in September 2020.[59] The Review was led by Dr Hilary Cass, former president of the Royal College of Paediatrics and Child Health. The Review's Interim Report was published in February 2022. Contrary to Laverne Cox's opinion, its starting point is that 'The care of

Protecting children from medical transition

137

... children and young people [needing support around their gender] is everyone's business'.[60]

The Final Report of the Cass Review, published on 10 April 2024, concluded with regard to puberty blockers that 'no changes in gender dysphoria or body satisfaction were demonstrated', that 'there is no evidence that puberty blockers buy time to think', and that 'because of the potential risks to neurocognitive development, psychosexual development and longer-term bone health, [puberty blockers] should only be offered under a research protocol'.[61] With regard to opposite-sex hormones, the Final Report recommended: 'NHS England should review the policy on masculinising/feminising [opposite-sex] hormones. The option to provide ... hormones from age 16 is available, but the Review would recommend *extreme caution*. There should be a clear clinical rationale for providing hormones at this stage rather than waiting until an individual reaches 18.'[62]

Without waiting for the Final Report of the Cass Review, and as a matter of clinical judgment (rather than a legal obligation imposed by a judicial or legislative decision), NHS England announced a new Clinical Policy on 12 March 2024: 'Puberty suppressing hormones (PSH) are not available as a routine ... option for treatment of children and young people who have ... gender dysphoria. ... [T]here is not enough evidence to support the safety or clinical effectiveness of PSH to make the treatment routinely available at this time.'[63] On 18 April 2024, two parts of NHS Scotland (NHS Greater Glasgow and Clyde, and NHS Lothian) announced that 'the prescription of puberty hormone suppressants ... to young people has been paused following the research findings of NHS England and the publication of the Cass Review'.[64] The Welsh Gender Service, provided by NHS Wales, is only available to persons aged 18 and over.[65] The decision taken by NHS England is similar to decisions taken in Finland in 2020 ('psychotherapy, rather than puberty blockers and cross-sex hormones, should

138   Transgender Rights vs Women's Rights

be the first-line treatment for gender-dysphoric youth')[66] and Sweden in 2021 ('The Karolinska Hospital ... has ended the practice of prescribing puberty blockers and cross-sex hormones to gender-dysphoric patients under the age of 18').[67]

The new Clinical Policy of NHS England protects children with gender dysphoria (not participating in a research trial) from medical treatment with puberty blockers. NHS England continues to prescribe opposite-sex hormones to persons who are 16 or 17,[68] but is reviewing its policy as part of its implementation of Recommendation 8 ('extreme caution') of the Cass Review.[69] On 18 April 2024, two parts of NHS Scotland (NHS Greater Glasgow and Clyde and NHS Lothian) announced that 'the prescription of ... gender affirming [opposite-sex] hormones to young people has been paused following the research findings of NHS England and the publication of the Cass Review'.[70] Surgery is not mentioned in these policies because the NHS does not offer it to persons under 18. It seems that comprehensive protection of children with gender dysphoria from the first and final stages of medical transition in NHS England, and from all three stages in NHS Scotland, has been achieved. But what about private providers of puberty blockers and opposite-sex hormones,[71] and private hospitals that might decide to change their policies and offer surgery to children who are 16 or 17,[72] and children under 16 who are *Gillick* competent? Is legislation needed to protect children from all public-sector or private-sector medical treatment for gender dysphoria?

Legislation to prohibit medical treatment of children with gender dysphoria

After the EWCA's September 2021 decision to dismiss Keira Bell's claim for judicial review, and the UK Supreme Court's April 2022 refusal of permission to appeal,[73] I real-

Protecting children from medical transition 139

ized that UK appellate courts do not want to get involved in deciding whether children with gender dysphoria should be protected from medical treatment. I began to think that the only effective and lasting solution would be an Act of the UK Parliament prohibiting such treatment throughout the UK. It makes sense if we think of other rules that protect persons under 18 from a harmful practice or substance. We do not allow persons under 18 to be sold cigarettes[74] or alcohol,[75] to be tattooed,[76] or (in England) to be injected with Botox or other cosmetic fillers.[77] Girls (and women) are protected from female genital mutilation. Neither they nor their parents may consent to it.[78] If we protect children in these ways, why should a child or the child's parents be allowed to consent to permanent changes to the child's body, caused by puberty blockers, opposite-sex hormones or surgery, which the child might later regret?

On 11 March 2024, former Prime Minister Elizabeth Truss introduced in the House of Commons a private member's (not Government) Bill[79] entitled the Health and Equality Acts (Amendment) Bill.[80] Clause 1(1) would create a new criminal offence throughout the UK:[81]

> A health care professional commits an offence if they prescribe, administer or supply a medicinal product to a child as part of a course of treatment for gender dysphoria for the purposes of – (a) stopping or delaying the normal onset of puberty, or (b) affirming the child's perception of their sex where that perception is inconsistent with the child's sex.

The Truss Bill does not refer to surgery, presumably because the NHS does not offer it to persons under 18. The human rights organization Sex Matters has proposed legislation against 'modern conversion therapy', going beyond the Truss Bill, that would '[o]utlaw all medical or surgical treatment of minors to modify their sexual characteristics[;] . . . [and]

140   Transgender Rights vs Women's Rights

[m]ake it an offence to take a child abroad to get around the prohibition of modern conversion therapy'.[82]

On 28 May 2024, the French Senate passed a bill prohibiting opposite-sex hormones and surgery for minors with gender dysphoria, but permitting puberty blockers, if at least two years have passed since the first consultation.[83]

On 29 May 2024, to extend to the private sector the NHS's ban on prescription of puberty blockers (outside a research trial that has yet to begin), the UK Government (Victoria Atkins, the Secretary of State for Health and Social Care in the former Conservative government) made an emergency order banning private prescriptions for puberty blockers in Great Britain (but not Northern Ireland) from 3 June to 2 September 2024.[84] On 30 July 2024, a claim for judicial review of the emergency order was dismissed by the EWHC.[85] On 21 August 2024, the UK Government (Wes Streeting, the Secretary of State for Health and Social Care in the new Labour government) extended the emergency order (and applied it to Northern Ireland as well as Great Britain) until 26 November 2024. The emergency order was extended again until 31 December 2024.[86] Following con-sultation of 'organisations . . . likely to be substantially affected' by the ban,[87] a permanent ban was introduced on 11 December 2024 (by Statutory Instrument 2024 No. 1319).

The ban does not refer to opposite-sex hormones (which NHS England is reviewing and which NHS Scotland has paused) or surgery, which is not available in the NHS and does not seem to be available in the private sector to persons under 18. For example, the Cadogan Clinic, 'London's Leading Cosmetic Surgery Specialists', offers 'FTM [female-to-male] Top Surgery' (a double mastectomy) to persons 18 and over,[88] and the London Transgender Clinic offers male-to-female 'gender confirmation surgery' to persons 18 and over.[89]

In the USA, where (unlike in the UK) healthcare is highly decentralized and there is a large private sector, 24 states have banned medication and surgical care for 'transgender youth'

Protecting children from medical transition 141

and 2 states have banned surgical care.[90] In view of the polarized nature of the debate about medical treatment of children with gender dysphoria (and male-to-female transgender participation in women's sports), it is not surprising that 25 of the 26 states are 'red states' (all but New Hampshire) carried by the Republican candidate for president in 2016. The states without bans are typically 'blue states' won by the Democratic candidate for president, in which the legislature is unlikely to pass a ban.

In a 'blue state' such as California, opponents of medical treatment felt obliged to bypass the legislature and appeal directly to voters, by proposing a ballot initiative for the November 2024 election: 'Minors cannot consent to sterilization or removing healthy body parts. To protect the future reproductive and sexual health of children into adulthood, puberty blockers, cross-sex hormones, mastectomies, and transitional genital surgeries for minors should not be allowed.'[91] The Protect Kids of California Act of 2024 would have provided that 'Health care providers are not permitted to provide sex-reassignment prescriptions or procedures on a patient under the age of 18 years' – meaning no puberty blockers, opposite-sex hormones or surgery 'for purposes of affirming a child's perceived gender if that perception is inconsistent with the child's biological sex'.[92] To make it harder to obtain the necessary number of signatures to put the initiative on the ballot, California's attorney general changed the title to 'Restricts Rights of Transgender Youth'.[93] His decision was upheld by a Superior Court judge.[94] On 28 May 2024, Protect Kids California announced:

> they collected an impressive 400,000 signatures ... but fell short of the 546,651 required to be collected within a 180 day timeframe to appear on the ballot. ... We plan to appeal the Superior Court Judge's decision, at which time we will decide how to proceed in the future. ... Had the measure qualified for the ballot, its proponents are confident it would pass.

142 Transgender Rights vs Women's Rights

Numerous polls have found that each tenant of the measure is supported by California voters.[95]

Some of the state bans are being challenged in federal courts. Two federal Courts of Appeals have allowed the bans in Kentucky and Tennessee[96] and the ban in Alabama[97] to come into force. In the Kentucky–Tennessee case, the majority found no unconstitutional discrimination:

> The Tennessee and Kentucky laws treat similarly situated individuals evenhandedly. And that is true however one characterizes the alleged classifications in the law, whether as premised on age, medical condition, or sex. ... The question is whether ... puberty blockers, hormone treatments, and surgeries – should be added to the [psychological] treatments [for gender dysphoria] available to those age 17 and under. This is a relatively new diagnosis with ever-shifting approaches to care ... [I]t is difficult for anyone to be sure about predicting the long-term consequences of abandoning age limits ... [L]ifetenured judges construing a difficult-to-amend Constitution should be humble and careful about announcing new ... rights that limit accountable elected officials from sorting out these medical, social, and policy challenges.[98]

The US Supreme Court agreed to review the Tennessee decision,[99] held a hearing on 4 December 2024, and is likely to decide in June 2025 whether it agrees with the conclusion of the Court of Appeals: federal law (including the US Constitution) permits each state to decide whether or not to prohibit medical treatment of children with gender dysphoria.

On 1 February 2024, Alberta became the first province in Canada to announce plans to protect children from medical transition (Egale launched a legal challenge on 9 December 2024):

> All gender reassignment surgeries for minors aged 17 and under will be prohibited. The use of puberty blockers and hormone

Protecting children from medical transition 143

therapies for the purpose of gender reassignment or affirmation will not be permitted for children aged 15 and under, except for those who have already commenced treatment. Mature teens, aged 16 and 17, may only choose to commence puberty blockers and hormone therapies for gender reassignment and affirmation purposes with parental, physician and psychologist approval.[100]

Is social transition harmless?

This is a difficult question. On the one hand, changes of clothing, hairstyle, name or pronouns at home and at school have no physical or other permanent consequences, and involve choices that I argued in chapter 4 (and will argue again in chapter 9) should generally be protected for adults under sex discrimination law. Why should children not enjoy the same choices? On the other hand, social transition at school could reinforce a child's transgender identity, make puberty harder to accept (it conflicts with the social 'change of sex') and cause the child to insist on medical treatment.[101] In the *AB* case on parental consent, the child (XY) had 'fully transitioned socially in all aspects of her life including legal paperwork' and had 'changed her name by deed poll'.[102] In her witness statement, she said: 'The visible and irreversible onset of male puberty was very and most distressing for me. It also meant that my life wouldn't be my life anymore and normal, where everyone knew and accepted me as female.'[103]

In *When Kids Say They're Trans*,[104] psychotherapists Sasha Ayad, Lisa Marchiano and Stella O'Malley offer detailed advice to parents with children who say that they are transgender. They observe that 'Social transition appears to set kids on a path to medical intervention, . . . [which] can have significant health consequences.'[105] They quote Lisa Selin Davis: 'We . . . have to accept and facilitate our kids' nonconformity, allowing

144　　　Transgender Rights vs Women's Rights

them to present as they please . . . while keeping them rooted in the reality of biological sex.'[106] They add:

> Accepting a little boy's preferences to dress up as a princess, while clearly stating that he is a boy and that he will grow up to be a man, will help him to accept himself and the immutability of sex. . . . Affirm that there is no right way to be a girl or a boy. Our bodies just are, and we don't get a say in them. But they don't dictate what we do, how we behave, what we're interested in, or whom we love.[107]

I agree. Social transition of children must be combined with honesty. Whatever the child feels inside, and whatever clothes she or he likes to wear, she or he will never have the body of the opposite sex. Children should be encouraged to accept the reality of their immutable birth sex (which might mean postponing some aspects of social transition) for as long as possible. Section 2 of the Truss Bill would have provided: 'A public authority [including a state school] in England must not take any steps [including use of language or access to facilities] to recognise . . . children as having a gender that is inconsistent with their sex.'[108]

8

Why transgender rights are not like LGB rights

On 5 December 2022, author and journalist Hadley Freeman spoke on BBC Radio 4's *Woman's Hour* about her decision to resign from the *Guardian* newspaper, partly because she was no longer allowed to write about transgender issues.[1] She said: 'there is a real feeling of fear because what Stonewall, and other [LGBT-rights] organisations like that, have been very successful at is saying that *[trans]gender rights are the same as gay rights.* And anyone who objects to any element of the [trans]gender activism is basically a homophobe.'[2] As we saw in chapters 2 and 3, it is not transphobic to question certain transgender demands, so it should not be LGB-phobic (a term I prefer to 'homophobic', because most LGB people do not like being called 'homos') to question political demands, be they transgender or LGB. But is it accurate to claim that transgender rights are 'the same as' LGB rights?

My initial doubts in the 1990s

In the 1990s, before the political coalition of LGB and transgender had begun to solidify, I had my doubts. I could not see what

146 Transgender Rights vs Women's Rights

LGB people and transgender people had in common. Indeed, I sensed that the two groups viewed each other with suspicion. Which minority did society consider stranger or more threatening? If the two worked together, the one seen as stranger or more threatening might 'drag down' the one seen as less strange or less threatening. It was not clear which minority might be 'dragged down'.

On the one hand, the non-transgender majority found it very hard to understand why a transsexual person (the term used at the time) would feel the need to use hormones and surgery to change her or his body. On the other hand, the number of transsexual persons was very small, which made them seem less threatening, and made them more likely to evoke sympathy. The number of LGB people was much larger and could conceivably grow, if having a same-sex relationship was a 'contagious idea' that could spread across society. At the time, a parent was much more likely to fear that their child might be lesbian or gay than that they might be transsexual.

The mutual suspicion that I sensed appeared to explain the separate lobbying and litigation organizations that existed in England and Wales. Stonewall worked on LGB rights only (from 1989 to 2015), while Press for Change (founded in 1992) worked on transgender rights. In Scotland, the LGBT coalition developed much earlier than in England and Wales, after the new Equality Network organized 'Equality for All: A One-Day Conference for Lesbian, Gay, Bisexual and Transgender People in Scotland' on 20 June 1997.[3]

A legal development that might have influenced the Scottish conference, and definitely caused me to 'try harder' to discover what LGB rights and transgender rights had in common, was *P. v. S. & Cornwall County Council*, a 1996 judgment of the CJEU (discussed in chapter 4), which held that an EU law prohibiting sex discrimination in employment 'precludes dismissal of a transsexual for a reason related to a gender reassignment'.[4]

Why transgender rights are not like LGB rights 147

Suddenly, transgender rights and LGB rights had a lot in common, because they both involved sex discrimination!

Cherie Booth, a barrister representing Lisa Grant, thought so too and asked an Industrial (now Employment) Tribunal to refer the pending case of *Grant* v. *South-West Trains* (also discussed in chapter 4) to the CJEU. The case concerned a rail company's refusal to provide free travel benefits to a female employee's unmarried female partner, even though the company provided them to a male employee's unmarried female partner. In May 1996, I began writing an article that explained why there was sex discrimination in the *Grant* case, as there had been in the *P.* case. The article was published in May 1997.[5] On 9 July 1997, I attended the hearing in the *Grant* case at the CJEU in Luxembourg, as an adviser to Lisa Grant's legal team, led by Cherie Booth (by then Queen's Counsel and the wife of the new British Prime Minister Tony Blair).[6]

The *Grant* case, which involved legal recognition of a same-sex partner for the purpose of employment benefits, was a more difficult one in 1996–8 than the *P.* case, which involved loss of employment. Same-sex marriage did not exist anywhere, while only five countries (Denmark, Iceland, the Netherlands, Norway and Sweden) had same-sex registered partnership (civil union). I warned Cherie Booth about this problem when I wrote to her on 14 May 1996: 'equal treatment of a same-sex couple, rather than a gay, lesbian or bisexual individual, will be seen as threatening traditional concepts of "marriage" and "family", and as having potentially sweeping consequences for employment and social security benefits. The Court may shy away from ordering these consequences.'

Unfortunately, my assessment proved to be correct. Despite the best efforts of Lisa Grant's legal team, the CJEU ruled against her on 17 February 1998, finding no sex discrimination, because her employer had treated a female employee with a female partner in the same way as it would have treated a male employee with a male partner.[7] I thought that the CJEU's judgment was

148   Transgender Rights vs Women's Rights

wrong (and was delighted when the US Supreme Court reached the opposite conclusion in the 2020 *Bostock* case, discussed in chapter 4). Fortunately, the negative effect of the *Grant* judgment was removed, less than three years later, by a new EU law prohibiting discrimination based on sexual orientation in employment.[8] The different outcomes in *P.* and *Grant* put transgender people and LGB people in separate categories in EU law: sex discrimination covered transgender people, while sexual orientation discrimination covered LGB people. In 2007, John Aravosis asked 'why transgendered people qualify as our siblings rather than our cousins'.[9] In 1996–8, I was straining to see transgender people as 'siblings' of LGB people. Today, as I will explain below, I would say 'cousins'.

The LGBT political coalition forms (1990s–2008)

In the beginning there was 'gay', as in the National Gay Task Force (founded in 1973 in New York),[10] the International Gay Association (IGA; founded in 1978 in Coventry, England) and the Gay Games (founded in 1982 in San Francisco, after a court ordered the organizers to stop calling them the 'Gay Olympic Games').[11] To make women more visible, 'gay' became 'lesbian and gay'. In 1985, the National Gay Task Force was renamed the National Gay and Lesbian Task Force.[12] In 1986, the IGA was renamed the International Lesbian and Gay Association (ILGA).[13] The National March on Washington for Lesbian and Gay Rights was held in 1979 and 1987. In 1993, it was renamed the 'March on Washington for Lesbian, Gay and Bi[sexual] Equal Rights and Liberation'.[14]

At what point was T for transgender added to LGB? Of course, a 'referendum' on this question was never held in LGB communities in the UK or the USA, or at the European or international levels. Use of LGBT by formerly LGB organizations and events began gradually at different times in different cities

Why transgender rights are not like LGB rights   149

and countries. It is hard to be more precise than 'in the 1990s'. One can only search for indicators of the gradual change. The 1993 March on Washington used LGB, whereas a poster for the 2000 Millennium March on Washington for Equality read: 'Join thousands of lesbians, gays, bisexuals and transgendered people.'[15] In 1999, the San Francisco-based Gay and Lesbian Historical Society was renamed the GLBT Historical Society, after hiring transgender historian Susan Stryker as its first executive director in 1998.[16] In my own publications, I used LGB in 1999, LGB with occasional references to LGBT in 2000 and 2001, and LGBT (69 times!) in 2002.

At the international level, LGBT appeared at ARC International's first International Dialogue in Geneva in December 2004[17] (to discuss lobbying at the United Nations level),[18] and at the International Conference on LGBT Human Rights of the 1st World Outgames in Montréal in July 2006.[19] The Preamble to the Yogyakarta Principles (drafted by experts meeting in Yogyakarta, Java, Indonesia in November 2006 and published in March 2007) referred to people who are 'lesbian, gay or bisexual' or 'transsexual, transgender or intersex', but the Principles did not use an abbreviation.[20] In November 2008, ILGA was renamed the 'International Lesbian, Gay, Bisexual, Trans and Intersex Association' (the short form remains ILGA World).[21]

In the USA, the Employment Non-Discrimination Act (ENDA), a bill prohibiting discrimination based on 'sexual orientation' (protecting LGB people), was introduced in each two-year session of the federal Congress beginning in 1994–5 (except for 2005–6). In 2007–8, there was a turning point when, for the first time, 'gender identity' (protecting transgender people) was added to the bill. It was later removed, causing great controversy among LGBT organizations, because there was more political support for 'sexual orientation' on its own. In the 2009–10 bill, 'gender identity' was reinstated.[22] Since then, Congress has not passed either ENDA or its successor – since 2015 – the Equality Act.[23]

150 Transgender Rights vs Women's Rights

The transgender-rights movement hijacks the LGB-rights movement (after 2015)

In chapter 1, I referred to 26 June 2015 (the date of the US Supreme Court's decision requiring same-sex marriage in all 50 states) as 'the turning point'. Before then, I would have described the presence of transgender people and their allies in the LGB-rights movement simply as a case of a smaller minority being helped by a larger minority with more political clout. It was a charitable act, which could not possibly have any negative consequences. Then, in October 2016, I attended the ILGA-Europe conference in Nicosia, Cyprus. For the first time, my participant's identification badge had a blank line for my pronouns.

In 2018, Helen Joyce described what followed the widespread introduction of same-sex marriage in Western Europe and North America:

> The final stage in the triumph of gender identity, over the past few years, has been its conversion into a political platform. The moment was opportune. The fight for same-sex marriage was over, and the groups that had campaigned for it, by now large, well-funded and politically powerful, were not averse to turning their attention to a fresh cause, not least because one would be needed if they were to survive. Many on the left were naturally inclined to believe in a new axis of oppression. Some on the right, including many conservatives, regretted having been slow to support same-sex marriage. This was a boat they were determined not to miss before it left dock.[24]

In a March 2024 interview with Katherine Brodsky, lesbian journalist Katie Herzog provided a similar explanation:

> The problem, as [Katie Herzog] sees it, is the radicalism and single-mindedness exhibited by trans-rights organizations,

many of which once presented themselves as representing the interests of the LGBT community more broadly. In her view, their mission creep can be explained by financial incentives: 'You get organizations like Human Rights Campaign, which pivoted away from gay marriage in 2015 . . . They had all this funding, and so they had to pivot . . . Part of that [was] just self-protection. You had jobs, you had a giant budget, you've got to do something. What's next on the list [of social issues]?' As a result, what started as a fight to protect trans people from discrimination in jobs and housing has morphed into a push to include trans women in all-female spaces, whether in prisons, changing rooms, or sports.[25]

Today, there is a transgender-rights movement and an LGBT-rights movement dominated by transgender concerns ('Tlgb' might be a more accurate abbreviation). LGBT-rights organizations generally support all transgender demands and do not see any conflicts with the rights of lesbian and bisexual women, or the rights of children who might grow up to be LGB adults (those conflicts were discussed in chapters 5, 6 and 7). Stonewall put it this way on 4 October 2018: 'The petition . . . asks us to acknowledge that there is a conflict between trans rights and "sex based women's rights". We do not and will not acknowledge this. . . . [W]hat we will not do is debate trans people's rights to exist.'[26] This common 'no conflicts' position of LGBT-rights organizations means that transgender rights get 'two bites of the cherry'.

In the UK, there is Press for Change (transgender rights) and Stonewall (LGBT rights). At the European level, there is Transgender Europe and the LGBT organization ILGA-Europe. At the international level, there are transgender organizations such as Global Action for Trans Equality, and LGBT organizations such as ILGA World and OutRight Action International. As of September 2024, the executive director of ILGA-Europe was transgender, as was the executive director

152   Transgender Rights vs Women's Rights

of ILGA World (who was formerly the executive director of Transgender Europe). In the USA, there are transgender organizations such as Advocates for Trans Equality, and LGBT organizations such as Human Rights Campaign, the National LGBTQ Task Force, Lambda Legal, and GLAD (GLBTQ Legal Advocates & Defenders).

In London, Trans+ Pride was held on 8 July 2023, a week after Pride in London on 1 July 2023, an LGBT event with no set of letters (to avoid the risk of offending a group by leaving out their letter). The slogan of Pride in London 2023 was 'Never March Alone: We March with Our Trans Family'. The accompanying campaign #NeverMarchAlone 'offer[ed] unwavering solidarity and focuse[d] on trans allyship, both within and from outside the wider LGBTQIA+ community'.[27] The message was clear: no disagreement, no debate. As a result, many lesbian women and gay men no longer feel welcome at their own Pride events.[28] In 2022, police removed a group of lesbian women from the LGBT Pride parade in Cardiff, Wales. They were 'displaying banners reading "transactivism erases lesbians" and "lesbians don't like penises"'.[29]

'Two bites of the cherry' also applies to flags. There is a transgender pride flag (blue, pink and white) and the constantly changing LGBT 'progress pride' flag, which consists of the original six-stripe rainbow flag for lesbian and gay pride, on which have been superimposed brown and black stripes (to show that the rainbow is not racist), blue, pink and white stripes (for transgender), and a purple circle on a yellow triangle (for intersex). Proposed additions include a red umbrella (for sex workers) and an infinity symbol (for autistic people).[30] As the symbols of more and more groups seeking representation march from left to right across the flag, the rainbow might at some point disappear.

'Transgender inclusion' extends beyond flags to the very private matter of dating. Stonewall defines 'homosexual' as 'someone who has a romantic and/or sexual orientation

Why transgender rights are not like LGB rights   153

towards someone of the same gender [identity]', not the same sex.[31] This view seems to have influenced dating apps. It was reported that Grindr, an app originally for gay and bisexual men seeking other men, 'prevents users from searching solely for Cisgender men and women'. Grindr explained: 'It was important to us to not further perpetuate discrimination and harm for the trans and nonbinary community.'[32] In practice, this means that gay men are expected to consider sexual activity with a person with a beard or moustache and a vagina.[33] Lesbian women report encountering male-looking 'lesbians' (most of whom have a penis) on dating apps for women seeking women.[34] In 2022, *Observer* columnist Sonia Sodha noted that 'lesbians are now being told by some activists that it is bigoted for them to say they are not attracted to trans women who are biologically male'.[35] In 2023, Kate Barker, CEO of LGB Alliance, described an attempt to shut down a lesbian speed-dating event in London, after it excluded a male-to-female transgender person.[36] Events for 'lesbians born female' in Australia have faced similar problems.[37]

Some sports clubs, originally founded as LGB, have enthusiastically embraced 'transgender inclusion' and the prioritization of transgender identity over birth sex. The Gender Policy of the Federation of Gay Games (FGG), which selects cities to host the quadrennial Gay Games, states that 'The FGG firmly believes that all participants should be able to take part in the Gay Games in the gender category they feel truly reflects their identity.'[38] In June 2022, shortly after FINA (now World Aquatics) announced that 'Male-to-female transgender [swimmers] . . . are eligible to compete in the women's category . . . [only] if . . . they have not experienced any part of male puberty', the FGG issued a press release: 'The decision by FINA to ban transwomen from competing with the gender they identify as is discriminatory and exclusive.'[39] At the EuroGames (the Gay Games of Europe) in Vienna in July 2024, participants in swimming and track and field could choose

154   Transgender Rights vs Women's Rights

between the categories 'Female* identified', 'Male* identified' and 'Non-binary'.[40]

Out To Swim, an LGBT swim club with branches in London, Brighton (where, when I was swimming with them, you were asked to state your pronouns before entering the water), and Bristol, states in its Social Media Policy that it 'will not tolerate ... any comments or content that are ... transphobic, homophobic, biphobic, femphobic, mascphobic, enbyphobic [relates to non-binary], genderphobic, dyadist [relates to intersex], ageist, racist, xenophobic, sexist, cissexist, misogynistic ... religiously intolerant'.[41] Of the 15 categories that relate to individual characteristics, 6 ('transphobic ..., femphobic, mascphobic, enbyphobic, genderphobic, ... cissexist') appear to relate to gender identity, whereas disability (including HIV status) is not mentioned. The club's shirts and sweatshirts feature the 'progress pride' flag. Versions with the original rainbow flag are not available.[42] A lesbian member who objected to seeing male genitals in the women's changing room was accused of being 'transphobic' and sent to mediation. At the end of the process, she no longer felt welcome and left the club.

When Out To Swim hosted the International LGBTQ+ Masters (age-group) Aquatics Championships (IGLA) in London in June 2023,[43] the registration form contained a compulsory question about pronouns, as well as two compulsory questions about gender identity under the heading 'Inclusion and Representation': 'How do you define your gender identity?' and 'Does your gender identity differ from the gender you were assigned at birth?' In March 2023, I wrote to the organizers: 'I have a birth sex (male). I do not have a gender identity. I do not state my pronouns ... I will be happy to register for IGLA 2023 when [these] questions are made optional.' I was told that the questions would remain compulsory because 'prefer not to say' was an option. I replied: 'I have been a member of Out To Swim for over 18 years ... It is sad that a club founded by lesbian women and gay men insists on excluding ... lesbian women and gay men who do not support "gender ideology". I will not be registering for IGLA.'

I had a better experience when I registered to swim at the Gay Games in Hong Kong in November 2023.[44] I wrote to them: 'I have registered as "Other" because I do not have a gender identity, only a birth sex (male). I could therefore not register as "Cisgender Male". Please add "Male" and "Female" [to Cisgender Male, Transgender Male, Cisgender Female and Transgender Female] ... Otherwise, your efforts to include participants who have a gender identity might end up excluding participants who do not have a gender identity.' They replied: 'we took your feedback very seriously. ... [O]ur IT team has made the appropriate changes in how our system asks for gender during the registration process. New registrants ... will be able to indicate the gender identity of their choice, including those that are "male" but not "cisgender male".'

A prior mistake: the LGB–paedophile political coalition (1970s–1994)

In July 1990, I attended the ILGA World Conference in Stockholm. I was astonished to see that the programme included a workshop on 'Paedophilia'. Out of curiosity, I went to it. Throughout it, I was thinking: 'If the outside world knew about this, there would be big problems.' I asked one of the paedophile speakers: 'What age of consent to sexual activity would you consider acceptable? 12, 10, 8?' He was not willing to specify a minimum age. This was consistent with the motion passed at the IGA Conference in Barcelona in 1980 (with the qualification that 'This Conference urges member-groups *to study whether or not to adopt the policy of abolition of all such laws*'):

156   Transgender Rights vs Women's Rights

1. Believing that all individuals should have the right to sexual self-determination irrespective of gender or age;
Considering that age of consent laws operate to oppress and not to protect;
This Conference calls for the abolition of all such laws. . . .
2. . . . Considering that our opponents use arguments concerning pedophilia against the idea of homosexual liberation;
. . .
Considering that the legal use of the concept of 'age of consent' is often a fiction because it suggests that real consent cannot be given under a certain age; . . .
Considering our distinctive ability, derived from our experience of oppression as gay men and lesbian women, to contribute to the discussion of the liberation of pedosexuality.[45]

Helen Joyce's book, *Trans: When Ideology Meets Reality*, reminded me that there had been an LGB–paedophile political coalition from the 1970s to 1994, which I had almost forgotten. Joyce mentions her interview with the journalist Eileen Fairweather, an expert on paedophiles: 'Paedophiles had so thoroughly infiltrated the gay movement by that time [1979] that if you dared criticise those calling for "child sexual liberation" you were branded anti-gay. Fairweather says she sees "the same intimidation and paralysis of intelligence" today, caused by the fear of being called transphobic.'[46]

The prominent gay commentator Andrew Sullivan has made the same connection between the former debate about child–adult sexual activity and today's transgender debate: 'Queering everything, as Foucault showed, means breaking down any and all prohibitions. It does not surprise me that a postmodern movement that began by saying that children can legitimately consent to sex with adults would eventually argue they can legitimately consent to having their bodies permanently altered before they even hit puberty.'[47] Sullivan cites petitions calling for the decriminalization of paedophilia

Why transgender rights are not like LGB rights 157

in the 1970s that were signed by Jean-Paul Sartre, Simone de Beauvoir, Michel Foucault and Jacques Derrida.[48]

In June 1994, I attended the ILGA World Conference in New York, during the celebrations of the twenty-fifth anniversary of the Stonewall riots. There, I witnessed the implosion of the LGB–paedophile political coalition. In July 1993, ILGA World had been granted consultative status as a non-governmental organization at the United Nations Economic and Social Council. Senator Jesse Helms, intending to punish the UN, responded with an amendment to a budget bill in the US Congress, which became law on 30 April 1994:

> 'Contributions for International Organizations' shall be reduced in the amount of $118,875,000 for each of the fiscal years 1994 and 1995, . . . unless the President certifies . . . that no . . . United Nations . . . agency grants any official status . . . to any organization which promotes, condones, or seeks the legalization of pedophilia, or which includes as a . . . member any such organization.[49]

Despite the expulsion of three paedophile-rights organizations from ILGA at the June 1994 World Conference (including the North American Man/Boy Love Association, which had been a member since 1984),[50] the consultative status of ILGA World was suspended in September 1994[51] and not reinstated until July 2011.[52]

How did this happen? When paedophile-rights organizations first joined ILGA World, the thinking was probably the same as when the LGBT political coalition formed: it was simply a case of a smaller minority being helped by a larger minority with more political clout. With the benefit of hindsight, the question that should have been asked was: 'What do we have in common?' Paedophile-rights organizations sought the abolition of the minimum age of consent to sexual activity with adults, i.e., *no age of consent.* LGB-rights organizations sought *an equal*

158　　　Transgender Rights vs Women's Rights

age of consent to sexual activity with adults, whether the sexual activity was male–female, male–male or female–female, and whether the age was 18, 16 or 14. This fundamental disagreement about the rights of children should have precluded the formation of the LGB–paedophile political coalition when it was first proposed. It was a mistake from day one.

I must stress here that I am not suggesting that having a transgender identity is in any way like being a paedophile: my comparison only concerns the fundamental disagreement that should have precluded a political coalition. When a paedophile acts on his or her sexual attraction to children, he or she harms the child and commits a crime. Sexually active paedophiles are universally reviled and have never received any significant political support anywhere. No law protects them from employment discrimination. When a transgender adult acts on her or his identity (outside the women-only spaces or categories discussed in chapter 6), she or he does not harm anyone. In many countries, transgender people have enjoyed increasing respect for their rights over the years, from legislatures, courts and the wider society. In EU countries, the UK, Canada and the USA, the law protects them against employment discrimination. The point of my comparison is that a political coalition between two groups requires a determination that they have enough in common and that there are no fundamental disagreements. This did not happen when the LGB–paedophile political coalition was formed in the 1970s, nor when the LGBT political coalition was formed in the 1990s.

What do LGB people and transgender people have in common?

In 2005, I wrote:

> What sexual orientation discrimination and gender identity discrimination have in common is that they are both 'minority'

Why transgender rights are not like LGB rights   159

forms of sex discrimination, which are often not recognised as sex discrimination because they involve what the majority sees as disturbing departures from traditional social sex roles (eg, in the case of a gay man, wishing to marry another man, or in the case of a transsexual woman who was born male, wishing to have her penis surgically removed). LGB individuals and transsexual individuals are therefore both members of 'sex discrimination minorities'.[53]

I would still describe LGB people and transgender people as 'sex discrimination minorities'. But, today, I would say that this makes us fairly distant 'cousins', rather than 'siblings'. What I was not focusing on in 2005 (because I could not foresee demands for 'self-identification' and for medical transition of children) was the dramatic difference between the two actions mentioned above: a man marrying another man vs a person born male asking to have their penis surgically removed.

There is a huge physical difference between acting on same-sex attraction and acting on transgender identity. Same-sex attraction is 'the possible dream'. An LGB individual need only find another same-sex-attracted person interested in her or him and give it a try. No hormones, surgery or changes to documents are required. If the individual decides that it was a big mistake, they have made no permanent changes and can go back to where they were.

Transgender identity is 'the impossible dream'. The transgender individual's strong belief that they are a person of the opposite sex on the inside does not make it so on the out-side. They will never have the reproductive organs of a person of the opposite sex, however much they might want them, and however unjust they might feel it is that they do not have them. If they use hormones or surgery to feminize or masculinize their bodies, the changes will often be irreversible.

Not only are LGB and T physically very different, they are also politically very different. LGB-rights organizations have

160 Transgender Rights vs Women's Rights

never campaigned to abolish marriage. Instead, they have petitioned courts and lobbied legislatures to end the exclusion of same-sex couples from legal (vs religious) marriage, a form of direct discrimination based on sexual orientation (disparate treatment in the USA). Because legal marriage does not require proof of an opposite-sex couple's capacity or desire to procreate without assistance, there was no reason to exclude loving same-sex couples willing to commit to each other.

The transgender-rights movement has sought to change neutral rules that apply to everyone (rules that make one's birth sex one's legal sex for life and that sometimes segregate individuals on the basis of birth sex), and recently to abolish legal sex altogether. These are much more radical demands. The neutral rules and the recording of birth sex are at most indirect discrimination based on transgender identity (disparate impact in the USA), and will often be justified as necessary to protect the rights of others (women).

Here is another way to explain the difference. LGB people are 'gender-nonconforming': an LGB person accepts their body and engages in their preferred behaviour (such as choice of clothing), even though it is not what society expects for a person of their sex. Many transgender people are in fact 'gender-conforming': they feel that they must use hormones or surgery to change their bodies to match their preferred behaviour (such as choice of clothing). For example, combining stubble or other facial hair with lipstick and a dress is not a 'convincing' presentation for a person born male who identifies as female and wants others to see them as a woman.

A popular LGB-people mantra, from the 1983 musical *La Cage aux Folles*, goes: 'I am what I am, and what I am, needs no excuses!'[54] The transgender version seems to be: 'I am what I am, and what I am, needs hormones and surgery!' We are told today that many transgender people can only live authentically in an inauthentic body. This form of 'gender conformity' appeals to some parents who cannot accept having a lesbian or

Why transgender rights are not like LGB rights   161

gay child,[55] and to some transgender adults who would rather be seen as a heterosexual person of the opposite sex than as lesbian or gay.[56] In Iran, some women attracted to women and some men attracted to men feel pressure to undergo surgery to 'convert' their attraction from same-sex to opposite-sex, thereby 'legalizing' it.[57]

A further difference between LGB people and transgender people relates to the demand that many transgender people impose on others: to 'validate' an individual's transgender identity by seeing them as a person of the opposite sex, however implausible that might be in a particular case. LGB persons do not ask others to believe anything that is contrary to biological science. A lesbian or gay couple in a park, holding hands with each other and holding the hand of their child, do not expect anyone to believe that the child was conceived by the fusion of two egg or two sperm cells. It is obvious that the conception and pregnancy involved (for some lesbian couples) a sperm donor, or (for some gay couples) an egg donor and a surrogate mother, or that the child was adopted. Lesbian and gay couples do not wear T-shirts saying: 'Same-sex parents are both genetic parents. Get over it!'[58]

I would argue that LGB people and transgender people do not have enough in common to form a political coalition: our differences are greater than our similarities. Are there any fundamental disagreements between the two groups? Today, many LGB people strongly disagree with many transgender people about change of legal sex (how easy it should be: chapter 5; and when there should be exceptions for women-only spaces and categories: chapter 6), and especially about medical transition of children (chapter 7). In my view, these fundamental disagreements preclude a 'no conflicts, no debate' political coalition of the kind that exists today.

Was the LGBT political coalition a mistake from the start? In questioning the former LGB–paedophile political coalition, I had the benefit of hindsight. What was obvious to me in

162   Transgender Rights vs Women's Rights

1990 – that this was a very bad idea – might not have been obvious to activists in the 1970s, when 'sexual liberation for all' was a fashionable idea and when sexual abuse of children (by priests and others) was not yet seen as a serious problem. My criticism of the LGBT political coalition also enjoys the benefit of hindsight. When the coalition began to form in the late 1990s, there were no laws permitting 'self-identification' and the treatment of children with puberty blockers was just beginning in the Netherlands (it had yet to reach the UK or the USA). It was hard for LGB-rights activists to foresee how far the demands of the transgender-rights movement would go.

Renato Sabbadini, former co-secretary general and later executive director of ILGA World, explained to me the historical connection between LGB and T, which gave rise to the political coalition, as follows:

> While it is true that if we consider LGB and T . . . today one finds very little in common, . . . this alliance made sense or was 'natural' in the past . . . [T]he gay movement in the Seventies . . . became the natural receptacle of 'deviant' people, i.e. mostly people with a history of betrayal of the expectations their families and society had vis-à-vis their sex and the culturally appropriate gender role associated with it. Homosexual males just happened to be the large majority of the 'deviants' and their meeting/socialising spaces naturally attracted anyone with a similarly troubled sexual history.

Does LGB need a 'divorce' from T?

If the potential problems in the LGBT 'marriage' could not be foreseen at the start, is it now clear that LGB needs a 'divorce' from T? Since the political coalition formed, dissenting views have been expressed from time to time. In 2007, John Aravosis asked 'How did the T get in LGBT?', a taboo question even then, when he supported passing the ENDA bill in the US Congress – including sexual orientation but not gender identity – as a matter of political compromise and incremental extension of anti-discrimination laws:

> over the past decade the trans revolution was imposed on the gay community from outside, or at least above, and thus it never stuck with a large number of gays who weren't running national organizations, weren't activists, or weren't living in liberal gay enclaves like San Francisco and New York. . . . A lot of gays have been scratching their heads for 10 years trying to figure out what they have in common with transsexuals . . . It's a fair question, but one we know we dare not ask. It is simply not p.c. in the gay community to question how and why the T got added on to the LGB, let alone ask what I as a gay man have in common with a man who wants to cut off his penis, [and] surgically construct a vagina . . . But when we are asked . . . to put our civil rights on hold . . . until America catches up on its support for trans rights, a lot of gay people don't feel . . . sufficiently vested in the T being affixed to the LGB, to agree to such a huge sacrifice for people they barely know.[59]

In 2016, Chris Bodenner asked: 'Why Is the T in LGBT?' One reader wrote: 'The T in LGBT has never rested easily with LG because the L & G tend to be gender/sex essentialists.'[60] By 'gender/sex essentialists', the reader presumably meant that lesbian women and gay men are more likely to think that an individual's birth sex (the physical reality of their body) determines whether they are a man or a woman.

In 2018, Jane Clare Jones observed wryly:

> Once more with feeling everyone: Trans rights are just like gay rights. . . . This parallel . . . has been leveraged for all its worth by the trans rights movement. The key thing to understand

164   Transgender Rights vs Women's Rights

about trans rights activism is that, unlike gay rights activism, it is not just a movement seeking to ensure that trans people are not discriminated against. It is, rather, a movement committed to a fundamental reconceptualization of the very idea of what makes someone a man or a woman.[61]

On 26 October 2019, Brad Polumbo dared to write a comment entitled 'It's Time for "LGB" and "T" to Go Their Separate Ways'.[62] He did so four days after a new organization, LGB Alliance, had been founded in London as an alternative to Stonewall:

> This week, Europe's biggest LGBT-rights organization, the London-based Stonewall charity, was publicly accused of subordinating LGB rights to the group's increasingly single-minded goal of replacing sex with gender . . . I am surprised that it has taken this long for such a formal breach to occur. The same pressures have been building everywhere, and it was only a matter of time before someone acted on them. . . . LGB rights and T activism have been revealed to be unnatural bedfellows, and it's inevitable that, as is happening in Britain, they will go their separate ways. . . . The redefinition of sex as gender is a step that most people . . . simply will never accept . . . So long as self-described 'LGBT' activists demand that a male with gender dysphoria is 'really' a female, many otherwise accepting people will remain opposed to, or at least skeptical of, the wider movement. . . . To say that these two causes – LGB and T – should separate isn't to say that one has value and the other does not. I am simply noting that their goals are at odds.

In 2021, Kathleen Stock reached a similar conclusion: 'gay and bisexual people should be the exclusive political project of gay activism, with separate campaigns for lesbians and gay men where their interests differ. Trans people should be the exclusive political project of a separate trans

Why transgender rights are not like LGB rights   165

activism.'[63] In 2023, Julie Bindel, Martina Navratilova and Kathleen Stock founded a new organization called the Lesbian Project.[64]

In 2022, Andrew Doyle, author of *The New Puritans*, saw nothing wrong with separate LGB activism:

> Given that gender identity is at best tangentially related to sexual orientation, the extension of the initialism beyond LGB seems futile. . . . [B]y gathering these disparate causes under the same aegis, campaigners have inadvertently stirred a brew of conflicting interests. This was . . . clearly demonstrated by the reaction to the establishment of LGB Alliance . . . [T]he hostility towards the group was frenetic. . . . [O]rganisations exclusively concerned with issues of transgenderism are not faced with accusations of homophobia for failing to represent gay people, and so why LGB Alliance should automatically be considered transphobic is not entirely clear.[65]

In 2024, Andrew Sullivan argued that 'It's time to return to reality, to say things plainly and to consign this increasingly meaningless acronym [LGBTQ+] to the dustbin of history'. He explained his reasoning:

> Transgender people are utterly different . . . with a wholly separate life experience. . . . The T section of the LGBTQ+ world . . . is comparatively tiny, at around 6 percent. . . . [T]he Human Rights Campaign . . . can . . . tweet . . . that 'the . . . anti-LGBTQ+ bathroom ban . . . passed in Utah' . . . was 'a coordinated attack on our existence'. But if 94 percent of the 'LGBTQ+ community' isn't transgender, how on earth can our existence be at stake? . . . [P]erhaps the greatest problem with the 'LGBTQ+' formula is that it implies there could never be any conflicting interests between gays, lesbians, trans people and 'queer' straights. . . . [Yet] the most controversial question in the 'LGBTQ+' space – the affirmation-only transing of

166   Transgender Rights vs Women's Rights

children with gender dysphoria – directly pits the interests of gay and lesbian kids against those of trans kids.[66]

Imagine a hypothetical LGBW political coalition, with LGBW standing for 'lesbian, gay, bisexual and wheelchair-user'. In such a coalition, activists would realize, before long, that most LGB people are not wheelchair-users and do not understand the challenges that wheelchair-users face. They would also realize that most wheelchair-users are heterosexual and do not understand the challenges that LGB people face. Eventually, the coalition would be dissolved, allowing LGB and W to defend their interests separately (with occasional joint campaigns when their interests overlap). It would be understood, as Brad Polumbo suggested, that neither cause had greater value than the other, but that the two causes were different. This might be the future of the LGBT political coalition.

A new political space: LGB-friendly but birth-sex-affirming (gender-critical)

Transgender-rights activists often chant 'L-G-B, with the T!' or 'No L-G-B without the T!' A significant part of the success of the transgender-rights movement has come from its attaching itself to the LGB-rights movement. The LGBT political coalition has supported the misleading assumptions, discussed above, that being transgender is just like being LGB, and that transgender demands are just like LGB demands. The political benefit for transgender people has come with a political cost: the loss of LGB people's freedom of expression and freedom to disagree with some transgender demands.

What the new organization LGB Alliance (of which I am a trustee)[67] and this book seek to create is a 'middle political space', between 'progressive' and 'conservative', for people who support LGB equality but have concerns about some

Why transgender rights are not like LGB rights 167

transgender demands. The counter-chant I would propose is: 'L-G-B is not like T, sometimes we might disagree!' At the moment, this political space is very small. Political polarization (especially in the USA) means that it is 'all or nothing'. Either you support all transgender demands or you are anti-LGBT.

It is true that most people who are 'gender-critical' (question some transgender demands) are also politically conservative. I can give two examples. In 2021, I read Ryan Anderson's book *When Harry Became Sally: Responding to the Transgender Moment*.[68] I agreed with almost everything he wrote about transgender issues: 'LGBT activists . . . emphasize a unity of purpose between the T and the LGB parts of their constituency – to the consternation of many gay and lesbian Americans who feel that "gender identity" and "sexual orientation" have little in common.'[69] His conclusion, Andrew Sullivan's and mine are the same:

> the transgender cause is portrayed as the next wave of civil rights and as a natural extension of the past decade of LGBT successes. If you support . . . gay rights, you have to support trans rights. If you support . . . marriage equality, you have to support trans equality. There's little willingness to recognize that the LGB and the T are radically dissimilar, especially as applied to children.[70]

But Ryan Anderson opposes same-sex marriage![71] How could I possibly agree with anything he writes? The simple answer is that 'politics makes strange bedfellows'. As Anderson put it: 'Just because we disagree about some things [such as same-sex marriage or the UK's leaving the EU or Israel–Palestine], . . . that does not mean we disagree about everything. And where we do agree, we can and should work together.'[72]

My second example is the pending federal court case of *Soule* v. *Connecticut Association of Schools*, in which teenage girls (now adult women) are challenging the 'transgender

168   Transgender Rights vs Women's Rights

inclusion' policy that allowed two male-to-female transgender athletes to compete against them in track and field and defeat them. The transgender athletes are supported by the very LGB-friendly ACLU.[73] The girls (now women) are supported by the very LGB-unfriendly Christian-rights organization Alliance Defending Freedom (ADF).[74] I usually agree with the ACLU and disagree with the ADF. But, in this case, I agree with the ADF and wish that the ACLU understood, as World Aquatics and World Athletics do, that fair competition in sports for women and girls requires the exclusion of persons who have gone through male puberty.

In her recent book *Who's Afraid of Gender?*,[75] Judith Butler rejects the possibility of a 'middle political space'. A feminist is either with Judith Butler and the forces of Gender (Good), or with the Vatican and the forces of Anti-Gender (Evil). She describes the targets of Anti-Gender as 'trans people', 'anyone seeking an abortion', 'all those waging equal wage campaigns', 'all those working to pass and conserve laws opposed to discrimination, harassment, and rape' and 'lesbian, gay, and bisexual people'.[76] The Anti-Gender movement is a wish for 'a patriarchal dream-order where ... white people hold uncontested racial supremacy'[77] and is 'part of fascism'.[78] The movement 'will target, if not eliminate, sexual and gender minorities'. It aims 'to make marriage exclusively heterosexual, to insist that whatever sex is assigned at birth stays in place, and to restrict abortion because the state knows better what limits should be placed on pregnant people's bodies'.[79]

Turning to birth-sex-affirming (gender-critical) feminists in the UK, she decrees that what she calls 'transphobic femi-nism' (or 'trans-exclusionary feminism') 'is not feminism'.[80] 'Their arguments establish a perhaps unwitting alliance with right-wing groups that would ... eradicate feminism ... In the context of trans people, [they] oppose ... rights to be protected from violence, and rights of access ... to health care without discrimination.'[81] Her claim about protection from violence is false, and her claim about healthcare only applies to medical treatment of persons under 18 for gender dysphoria. She concedes that 'there are serious discussions to be had about what kind of health care is wise for young people, and at what age'.[82]

I reject this false choice between the 'Judith Butler package' of political positions and the 'Vatican package'. Questioning some transgender demands does not mean that one is against abortion, equal pay for women, laws against discrimination or harassment or rape, or same-sex marriage, or that one is for white supremacy. Every individual is free to choose the positions in the 'Judith Butler package' and the 'Vatican package' that are consistent with the individual's principles.

When my seminar at the McGill University Faculty of Law was disrupted by protesters on 10 January 2023 (see chapter 3), I realized that those who accuse LGB Alliance of being an 'anti-trans hate group' have it the wrong way around. LGB Alliance does not promote hatred of transgender people. But the transgender-rights movement promotes hatred of LGB Alliance. Why is this? Because LGB Alliance has committed the crime of high treason. It has done so by distancing itself from the transgender-rights movement, and by reserving the right to disagree with some transgender demands. LGB Alliance has been punished severely for this crime through constant false labelling as an 'anti-trans hate group'.

The greatest punishment came in June 2021 when, shortly after being registered as a charity by the Charity Commission for England and Wales, LGB Alliance was dragged into the appeal of the Commission's decision by another charity, Mermaids (a transgender-rights organization which specializes in supporting children with gender dysphoria and their parents). Never before had a charity appealed the registration of another charity. LGB Alliance and Mermaids disagree about 'self-identification' and medical transition of children. But it is perfectly normal for two charities to disagree. Stonewall and the Christian Institute have disagreed for many years about

170 Transgender Rights vs Women's Rights

many issues, but neither has challenged the other's registration as a charity. It was obvious from the start that Mermaids did not have legal 'standing' to bring the appeal, because it was not a 'person who is or may be affected by the decision'.[83] Its political disagreements with LGB Alliance did not give it standing. But two years of litigation followed. A great deal of money was wasted on fees paid to barristers and solicitors, which could have been spent on charitable work. According to the CrowdJustice pages of the two sides, nearly £300,000 was pledged by supporters.[84]

On 6 July 2023, the Charity Tribunal dismissed the appeal: 'the fact that Mermaids and those they support have been affected emotionally and/or socially is insufficient to provide them with standing to bring this appeal, no matter the depth of the feelings resulting from the Decision or the strength of their disagreement.'[85] With regard to LGB Alliance's public criticism of Mermaids, the Tribunal observed:

> One charity may, in principle, publicly object to the way in which another charity chooses to achieve its charitable objects. ... [T]here is no legal right to be free from criticism by those who disagree with you or to prevent those who hold beliefs that the law recognises as protected from expressing themselves or seeking to persuade others to their point of view.[86]

The Tribunal's decision supported the freedom of LGB Alliance to criticize the transgender-rights movement, which was one of the reasons why LGB Alliance was founded.

Returning to the start of this chapter, my advice to Hadley Freeman would be as follows: 'LGB is not like T. You can support LGB rights and most transgender rights, while questioning some transgender demands. You are not LGB-phobic and you are not transphobic. You are rightly concerned about the impact of some transgender demands on the rights of women and children.'

9

From conflicts to co-existence between transgender rights and women's and children's rights

As mentioned in chapter 1, the political tensions surrounding transgender rights today are the result of what I would call 'abuse of sympathy', which has led to an 'escalation of demands', especially since 2002. These demands have gone from (i) change of legal sex after surgery, to (ii) change of legal sex without medical treatment but with safeguards, to (iii) change of legal sex based on 'self-identification' with no safeguards, to (iv) removing sex from birth certificates, so that there is no legal sex to change. There have also been demands to enter women-only spaces and categories (including sports), and to permit the medical transition of children with gender dysphoria. As explained in chapters 5, 6 and 7, these demands conflict with the rights of women and children. How can we resolve these conflicts, in the hope of achieving co-existence between transgender rights and women's and children's rights?

Sympathy for people with gender dysphoria

A non-transgender person can only imagine what it is like for a transgender person to feel strongly that she is a woman (he is a man) on the inside but realize that, on the outside, her body

172   Transgender Rights vs Women's Rights

is male (his body is female) and that this is how others see her (him). Sympathy is the only humane reaction to hearing that this incongruence between inner feelings and outer body can cause a transgender person severe mental distress, to the point of considering suicide, and that they might consider it necessary to use hormones and surgery to change their body, to make it resemble more closely what they feel inside. The challenge for society is to do whatever it can to make the transgender person's life easier, while avoiding conflicts with the rights of others. These conflicts may arise because the rest of society can only see and hear the outer body (the person's birth sex), not the inner feelings (the person's transgender identity), whether the person has used hormones and surgery or not.

Unreasonable demands have reduced sympathy

By focusing only on the interests of transgender people, and failing to consider the rights of others (women and children), transgender-rights activists have made some demands that most people in most countries would probably consider unreasonable (unlike the uncontroversial and entirely reasonable demands discussed in chapter 4). These unreasonable demands have mainly been made since 2010. They include change of legal sex after 'self-identification' (open to any man, with no safeguards), entry into women-only spaces and categories (including sports), and use of puberty blockers, opposite-sex hormones or surgery to treat children with gender dysphoria. These unreasonable demands have reduced public sympathy for transgender people and shone a spotlight on what I would call 'transgender exceptionalism'. In the US, the Pew Research Center found that the percentage of adults agreeing that 'whether a person is a man or a woman is determined by sex assigned at birth' rose from 54 per cent in 2017 to 60 per cent in 2022.[1]

Transgender exceptionalism

I can think of five features of transgender demands that are exceptional and tend to confirm that the demands are unreasonable (or make it harder for the public to understand them).

First, the demand that legal sex should be based on 'self-identification' is exceptional. Other important facts about an individual's birth are fixed and cannot be changed by 'self-identification': the individual's date of birth, place of birth and genetic parents. The individual's date of birth determines their age. In 2018, a court in the Netherlands rejected a man's attempt to change his date of birth, because he wanted to reduce his age from 69 to 49.[2] In some countries, the individual's place of birth will determine their citizenship. This is the case in, for example, Canada, the USA and Mexico. A person born elsewhere may not 'self-identify' as a citizen of one of these countries by changing their place of birth. An individual's genetic parents, whose names often appear on the individual's birth certificate, determine the individual's racial or ethnic origins, which (especially if the two parents are of the same racial or ethnic origins) will often determine the individual's likely physical appearance. In *Trans: When Ideology Meets Reality*, Helen Joyce notes the 'revealing comparison between gender self-identification, which is social-justice dogma, and racial self-identification, which is taboo'.[3] In the USA, it is socially unacceptable for people born to white parents to 'self-identify' as black.[4] In both the USA and Canada, people have been accused of falsely claiming indigenous ancestry.[5] You do not hear the slogan 'White black women are black women.'

In chapter 5 (Option D), I noted a number of legal statuses that can only be obtained if certain conditions are satisfied: permission to cross an international border, a new citizenship, refugee status, approval as an adoptive parent, entitlement to disability benefits, or the status of conscientious objector to

174   Transgender Rights vs Women's Rights

military service. In none of these situations is it sufficient to 'self-identify' as a person with the legal status.

Second, if one considers groups typically protected by anti-discrimination legislation, such as women, racial or ethnic minorities, religious minorities, disabled persons, older persons or LGB people, none of them requires medical treatment to 'affirm' their identity or live their particular difference 'authentically'.

Third, apart from gender dysphoria, there does not appear to be any mental-health condition for which the standard treatment is hormones or surgery to change the individual's body.[6] I say 'mental-health condition', without intending to stigmatize gender dysphoria or transgender people in any way, because hormones and surgery are used to improve a transgender person's mental health, rather than their physical health, given that there is no physical need to remove or change healthy body parts.

Fourth, 'self-identification' with regard to legal sex has led to a demand for 'self-prescription' of hormones and surgery as part of 'self-determination', without 'gatekeeping'. 'Because I want it' is not usually sufficient to justify medical treatment, especially if it is not considered cosmetic surgery and if it is paid for by a public health insurance system. The 2016 report on 'Transgender Equality' of the UK House of Commons' Women and Equalities Committee supported 'self-identification' of legal sex but not 'self-prescription' of medical treatment based on 'informed consent', as in Argentina:[7]

> Many people now favour the adoption instead of a model involving only the granting of informed consent, which is said to be used by some providers of private care in the USA. However, we are unconvinced of the merits of . . . [this] model. . . . [It] is less appropriate for a medical intervention as profound and permanent as genital . . . surgery. Clinicians do have a responsibility to observe ethical and professional standards

From conflicts to co-existence 175

... In addition, clinicians practising in the [National Health Service] have a duty to ensure that the service's finite resources are spent appropriately and effectively. All of the foregoing obligations are incompatible with simply granting on demand whatever treatment patients request.[8]

Fifth, the 'gender-affirming' approach to treatment of children with gender dysphoria considers the child's declaration of her or his 'transgender identity' as definitive and permanent. The child 'knows' who she or he is and 'is not going through a phase'. The authors of *When Kids Say They're Trans* reject this exceptional approach:

The affirmative approach doesn't accord well with treatments for any other mental health issue – therapists don't usually simply agree with a patient's self-diagnosis and green-light whatever treatments the patient wishes. According to the affirmative approach, not only therapists are meant to affirm; everyone in the child's life is meant to validate and even celebrate the child's perception that she is a boy [or he is a girl]. This includes teachers, friends, family – and parents. ... [T]he paradigm of the affirmative model is that some kids are 'truly trans'. ... We believe it is better to address the causes of the [gender-related] distress rather than its symptoms [the child's belief that she or he is a person of the opposite sex].[9]

Transgender-rights activists should take an honest look at their movement's exceptionalism, which has contributed to its unreasonable demands and to today's political tensions.

How to move from conflicts to co-existence?

The main cause of political tension is the insistence of many transgender people (or of activists representing them) that

176 Transgender Rights vs Women's Rights

others must see them as persons of the opposite sex, regardless of any evidence to the contrary, including the biological fact of their birth sex. As the former Stonewall T-shirts say: 'Trans women are women. Get over it! Trans men are men. Get over it!'[10] It is likely that the majority of non-transgender people do not believe these two statements, and unlikely that they will 'get over it'.

Co-existence would be easier if transgender persons could accept that they are 'in between'. Their transgender identity makes them different from non-transgender persons of their birth sex, but they have not become, and can never become, persons of the opposite sex. I will develop this proposal below. It involves two parts: a 'concession' by transgender people to improve their relations with the rest of society, and a 'concession' by society to make the lives of transgender people easier. The two parts are: (i) an end to demands that others 'validate' a transgender person's identity; and (ii) greater social acceptance (promoted by clear sex discrimination law) that an individual's appearance need not match their birth sex. In some ways, my proposal resembles that of James Lindsay and Helen Pluckrose in 2017, 'An argument for a liberal and rational approach to transgender rights and inclusion': 'For trans activists, this requires accepting that they cannot dictate the language that other people use [or] the beliefs they have about gender . . . A liberal attitude on the part of trans people requires accepting that other people may or may not support your gender identity. If you are discriminated against or intimidated, you should be able to expect protection from a liberal society.'[11]

An end to demands that others 'validate' a transgender person's identity

I think it would be better for the acceptance of transgender people in society, and for transgender people themselves, if

From conflicts to co-existence 177

they were to stop demanding that others (including the state
– see chapter 5) 'validate' their transgender identities. Gender
identity is a personal matter, like political or religious identity.
A transgender person should not expect everyone to share
their belief that they are a person of the opposite sex (if they
hold that belief), any more than they should expect everyone
to share their political or religious beliefs. As Helen Joyce puts
it: 'Gender self-identification is a demand for validation by
others. The label is a misnomer. It is actually about requiring
others to identify you as a member of the sex you proclaim.'[12]
The focus, as I will explain in the next section, should be on
combatting hostile reactions to the difference between an individual's appearance and the appearance that others expect to
see, because of the individual's birth sex.

An obligation to 'validate' a transgender person's identity
is bad for society and bad for transgender people. It is bad
for (causes tensions in) society because it is not an obligation
that can reasonably be imposed on non-transgender people,
many of whom resent being told that they must deny biological
reality to protect the feelings of a transgender person. Respect
for the feelings (gender identity) of a fellow human being does
not mean sharing their belief that they are a person of the
opposite sex and that their subjective gender identity trumps
their objective birth sex in all circumstances.

It is also bad for transgender people because, as psychologists advise, it is not good for an individual's mental health to
seek validation from others.[13] It occurred to me that, when a
transgender person says 'You're erasing my existence!', they
probably mean 'You don't believe that I'm a person of the
opposite sex!' If the transgender person knows that they are
a person of the opposite sex, why does it matter what other
people think? Some people will share the transgender person's
belief, others will not.

Some male-to-female transgender persons accept
that they remain biologically male, despite medical

178   Transgender Rights vs Women's Rights

transition. In 2015, in a comment entitled 'The trans women who say that trans women aren't women: meet the apostates of the trans rights movement', Michelle Goldberg quoted from a blog post by male-to-female transgender person Helen Highwater:

> Though 'trans women are women' has become a trans rights rallying cry, Highwater writes, it primes trans women for failure, disappointment, and cognitive dissonance. She calls it a 'vicious lie'. 'It's a lie that sets us up to be triggered every time we are called he, or "guys" or somebody dares to suggest that we have male biology,' she [wrote]. 'Even a cursory glance from a stranger can cut to our very core. The very foundations of our self-worth are fragile.'[14]

Goldberg added:

> From the perspective of the contemporary trans rights movement, this is close to blasphemy. ... Gender-critical trans women have different theories about why they were driven to transition, but in general, they don't think they were actually women all along. ... [They] are a uniquely despised group: [t]hey experience the discrimination all trans people are subject to as well as the loathing of the trans rights movement and its allies.[15]

Goldberg also quoted Aoife Assumpta Hart: "'I'm speaking as someone who was traumatized by decades of an insoluble war within my own brain between thinking I was one thing [a woman] and physically being another [a man]," Hart [said]. She began her transition in 2011, after a failed suicide attempt ... [In 2015, she said:] "You can't identify your way out of your body. Genderism is a myth that suggests that's possible.'"[16]

In 2024, Debbie Hayton (born male and the father of three children) published her memoir *Transsexual Apostate: My*

From conflicts to co-existence

Journey Back to Reality.[17] She writes that, in 2017 and 2018 (after genital surgery in 2016):

> for the first time in my life, I began to understand myself. Transition [social then medical] . . . never gave me the freedom that I craved. Not only did I need to convince myself that I was a woman, I needed other people to believe it . . . Looking back, it was a fool's game that left me at the mercy of other people's words, thoughts and feelings. Now, I really was free. I knew why I had transitioned [autogynephilia] . . . I no longer needed the rest of humanity to affirm the fantasy that I was somehow the opposite sex.[18]

Hayton accepts that her body is male and, in 2019, wore a T-shirt saying: 'Trans women are men. Get over it!'[19] She was accused of 'hate speech' and faced expulsion from the LGBT Committee of the UK's Trades Union Congress.[20] Nor does she believe that she has a gender identity, or that anyone needs one.[21] She concludes her book by asking: 'Why would anyone want to be defined by a transgender identity, when they could just be themselves?'[22]

Greater social acceptance that an individual's appearance need not match their sex

Both in Sweden in 1972 and in the ECtHR in *B. v. France* in 1992 (see chapter 5), the focus should not have been on permitting change of legal sex through national legislation, or on requiring change of legal sex under the European Convention on Human Rights, but instead on combatting hostile reactions to the difference between an individual's appearance and the appearance that others expect to see, because of the individual's birth sex. As Debbie Hayton puts it: 'Trans people can be protected against harassment and discrimination – and hate

180   Transgender Rights vs Women's Rights

speech – without imposing the pretence that we are somehow the same as the other sex. And, crucially, [without] impinging on the rights of women.'[23]

In chapter 4, in the section on 'Freedom of "gender expression" (choices of clothing, hairstyle, jewellery and make-up)', I noted that, since I published an article in 1997, part of which dealt with dress codes,[24] I have supported the right of any person, regardless of birth sex, to wear any form of clothing, jewellery or make-up, or choose any hairstyle, that is available to a person of the opposite sex. I also noted that, because challenges to sex-specific dress codes are infrequent, the argument that they are prohibited as direct sex discrimination (disparate treatment) has yet to be accepted by the ECtHR, the CJEU, the UK Supreme Court or the US Supreme Court, but has been accepted by the Hong Kong Court of Final Appeal (with regard to rules about hair length for male and female prisoners).

What is needed to protect transgender people, and anyone whose choice of clothing, jewellery, make-up or hairstyle departs from social expectations, is legislation or judicial decisions clearly prohibiting (as direct sex discrimination) an employer's refusal to permit employees of one sex to wear what is acceptable for employees of the opposite sex. Given that court challenges to dress codes are rare (most employees reluctantly comply with the dress code or find another job), the best solution would be amendments to the Equality Act 2010 in Great Britain, the Civil Rights Act of 1964 (Title VII) in the USA, and similar legislation in other countries, states and provinces that would expressly prohibit sex-specific dress codes (including with regard to access to goods and services). Similar amendments could protect the right of any person to choose a 'female' name or a 'male' name, regardless of the person's birth sex (as has long been the case in England and Wales).[25] Clear sex discrimination law would help to promote greater social acceptance that an individual's appearance need not match their birth sex.

My 1997 article (the part on dress codes) drew on a 1995 article by Professor Mary Anne Case, in which she wrote: 'Sex-specific grooming codes violate the plain language of Title VII ... [I]t is important that the protections of Title VII be seen as extending even to men in dresses. ... [U]nfortunately, the world will not be safe for women in frilly pink dresses ... unless and until it is made safe for men in dresses as well.'[26] Despite Professor Case's article and mine (and others) defending the legal right of men to wear dresses (when women may do so), it is not common to see a man in a corporate office or a law firm wearing a frilly pink dress. Why is this? Why are men not exercising their 'freedom of dress'? It occurred to me that it might be simply a matter of convenience. Most men know that others see them as male, because of what can be seen of their bodies and because of their voices. Most women know that others see them as female, because of what can be seen of their bodies and because of their voices. Choosing 'male' or 'female' clothing merely confirms what others presume to be the case and avoids confusion. (Of course, society is used to women wearing dresses or trousers, so women's choices of clothing are less restricted than men's.) But the fact that only a small minority of men will choose to wear dresses to work does not mean that this right should not be clearly protected. It is also true that a small minority of individuals choose to marry a person of the same sex.

If we could achieve greater social acceptance that an individual's appearance need not match their birth sex, with the assistance of clear sex discrimination law, would that make it unnecessary to change the reference to 'male' or 'female' in a passport or driver's licence? Arguably, if you look like your photo, that should be enough, regardless of whether your document says F or M. Public and private employees checking identification documents could be trained not to question a document solely because the photo does not match the employee's expectation regarding the appearance of a person

182   Transgender Rights vs Women's Rights

whose birth sex, according to the accurate information in the document, is male or female.

An individual's 'appearance' to others includes the sound of their voice. A transgender person with a male-sounding voice, wearing clothing associated with women, might encounter discrimination, which should be clearly prohibited, whether on the basis of 'sex', 'gender reassignment' or 'gender identity'. In Québec, the Human Rights Tribunal ruled on 10 June 2024 that a male-to-female transgender person had been denied employment on the basis of gender identity:[27] 'the manager noticed the woman's voice had a masculine timbre and asked if she was trans. When the woman confirmed she was, the manager said he couldn't hire her. . . . [He] said the bar's clientele was "old-fashioned", and he didn't want to have to defend the woman every day.'

Would greater social acceptance help more transgender adults to accept their bodies?

In chapter 7, I concluded that medical transition (use of puberty blockers, opposite-sex hormones or surgery) should be prohibited for children (persons under 18). But transgender adults must be allowed to seek medical treatment to change their bodies, if they consider it necessary. In 1995, after a criminal prosecution for sado-masochism (which later reached the ECtHR),[28] the Law Commission recommended reform of the criminal law of England and Wales on consent to make it clear that 'the intentional causing of any injury to another person *other than seriously disabling injury* . . . should not be criminal if . . . the other person consented to injury of the type caused'. The report includes an exception, applying to injury 'of whatever degree of seriousness', for 'proper medical treatment or care administered with the consent of [the adult patient]', which includes 'surgical operations performed

From conflicts to co-existence   183

for the purposes of enabling a person to change his or her sex'.[29]

If society became more accepting of male-looking/male-sounding persons wearing clothing, make-up and hairstyles associated with women, or female-looking/female-sounding persons wearing clothing and hairstyles associated with men, would more transgender people decide that they do not need to transition medically, thereby avoiding the potential complications of surgery or side effects of life-long hormone use?[30] Hannah Winterbourne, a male-to-female transgender army officer who transitioned socially in 2012 and had surgery in 2015, said: 'I transitioned because it is who I am. There is no choice. You can no more choose than you can choose to be black or white or left handed.'[31]

Others argue that 'no one is born in the wrong body' and that medical treatment is for mental distress, not for a problem with the transgender person's body. Peter Gajdics, a gay man, does not agree that 'someone can be born into the "wrong body". [This] implies that there is a "right body" – [but] all [we] ever know is the body we were born into. Bodies are not right or wrong; they just are. Experiencing distress with the body we were born into is something else.'[32] Similarly, in *Defending Women's Spaces*, Karen Ingala Smith asks:

> Resisting sex stereotypes and gender norms is a feminist issue and a trans one too, and yet we are divided between those who think that the answer lies in changing the individual and those who believe that we need to change society, to abolish not entrench gender. How can it be that a body needs to be altered chemically and surgically to fit the prison of gender, rather than the bars of the cells be ripped down?[33]

As Helen Joyce puts it: 'These redefinitions ... define womanhood as stereotypes enacted by people of different body types [female or male], rather than a body type [female] that need

184   Transgender Rights vs Women's Rights

not in any way limit the behaviour of the people who possess it.'[34]

When I read *The Myth of the Wrong Body* by Miquel Missé, a female-to-male transgender person born in Barcelona, I was surprised to learn that someone with a very different perspective had reached conclusions similar to mine, regarding medical treatment of children and adults with gender dysphoria: 'we knew that we wanted to denounce ... the perpetual medical treatment of trans people, which concealed an asphyxiating, normalizing gender system.'[35] He is concerned that:

> the intense focus placed on transgender minors has hijacked trans movements and politics ... Boys with feminine gender expressions and girls with masculine gender expressions have probably always existed. What is new is the labeling of these children as transgender minors. ... Just as with trans adults before, the medical model has a solution for being transgender in minors. Now they talk about hormonal blockers. What a surprise, another medical solution based in the modification of trans people's bodies. ... Once again, the suffering of trans people is resolved by altering the body, and that is the underlying idea that I think we need to challenge.[36]

Missé criticizes the focus on a transgender person 'passing' as a person of the opposite sex, ideally one who is 'beautiful and sexy':[37] 'Up to what point are we going to swallow the lie that surgery is the solution to the suffering, when in fact we know it's a structural problem caused by the rigidity of the gender system?'[38] He hopes 'to transform many trans people's need to change their bodies'.[39] Regarding 'the wrong body', he writes:

> I often ask cis persons if they think it's possible to be born trapped in the wrong body. Their unwillingness to respond speaks volumes. Then I say that I don't think it's possible, and suddenly the oxygen rushes back into the room. Many people

suddenly say: 'If you say it, then I can say it too', 'I didn't dare to say it because I'm not trans' . . . Creating a bubble of exceptionality around transgendered individuals that makes most people prefer not to speak out critically . . . is the worst thing that we can do for the trans movement.[40]

Similarly, Corinna Cohn, a male-to-female transgender person who had surgery at 19, urges young transgender adults considering medical treatment to 'slow down': 'You may yet decide to make the change. But if you explore the world by inhabiting your body as it is, perhaps you'll find that you love it more than you thought possible.'[41]

No one chooses their birth sex or their body. Making changes to your body to improve your mental health is counter-intuitive. People reciting the Serenity Prayer of Alcoholics Anonymous ask for 'the serenity to accept the things I cannot change'.[42] Is it better to accept your reproductive organs and secondary sex characteristics than try to change them?

Biology (your body) is not destiny: putting aside roles in human reproduction, a woman can do anything she wants in life, as can a man. Similarly, feelings (your gender identity) are not destiny: you do not have to change your body. Might the best option for many transgender people be to express their feelings about their 'true gender', while accepting their bodies and their birth sex? Could this 'middle option' be better than suppressing these feelings (which could have a negative effect on their mental health), or acting on these feelings by rejecting their bodies and their birth sex and seeking to change their bodies (which could have a negative effect on their physical health, because of complications of surgery or side effects of hormones)?

Conclusion

Throughout this book, and especially in this chapter, I have tried to show 'tough love' for transgender people. I have proposed a model for co-existence which I think could reduce conflict and division and which could be implemented, eventually, in every country in the world. Because same-sex marriage does not affect heterosexual people, it can eventually be introduced in every country in the world, including Jamaica, Venezuela, Nigeria, Uganda, Hungary, Russia, Saudi Arabia, Iran, India and China. But the model of 'Trans women are women', 'Trans women in women's prisons', 'Trans women in women's sports' and 'Trans children need medical treatment', which has caused a strong political backlash in North America, Western Europe and Australasia, is not one that can spread across the world. The only model of transgender rights that can do so is one that respects 'the rights of others' – the rights of women and children.

Notes

1 How did we get here? From sympathy for transsexuals (1972) to a call to remove sex from birth certificates (2017)

1 See https://twitter.com/MForstater/status/1044588721423638529 (25 September 2018).

2 See https://twitter.com/jk_rowling/status/1207646162813100033.

3 See www.france24.com/en/live-news/20211122-j-k-rowling-reveals-death-threats-over-transgender-row; the podcast 'The Witch Trials of J. K. Rowling'; J. K. Rowling, 'Wheesht for the witch burners' in Susan Dalgety & Lucy Hunter Blackburn (eds.), *The Women Who Wouldn't Wheesht: Voices from the Frontline of Scotland's Battle for Women's Rights* (Constable, 2024).

4 See www.lefigaro.fr/international/bruxelles-une-conference-sur-le-transgenrisme-perturbee-par-des-jets-d-excrements-20221216; Eliacheff & Masson, *La fabrique de l'enfant transgenre: Comment protéger les mineurs d'un scandale sanitaire?* (Observatoire, 2022).

5 See https://elizamondegreen.substack.com/p/this-is-what-no-debate-looks-like.

6 I will use this term and 'female-to-male transgender person'. These neutral and respectful terms are used in the Hate Crime and Public Order (Scotland) Act 2021, section 11(7). I will not use the terms 'trans woman' and 'trans man', which imply that birth sex is irrelevant.

7 See www.gov.uk/government/news/new-transgender-prisoner-policy-comes-into-force.

188   Notes to pp. 2–6

8   See https://leginfo.legislature.ca.gov/faces/billTextClient.xhtml?bill_id =201920200SB132 (emphasis added).

9   See section 195(2).

10   See 'Transgender track stars speak out as critics allege unfair advantage' (*ABC News*, 22 June 2018), https://youtu.be/sHqiG_hrbsc; www.aclu .org/press-releases/appeals-court-declines-to-rule-against-connecti cuts-inclusive-policy-for-transgender-athletes; https://adflegal.org/case /soule-v-connecticut-association-schools.

11   See *West Virginia* v. *B.P.J.*, www.ca4.uscourts.gov/opinions/231078 .p.pdf (Fourth Circuit, 16 April 2024); https://ago.wv.gov/Documents /7.11%20BPJ%20Petition%20final.pdf (petition for review by Supreme Court); www.supremecourt.gov/search.aspx?filename=/docket/docket files/html/public/24-43.html.

12   See www.nbcnews.com/nbc-out/out-news/transgender-athlete-wins -discrimination-case-usa-powerlifting-rcna72879 (2 March 2023); https://casetext.com/case/cooper-v-usa-powerlifting (18 March 2024).

13   See Carole Hooven, www.thefp.com/p/carole-hooven-why-i-left-harvard (17 January 2024); 'Academic freedom is social justice: sex, gender, and cancel culture on campus' (2023) 52 *Archives of Sexual Behavior* 35, https://link.springer.com/article/10.1007/s10508-022-02467-5.

14   See Peter Dunne, 'Transgender sterilisation requirements in Europe' (2017) 25 *Medical Law Review* 554.

15   See https://hudoc.echr.coe.int/?i=001-57770 (25 March 1992).

16   See Cass. ass. plén., 11 December 1992, no. 91-11.900.

17   See https://hudoc.echr.coe.int/?i=001-60596 (11 July 2002).

18   Ibid., paras. 55, 78, 90.

19   See www.washingtonpost.com/dc-md-va/2023/03/23/transgender- adults-transitioning-poll: 'Less than a third have used hormone treatments or puberty blockers, and about 1 in 6 have undergone gender-affirming surgery or other surgical treatment to change their physical appearance.'

20   See http://yogyakartaprinciples.org/wp-content/uploads/2016/08/prin ciples_en.pdf.

21   See *Ley* (Law) 26.743 of 9 May 2012, www.argentina.gob.ar/norma tiva/nacional/ley-26743-197860/texto, Article 3; https://globalhealth .usc.edu/wp-content/uploads/2017/03/english-translation-of-argen tina_s-gender-identity-law-as-approved-by-the-senate-of-argentina-on -may-8-2012.pdf.

22   See https://transrightsmap.tgeu.org/home/legal-gender-recognition/ cluster-map. It is not clear whether Germany's 2024 law can be

Notes to pp. 6–11

considered 'self-identification'. It does not require a diagnosis but does include a three-month waiting period (unlike in Argentina and Ireland). Sweden's 2024 law requires a certificate from a doctor (unlike in Argentina and Ireland).

23 See https://hudoc.echr.coe.int/?i=001-172913 (6 April 2017).

24 Ibid., para. 143.

25 Ibid., paras. 72, 135.

26 As of 3 January 2025, eleven states require surgery: Alabama, Arizona, Arkansas, Georgia, Kentucky, Louisiana, Missouri, Nebraska, North Dakota, Wisconsin and Wymong. Six states that do not permit the sex on an individual's birth certificate to be changed: Florida, Kansas, Montana, Oklahoma, Tennessee and Texas.

27 See http://yogyakartaprinciples.org/wp-content/uploads/2017/11/A5 _yogyakartaWEB-2.pdf.

28 See www.icc-cpi.int/sites/default/files/RS-Eng.pdf, Article 7(3).

29 Helen Joyce calls this 'gender-as-stereotypes' (*Trans: When Ideology Meets Reality*, Oneworld, 2021, p. 115). My 'gender as behaviour' combines Alex Byrne's 'gender as femininity/masculinity' and 'gender as social roles' (*Trouble with Gender: Sex Facts, Gender Fictions*, Polity, 2024, pp. 36–40), or Kathleen Stock's GENDER2 ('masculinity' and 'femininity') and GENDER3 ('manhood' and 'womanhood') (*Material Girls: Why Reality Matters for Feminism*, Fleet, 2021, p. 38).

30 See https://rm.coe.int/168008482e, Article 3(c).

31 See Judith Butler, *Gender Trouble: Feminism and the Subversion of Identity* (Routledge, 1990), pp. 4, 8.

32 Ibid., p. 5.

33 Ibid., p. 9.

34 Ibid., p. 25.

35 Ibid., pp. 190–1.

36 Ibid., p. 200.

37 Ibid., p. 203.

38 See Raquel Rosario Sánchez, www.spiked-online.com/2021/09/16/how -judith-butlers-gender-theories-sidelined-women.

39 See R. Wintemute, 'Recognising new kinds of direct sex discrimination: transsexualism, sexual orientation and dress codes' (1997) 60 *Modern Law Review* 334, https://onlinelibrary.wiley.com/doi/10.1111/ 1468-2230.00084.

40 See Robert Wintemute, 'Lesbian and gay inequality 2000: the potential of the Human Rights Act 1998 and the need for an Equality Act 2002' [2000] *European Human Rights Law Review* 603.

41 Equality Act 2010, section 10.

42 See Noa Ben-Asher, 'Transforming legal sex', *North Carolina Law Review* (forthcoming, 2024), https://papers.ssrn.com/sol3/papers.cfm?abstract_id=4344840 ('the trend in U.S. law is toward viewing gender identity, defined as "an individual's own internal sense of whether they are a man, a woman, or nonbinary," as a central characteristic of legal sex').

43 See https://quillette.com/2018/12/04/the-new-patriarchy-how-trans-radicalism-hurts-women-children-and-trans-people-themselves.

44 See Stonewall UK, https://twitter.com/stonewalluk/status/1207972598384082946?lang=en (20 December 2019).

45 See https://twitter.com/charilaou_alex/status/1684598307849445377.

46 See R. Wintemute, *Sexual Orientation and Human Rights* (Oxford University Press, 1995/7).

47 539 US 558, www.law.cornell.edu/supct/html/02-102.ZS.html (26 June 2003).

48 *Bostock* v. *Clayton County* 590 US 644 (2020).

49 See www.law.cornell.edu/supremecourt/text/14-556 (26 June 2015).

50 See Simon Edge, *The End of the World Is Flat* (Lightning Books, 2021).

51 See www.stonewall.org.uk/resources/key-dates-lesbian-gay-bi-and-trans-equality.

52 See https://time.com/magazine/us/135460/june-9th-2014-vol-183-no-22-u-s. See also https://en.wikipedia.org/wiki/Elliot_Page#/media/File:Elliot_Page_Time_Magazine.jpg (29 March – 5 April 2021 issue).

53 See https://youtu.be/JaqLG3myKUk.

54 See www.vanityfair.com/hollywood/2015/06/caitlyn-jenner-bruce-cover-annie-leibovitz.

55 Butler, *Gender Trouble*, at p. xxvii of 'Preface (1999)'.

56 See www.bbc.co.uk/news/uk-england-57853385, quoting Nancy Kelley of Stonewall: 'when dating, [if] you are writing off ... people of colour ... or trans people, then it's worth considering how societal prejudices may have shaped your attractions.'

57 R. Wintemute, 'Sexual orientation and gender identity' in Colin Harvey (ed.), *Human Rights in the Community* (Hart Publishing, 2005), p. 176.

58 Gender Recognition Act 2015.

59 Gender Recognition Act 2004, section 4(2) (as amended in 2013).

60 See https://thecritic.co.uk/issues/april-2021/the-trans-rights-that-trump-all.

Notes to pp. 21–30   191

61 See https://lgballiance.org.uk.
62 See www.dailymail.co.uk/news/article-10118587/Boris-Johnson-wades -culture-war-backing-controversial-LGB-Alliance-group.html (video 'Protesters chant outside LGB Alliance conference in London').
63 (Fleet, 2021).
64 (Oxford University Press, 2022).
65 (Polity, 2024).
66 (Constable, 2024).
67 (Polity, 2024).

2 Transgender rights vs women's rights: why the human rights of two groups often conflict

1 See Articles 8(2), 9(2), 10(2) and 11(2).
2 See Articles 12, 18(3), 19(3)(a), 21 and 22(2).
3 See Articles 3 and 15 of the European Convention on Human Rights.
4 See *Bouyid* v. *Belgium*, https://hudoc.echr.coe.int/fre?i=001-157670 (28 September 2015).
5 See *W. P.* v. *UK*, https://hudoc.echr.coe.int/eng?i=001-74270 (13 May 1980).
6 See *Evans* v. *UK*, https://hudoc.echr.coe.int/fre?i=001-80046 (10 April 2007), para. 90.
7 See *von Hannover* v. *Germany*, https://hudoc.echr.coe.int/?i=001-61853 (24 June 2004), para. 77.
8 See *Couderc & Hachette Filipacchi Associés* v. *France*, https://hudoc. echr.coe.int/fre?i=001-158861 (10 November 2015), para. 108.
9 Equality Act 2010, Schedule 9, para. 2(4)(a).
10 Schedule 9, para. 3.
11 Schedule 9, para. 1(1). See also Equality Act 2010, sections 15, 20 and 21.
12 Equality Act 2010, section 13(2). See also *Prigge* v. *Lufthansa*, Case C-447/09, Court of Justice of the European Union (13 September 2011).
13 Schedule 3, para. 25A.
14 See (2002) 1 *Journal of Law and Equality* 125.
15 Ibid., 141–2.
16 See *Eweida & Others (Ladele)* v. *UK*, https://hudoc.echr.coe.int/fre?i= 001-115881 (15 January 2013).
17 See *Bull* v. *Hall*, www.supremecourt.uk/cases/uksc-2012-0065.html (27 November 2013). See also Robert Wintemute, 'Accommodating religious beliefs: harm, clothing or symbols, and refusals to serve others' (2014) 77 *Modern Law Review* 223.

192 Notes to pp. 30–38

18 Equality Act (Sexual Orientation) Regulations 2007, reg. 14(2), now Equality Act 2010, Schedule 23, para. 2(2).

19 See Marriage (Same Sex Couples) Act 2013, sections 1(3), 1(4).

20 Sections 2, 4 and 5.

21 See *Pemberton* v. *Inwood*, www.bailii.org/ew/cases/EWCA/Civ/2018/564.html (22 March 2018), applying Equality Act 2010, Schedule 9, para. 2(1)(a).

22 See *Lee* v. *Ashers Baking* [2016] NICA 39, www.judiciaryni.uk/judicial-decisions/2016-nica-39 (24 October 2016), para. 67.

23 See [2018] UKSC 49, www.supremecourt.uk/cases/uksc-2017-0020.html (10 October 2018), paras. 22–3, 25, 34.

24 See Robert Wintemute, 'Message-printing businesses, non-discrimination and free expression: Northern Ireland's "Support Gay Marriage" cake case' (2015) 26 *King's Law Journal* 348–56.

25 [2018] UKSC 49, paras. 47–8, 54–7, 62.

26 See *Masterpiece Cakeshop* v. *Colorado Civil Rights Commission*, 584 US 617, www.supremecourt.gov/opinions/17pdf/16-111_j4el.pdf (4 June 2018).

27 See *303 Creative* v. *Elenis*, 600 US 570, www.supremecourt.gov/opinions/22pdf/21-476_c185.pdf (30 June 2023).

28 See www.bbc.co.uk/news/world-us-canada-49571207.

29 See Robert Wintemute, 'Europe's last colony: 1918 Palestine's Arab majority, Jewish immigration, and the justice of founding Israel outside Europe' (2012) 21 *Social and Legal Studies* 121–34.

30 See Robert Wintemute, 'Israel–Palestine through the lens of racial discrimination law: is the South African apartheid analogy accurate, and what if the European Convention applied?' (2017) 28 *King's Law Journal* 89–129. See also www.aljazeera.com/opinions/2018/5/17/gaza-is-israels-soweto.

31 See *Brown* v. *Board of Education of Topeka*, 347 US 483 (1954).

32 Equality Act 2010, Schedule 3, paras. 26–8.

33 See *City of Cleburne* v. *Cleburne Living Center, Inc.*, 473 US 432 (1985).

3 Transphobia: what is it, and what is instead protected political expression?

1 See https://dictionary.cambridge.org/dictionary/english/transphobia.

2 Sentencing Act 2020, section 66.

3 Hate Crime and Public Order (Scotland) Act 2021, section 4(3).

4 See www.holocaustremembrance.com/resources/working-definitions-charters/working-definition-antisemitism.

5 See https://transactual.org.uk/transphobia.

Notes to pp. 39–43

6 See www.gov.uk/government/statistics/hate-crime-england-and-wales-2022-to-2023/hate-crime-england-and-wales-2022-to-2023. In 2022–3, police in England and Wales recorded 4,732 hate crimes with 'transgender' as the motivating factor, an increase of 210% compared with the total of 2,253 in 2018–19. They recorded 24,102 hate crimes with 'sexual orientation' as the motivating factor, an increase of 170% compared with the total of 14,161 in 2018–19.

7 See www.facebook.com/events/s/protest-against-mcgill-univers/940420110675026.

8 See https://docs.google.com/document/d/1tRxRwYvrsT4vvYs85ATIzcDCtSIpy0YggpSKAkYDbMc/edit?fbclid=IwAR3x62tV8avZIwL5BbEWCpZFdDTKqNGIp20TzkC2JbXnTk5sze8iGfQsn4E.

9 See https://montrealgazette.com/news/local-news/trans-activists-plan-protest-against-controversial-speaker-at-mcgill.

10 See www.ledevoir.com/societe/777261/societe-des-manifestants-veulent-defier-la-venue-d-un-conferencier-juge-transphobe.

11 See https://lgballiance.org.uk/resources (Freedom of Speech, videos).

12 See https://youtu.be/orCiHYtlmg0.

13 See also https://elizamondegreen.substack.com/p/this-is-what-no-debate-looks-like; https://quillette.com/2023/01/12/feminists-tried-to-meet-at-mcgill-law-school-fortunately ('A mob stormed a feminist event at McGill Law School – in defence of gender justice, of course'); www.dailymail.co.uk/news/article-11626357/Protestors-shut-McGill-University-event-transgender-zealots-shutting-free-speech.html ('Proving my point! Speaker thanks militant transgender protestors for shutting down his event at McGill University – where he was to talk about how trans zealots RUIN free speech').

14 *Handyside* v. *United Kingdom*, https://hudoc.echr.coe.int/?i=001-57499 (7 December 1976), para. 49.

15 *Cohen* v. *California*, www.law.cornell.edu/supremecourt/text/403/15 (7 June 1971).

16 *Texas* v. *Johnson*, www.law.cornell.edu/supremecourt/text/491/397 (21 June 1989).

17 *Snyder* v. *Phelps*, 562 US 443, www.law.cornell.edu/supct/html/09-751.ZO.html (2 March 2011).

18 *Matal* v. *Tam*, 582 US 218, www.supremecourt.gov/opinions/16pdf/15-1293_1o13.pdf (19 June 2017).

19 See www.thecoddling.com/copy-of-read-ch-1-on-antifragility.

20 Helen Pluckrose and James Lindsay, *Cynical Theories* (Swift Press, 2021), p. 237.

194 Notes to pp. 43–47

21 Ibid., p. 183.
22 Ibid., p. 221.
23 See www.economist.com/leaders/2021/09/04/the-threat-from-the-illi beral-left.
24 See www.theguardian.com/society/2022/nov/01/its-out-of-order-gen-z-speak-up-on-cancel-culture-and-young-illiberal-progressives, reporting on 'Beyond Z: The real truth about British youth', https://assets-corporate.channel4.com/_flysystem/s3/2023-02/Channel%204%20-%20 Beyond%20Z%20report%20-%20FINAL%20%28Accessible%29.pdf.
25 See www.theguardian.com/commentisfree/2022/nov/04/gen-z-intoler ant-poor-illiberal.
26 Andrew Doyle, *The New Puritans: How the Religion of Social Justice Captured the Western World* (Constable, 2022), p. 45.
27 See www.bostonglobe.com/2023/04/12/opinion/harvard-council-aca demic-freedom; https://sites.harvard.edu/cafh. In the UK, see the Committee for Academic Freedom, https://afcomm.org.uk.
28 See https://quillette.com/2023/05/05/fear-and-self-censorship-in-higher-education.
29 See https://law.stanford.edu/wp-content/uploads/2023/03/letter-from -Stanford.pdf.
30 See https://law.stanford.edu/wp-content/uploads/2023/03/Next-Steps -on-Protests-and-Free-Speech.pdf.
31 See *Plattform 'Ärzte für das Leben'* v. *Austria*, https://hudoc.echr.coe. int/?i=001-57558 (21 June 1988) (emphasis added).
32 See 'Free speech doesn't mean hecklers get to shut down campus debate', www.washingtonpost.com/opinions/2022/03/24/free-speech-doesnt-mean-hecklers-get-shut-down-campus-debate (24 March 2022).
33 See 'UC Irvine's free speech debate', www.latimes.com/archives/la-xpm -2010-feb-18-la-oe-chemerinsky18-2010feb18-story.html (18 February 2010).
34 See https://adulthumanfemale.info.
35 See www.theguardian.com/society/2023/apr/26/edinburgh-university -cancels-film-screening-after-trans-rights-protest.
36 See Sex Matters, 'Women will not be silenced', https://youtu.be/RLzoY NuJxoo (23 November 2023). See also https://quillette.com/2023/03/28 /an-auckland-mob-shut-down-a-womens-rights-activist-and-proved -her-point and www.spectator.co.uk/article/the-shameful-persecution -of-posie-parker-in-new-zealand (25 March 2023).
37 See www.ohchr.org/en/special-procedures/sr-violence-against-women.

Notes to pp. 47–53

38 See www.ohchr.org/sites/default/files/documents/issues/women/sr/ statements/2023-05-19-statement-sr-vawg.pdf.
39 See www.gov.uk/government/publications/hate-crime-laws-final-report.
40 Ibid., para. 13.47.
41 See https://twitter.com/MForstater/status/1044588721423638529 (25 September 2018).
42 See section 10(2).
43 *Forstater* v. *CGD Europe*, Employment Tribunal, 18 December 2019, www.gov.uk/employment-tribunal-decisions/maya-forstater-v-cgd-europe-and-others-2200909-2019, paras. 5.1, 85, 90.
44 See Robert Wintemute, 'Belief vs. action in *Ladele*, *Ngole* and *Forstater*' (March 2021) 50 *Industrial Law Journal* 104, https://academic.oup.com /ilj/article-abstract/50/1/104/6079282, p. 116.
45 See www.bbc.co.uk/news/uk-57281448.
46 *Forstater* v. *CGD Europe*, Employment Appeal Tribunal, 10 June 2021, https://assets.publishing.service.gov.uk/media/60c1cce1d3bf7f4bd98 14e39/Maya_Forstater_v_CGD_Europe_and_others_UKEAT0105_20 _JOJ.pdf. Compare Simon Edge, *In the Beginning* (Eye Books, 2023).
47 Ibid., paras. 78–9.
48 Ibid., para. 4.
49 See www.judiciary.uk/wp-content/uploads/2022/08/Forstater-JR-AG .pdf (6 July 2022).
50 See https://assets.publishing.service.gov.uk/media/649eeb7e06179b001 13f76a6/Ms_M_Forstater__vs__CGD_Europe.pdf (30 June 2023).
51 See www.theguardian.com/world/2021/oct/28/sussex-professor-kath leen-stock-resigns-after-transgender-rights-row; www.dailymail.co.uk /news/article-10172813/KATHLEEN-STOCK-reveals-really-like-vili fied-beliefs.html.
52 See www.theguardian.com/commentisfree/2024/jan/26/law-clear-can not-be-sacked-gender-critical-views-women-sex. See also *Adams* v. *Edinburgh Rape Crisis Centre*, www.gov.uk/employment-tribunal-deci sions/r-d-adams-v-edinburgh-rape-crisis-centre-4102236-slash-2023. _v_Edinburgh_Rape_Crisis_Centre_-_4102236.2023_-_Judgment.pdf (14 May 2024).
53 See www.thecrimson.com/article/2023/12/29/steinberg-weaponizing -antisemitism.
54 See www.metroweekly.com/2018/10/alison-moyet-says-she-suppo rts-trans-people-after-inadvertently-signing-anti-transgender-letter (emphasis added).
55 See https://youtu.be/clyo9IBivso.

196 Notes to pp. 55–60

4 Common ground: transgender rights that are not questioned

1 See https://hudoc.echr.coe.int/eng?i=001-107331 (8 November 2011).
2 As a matter of courtesy, I will use the applicant's preferred pronouns.
3 *Halat*, note 1, para. 6.
4 Ibid., para. 43.
5 Ibid., paras. 47–9.
6 Ibid., paras. 55–7.
7 Ibid., para. 68.
8 See *Alekseyev* v. *Russia*, https://hudoc.echr.coe.int/eng?i=001-101257 (21 October 2010), para. 84 (emphasis added).
9 See https://hudoc.echr.coe.int/?i=001-57473 (22 October 1981).
10 539 US 558, www.law.cornell.edu/supct/html/02-102.ZS.html (26 June 2003).
11 Legislation was amended as follows: Canada (2017), Alberta (2015), British Columbia (2016), Manitoba (2012), New Brunswick (2017), Newfoundland (2013), Northwest Territories (2002), Nova Scotia (2012), Nunavut (2017), Ontario (2012), Prince Edward Island (2013), Québec (2016), Saskatchewan (2014) and Yukon (2017).
12 See Directive 76/207/EEC (1976).
13 See Case C-13/94, https://curia.europa.eu/juris/liste.jsf?num=C-13/94 (30 April 1996), paras. 20–1.
14 See Directive 2004/113/EC.
15 See *Grant* v. *South-West Trains*, Case C-249/96, https://curia.europa.eu/juris/liste.jsf?&num=C-249/96 (17 February 1998).
16 See Directive 2000/78/EC.
17 See COM(2008) 426 final, https://eur-lex.europa.eu/legal-content/en/ALL/?uri=CELEX%3A52008PC0426 (2 July 2008).
18 See Sex Discrimination (Gender Reassignment) Regulations 1999, amending the Sex Discrimination Act 1975.
19 See 590 US 644, www.supremecourt.gov/opinions/19pdf/17-1618_hfci.pdf (15 June 2020).
20 See ibid., Justice Kavanagh's dissenting opinion, footnotes 7 and 8 (Wisconsin). Virginia's 11 April 2020 law is not listed because it was scheduled to come into force 1 July 2020.
21 See A. Koppelman, 'Why discrimination against lesbians and gay men is sex discrimination?' (1994) 69 *New York University Law Review* 197; R. Wintemute, 'Sexual orientation discrimination as sex discrimination' (1994) 39 *McGill Law Journal* 429; R. Wintemute, 'Recognising new kinds of direct sex discrimination: transsexualism, sexual orientation and dress codes' (1997) 60 *Modern Law Review* 334; R. Wintemute, 'Sex

Notes to pp. 61–66 197

discrimination in *MacDonald* and *Pearce*' (2003) 14 *King's College Law Journal* 267.

22 *Bostock*, Justice Gorsuch, pp. 2 and 9.

23 Ibid., p. 31.

24 Ibid., Justice Alito, pp. 1–4, 45–8.

25 See Directive 2000/78, Article 2(3) (sexual orientation); Directive 2006/54, Article 2 (sex, including gender reassignment).

26 See *Meritor Savings Bank* v. *Vinson*, 477 US 57 (1986) (opposite-sex sexual harassment); *Oncale* v. *Sundowner Offshore Services*, 523 US 75 (1998) (same-sex sexual harassment).

27 Directive 2006/54, Article 14(2).

28 Section 703(e)(1) of Title VII, 42 USC section 2000e-2(e)(1).

29 See https://hudoc.echr.coe.int/?i=001-60596 (11 July 2002).

30 See *Hämäläinen* v. *Finland*, https://hudoc.echr.coe.int/fre?i=001-145768 (16 July 2014).

31 See www.law.cornell.edu/supremecourt/text/14-556 (26 June 2015).

32 See https://hudoc.echr.coe.int/fre?i=001-222750 (17 January 2023).

33 See *Hämäläinen* v. *Finland*, https://hudoc.echr.coe.int/fre?i=001-145768 (16 July 2014).

34 See *Salgueiro da Silva Mouta* v. *Portugal*, https://hudoc.echr.coe.int/eng?i=001-58404 (21 December 1999).

35 See *E. B.* v. *France*, https://hudoc.echr.coe.int/?i=001-84571 (22 January 2008).

36 See *X & Others* v. *Austria*, https://hudoc.echr.coe.int/?i=001-116735 (19 February 2013) (countries in which unmarried opposite-sex couples may adopt each other's children); *D. B. & Others* v. *Switzerland*, https://hudoc.echr.coe.int/?i=001-220955 (22 November 2022) (countries in which only married opposite-sex couples may adopt each other's children).

37 See *A. M. & Others* v. *Russia*, https://hudoc.echr.coe.int/fre?i=001-210878 (6 July 2021).

38 Wintemute, 'Recognising new kinds of direct sex discrimination'.

39 590 US 644, www.supremecourt.gov/opinions/19pdf/17-1618_hfci.pdf (15 June 2020), Justice Gorsuch, p. 31.

40 [2020] HKCFA 37, https://legalref.judiciary.hk/lrs/common/ju/ju_frame.jsp?DIS=132118 (27 November 2020).

41 Ibid., paras. 52–3.

42 490 US 228, www.law.cornell.edu/supremecourt/text/490/228 (1 May 1989), para. 20.

198 Notes to pp. 66–72

43 Ibid., paras. 55, 57. See also www.ca4.uscourts.gov/opinions/2010 01A.P.pdf (14 June 2022, pp. 33–5; the 14th Amendment to the US Constitution does not permit a public school to require girls to wear skirts), which the US Supreme Court declined to review on 26 June 2023.

44 See www.bbc.co.uk/news/uk-45082801 (6 August 2018).

45 See https://corporate.virginatlantic.com/gb/en/media/press-releases /virgin-atlantic-updates-gender-identity-policy.html (28 September 2022). See also https://youtu.be/a1eOmsEG01k.

46 See www.dailymail.co.uk/news/article-11412439/British-Airways-allow -male-pilots-cabin-crew-wear-make-up.html (10 November 2022).

5 Changing your legal sex: should it be possible and how easy should it be?

1 R. Wintemute, 'Sexual orientation and gender identity' in C. Harvey (ed.), *Human Rights in the Community* (Hart Publishing, 2005), p. 176.

2 See R. Wintemute, 'Recognising new kinds of direct sex discrimination: transsexualism, sexual orientation and dress codes' (1997) 60 *Modern Law Review* 334.

3 See https://publications.parliament.uk/pa/cm201516/cmselect/cmwo meq/390/390.pdf, para. 62.

4 See Debbie Hayton, *Transsexual Apostate: My Journey Back to Reality* (Forum, 2024), p. 217.

5 See https://assets.publishing.service.gov.uk/government/uploads/sys tem/uploads/attachment_data/file/721725/GRA-Consultation-docu ment.pdf.

6 See https://database.ilga.org/legal-gender-recognition. The 78 member states are: Andorra, Angola, Argentina, Armenia, Australia, Austria, Bahrain, Bangladesh, Belarus, Belgium, Bhutan, Bolivia, Bosnia and Herzegovina, Botswana, Brazil, Canada, Chile, China, Colombia, Croatia, Cuba, Cyprus, Czechia, Denmark, Ecuador, Estonia, Eswatini, Finland, France, Georgia, Germany, Greece, Iceland, India, Indonesia, Iran, Ireland, Israel, Italy, Japan, Kazakhstan, Latvia, Lithuania, Luxembourg, Malta, Mexico, Moldova, Mongolia, Montenegro, Mozambique, Namibia, Nepal, Netherlands, New Zealand, North Macedonia, Norway, Pakistan, Panama, Poland, Portugal, Romania, Serbia, Singapore, Slovakia, Slovenia, South Africa, South Korea, Spain, Sri Lanka, Sweden, Switzerland, Tajikistan, Türkiye, Ukraine, United Kingdom, Uruguay, Uzbekistan and Vietnam.

7 The 75 member states are: Albania, Algeria, Antigua and Barbuda, Azerbaijan, Bahamas, Barbados, Belize, Benin, Brunei, Bulgaria, Burundi, Cambodia, Cameroon, Cape Verde, Congo (Democratic Republic of), Dominica, Dominican Republic, Egypt, El Salvador, Ethiopia, Fiji, Gambia, Ghana, Grenada, Guatemala, Guyana,

Notes to pp. 72–75 199

Haiti, Honduras, Hungary, Iraq, Jamaica, Jordan, Kenya, Kiribati, Kuwait, Lesotho, Liberia, Liechtenstein, Malawi, Malaysia, Maldives, Marshall Islands, Mauritius, Monaco, Morocco, Myanmar, Nicaragua, Nigeria, Oman, Paraguay, Peru, Philippines, Qatar, Russia, Rwanda, Saint Lucia, Samoa, San Marino, Saudi Arabia, Seychelles, Somalia, Suriname, Tanzania, Thailand, Tonga, Trinidad and Tobago, Tunisia, Turkmenistan, Uganda, United Arab Emirates, Vanuatu, Venezuela, Yemen, Zambia, and Zimbabwe.

8 The 39 member states are: Afghanistan, Burkina Faso, Central African Republic, Chad, Comoros, Congo (Republic of), Costa Rica, Djibouti, East Timor, Equatorial Guinea, Eritrea, Gabon, Guinea, Guinea-Bissau, Ivory Coast, Kyrgyzstan, Laos, Lebanon, Libya, Madagascar, Mali, Mauritania, Micronesia, Nauru, Niger, North Korea, Palau, Papua New Guinea, Saint Kitts and Nevis, Saint Vincent and the Grenadines, Sao Tome e Principe, Senegal, Sierra Leone, Solomon Islands, South Sudan, Sudan, Syria, Togo, and Tuvalu.

9 Argentina, Belgium, Brazil, Colombia, Denmark, Finland, Iceland, Ireland, Luxembourg, Malta, New Zealand, Norway, Portugal, Spain, Switzerland and Uruguay.

10 Section 16(3) of the Births, Deaths and Marriages Registration Act 1999 is clear: 'The Registrar, in registering the birth of a person, is to register the sex of the person as being either male or female.' Under section 28C, a 'gender' may later be registered. Birth certificates may be ordered with or without 'all registered gender details'. See www.justice.tas.gov.au/bdm/forms/forms/one/Birth-Certificate-Application-Form.pdf.

11 Helen Joyce, *Trans: When Ideology Meets Reality* (Oneworld Publications, 2021).

12 See https://quillette.com/2018/12/04/the-new-patriarchy-how-trans-radicalism-hurts-women-children-and-trans-people-themselves.

13 See https://quillette.com/2020/06/07/jk-rowling-is-right-sex-is-real-and-it-is-not-a-spectrum, citing Leonard Sax, 'How common is intersex?' https://pubmed.ncbi.nlm.nih.gov/12476264 (2002). See also Zachary Elliott, *Binary: Debunking the Sex Spectrum Myth* (Paradox Press, 2023); Alex Byrne, *Trouble with Gender* (Polity, 2024), pp. 63–78.

14 See https://hudoc.echr.coe.int/fre?i=001-60596 (11 July 2002), para. 82.

15 See https://publications.parliament.uk/pa/ld200203/ldjudgmt/jd0304 10/bellin-1.htm (10 April 2003), para. 8.

16 Ibid., para. 40.

17 The neutral and respectful terms 'male-to-female transgender person' and 'female-to-male transgender person' are used in the Hate Crime and Public Order (Scotland) Act 2021, section 11(7).

200 Notes to pp. 76–81

18 See https://youtu.be/7B8Q6D4a6TM (23 October 2015).
19 See https://fairplayforwomen.com/wp-content/uploads/2018/11/gender_recognition_act-1.pdf (table 2).
20 See https://abcnews.go.com/blogs/headlines/2014/02/heres-a-list-of-58-gender-options-for-facebook-users.
21 See https://hudoc.echr.coe.int/eng?i=001-57770 (25 March 1992), para. 63.
22 Ibid., paras. 43, 45, 59 (emphasis added).
23 Ibid., para. 60 (emphasis added).
24 Ibid., para. 50.
25 Ibid., para. 47.
26 See https://tgeu.org/issues/legal-gender-recognition.
27 See https://eur-lex.europa.eu/legal-content/EN/TXT/?uri=CELEX%3A61994CJ0013 (30 April 1996).
28 See Article 119, Treaty of Rome (1957).
29 See Directive 76/207/EEC.
30 See Treaty on the Functioning of the European Union, Article 19 (added in 1997).
31 See https://yalebooks.co.uk/book/9780300022995/sexual-harassment-of-working-women.
32 See Laura Carlson, 'The metamorphosis of Swedish discrimination law', www.diva-portal.org/smash/get/diva2:305771/FULLTEXT01.pdf(book chapter, 2010), pp. 93–4; https://su.diva-portal.org/smash/record.jsf?pid=diva2%3A305771&dswid=339 (details of book).
33 See, e.g., Tennessee Vital Records Act, Tenn. Code. Ann. Sec. 68-3-304(d), https://law.justia.com/codes/tennessee/2010/title-68/chapter-3/part-2/68-3-203: 'The sex of an individual shall not be changed on the original certificate of birth as a result of sex change surgery.'
34 See www.theguardian.com/world/2023/jul/24/vladimir-putin-signs-law-banning-gender-changes-in-russia.
35 See www.feministcurrent.com/2018/09/14/never-mind-reforming-gender-recognition-act-theres-no-need-gender-recognition-certificates.
36 See https://hudoc.echr.coe.int/fre?i=001-60596 (11 July 2002), paras. 17, 19, 95.
37 See *Association Belge des Consommateurs Test-Achats* (CJEU, Case C-236/09, 1 March 2011), declaring invalid the exception permitting sex discrimination in insurance premiums from 21 December 2012.
38 See Marriage (Same Sex Couples) Act 2013 (England and Wales, in force on 13 March 2014); Marriage and Civil Partnership (Scotland) Act 2014 (in force on 16 December 2014); Marriage (Same-sex Couples) and Civil Partnership (Opposite-sex Couples) (Northern Ireland) Regulations 2019 (in force on 13 January 2020).
39 See https://assets.publishing.service.gov.uk/media/5a7f02e640f0b62305b84929/spa-timetable.pdf (table 2, 6 November 2018).

Notes to pp. 81–88   201

40 See www.gov.uk/government/publications/gender-recognition-certifi cate-applications-and-outcomes/gender-recognition-certificate-applications-and-outcomes (main tables).
41 See www.theguardian.com/news/audio/2020/oct/08/understanding -the-fight-over-trans-rights-part-1 (20:00–20:40).
42 See https://hudoc.echr.coe.int/?i=001-57641 (27 September 1990), para. 12.
43 See www.gov.uk/changing-passport-information/gender.
44 In *R. (on the application of Elan-Cane)* v. *Secretary of State for the Home Department* [2021] UKSC 56, the UK Supreme Court ruled that the European Convention does not require the UK Government to issue an 'X' passport to a 'non-binary' person.
45 See www.gov.uk/id-for-driving-licence.
46 See https://assets.publishing.service.gov.uk/media/6603f95cf9ab410 01aeea361/ins57p-information-on-driving-licences.pdf (p. 3).
47 See Sentencing Act 2020, section 66 (England and Wales). See also Hate Crime and Public Order (Scotland) Act 2021, section 1(2)(f).
48 See https://legalref.judiciary.hk/lrs/common/ju/ju_body.jsp?DIS= 150362&AH=&QS=&FN=&currpage= (6 February 2023), paras. 38, 115.
49 See https://hudoc.echr.coe.int/?i=001-172913 (6 April 2017), paras. 135, 154 (operative para. 5).
50 Ibid., paras. 68, 70–2.
51 Ibid., para. 131.
52 See https://hudoc.echr.coe.int/eng?i=001-60596 (11 July 2002), paras. 78, 91.
53 See *Hansard*, HL, vol. 656, cols. 369–70, 29 January 2024, https:// api.parliament.uk/historic-hansard/lords/2004/jan/29/gender-recognition-bill-hl.
54 Ibid., col. 371.
55 Ibid., col. 375.
56 Ibid.
57 Ibid., cols. 375–6.
58 See *Hansard*, HL, vol. 656, cols. 621–2, 3 February 2024, https://han sard.parliament.uk/Lords/2004-02-03/debates/3e850411-93f0-41cc-aa3f-9ec3dbc8f4aa/GenderRecognitionBillHl.
59 See *Hansard*, HL, vol. 418, col. 65, 23 February 2024, https:// api.parliament.uk/historic-hansard/commons/2004/feb/23/gender-recognition-bill.
60 Ibid.
61 See www.pfc.org.uk/GRA2004.html.
62 See https://publications.parliament.uk/pa/jt200203/jtselect/jtrights/ 188/188.pdf, p. 14.
63 See Gender Recognition Act 2004, section 2(1).

64 See www.huffingtonpost.co.uk/entry/meet-the-trans-woman-queer ing-gender-with-her-full-beard_n_55affb34e4b0a9b948538d24.

65 See www.feministcurrent.com/2018/09/14/never-mind-reforming-gen der-recognition-act-theres-no-need-gender-recognition-certificates.

66 See www.telegraph.co.uk/news/2022/12/02/scottish-parliament-should -leave-gender-recognition-act.

67 See *Ley* (Law) 26.743 of 9 May 2012, www.argentina.gob.ar/norma tiva/nacional/ley-26743-197860/texto, Article 3; https://globalhealth .usc.edu/wp-content/uploads/2017/03/english-translation-of-argent ina_s-gender-identity-law-as-approved-by-the-senate-of-argentina-on -may-8-2012.pdf.

68 See www.gba.gob.ar/registrodelaspersonas/otros_tramites/identidad _de_genero.

69 Gender Recognition Act 2015, https://revisedacts.lawreform.ie/eli/2015 /act/25/revised/en/html (22 July 2015).

70 See www.thepinknews.com/2023/01/27/trans-self-id-gender-recog nition-ireland.

71 See www.spiked-online.com/2020/10/23/the-rise-and-fall-of-stonewall.

72 'Transgender Equality', 2015 HC 390, https://publications.parliament .uk/pa/cm201516/cmselect/cmwomeq/390/390.pdf, p. 6.

73 Ibid., pp. 79–80 (para. 7).

74 See https://assets.publishing.service.gov.uk/government/uploads/syst em/uploads/attachment_data/file/721725/GRA-Consultation-docume nt.pdf.

75 See www.gov.uk/government/speeches/response-to-gender-recog nition-act-2004-consultation. For a detailed discussion of political developments during this period (2016–20), see the judgment on a judicial review of the 2004 Act in Northern Ireland, [2021] NIQB 48, www.judiciaryni.uk/sites/judiciary/files/decisions/JR111%20Appli cation%20for%20Judicial%20Review.pdf.

76 See www.parliament.scot/-/media/files/legislation/bills/s6-bills/gen der-recognition-reform-scotland-bill/stage-3/bill-as-passed.pdf.

77 Ibid., sections 3, 4.

78 See Gender Recognition Reform (Scotland) Bill (Prohibition on Submission for Royal Assent) Order 2023, www.legislation.gov.uk/uksi /2023/41/contents/made, Schedule 2, paras. 1, 4, 10.

79 See James Kirkup, www.spectator.co.uk/article/how-self-id-helped-bring-down-nicola-sturgeon (15 February 2023).

80 See https://news.sky.com/story/keir-starmer-says-99-9-of-women-havent-got-a-penis-as-he-faces-questions-over-trans-rights-12848438 (2 April 2023); https://youtu.be/r81aZGJHDeM (26 September 2021).

81 See www.theguardian.com/commentisfree/2023/jul/24/labour-will-lead-on-reform-of-transgender-rights-and-we-wont-take-lectures-from-the-divisive-tories.

Notes to pp. 92–97   203

82 See www.stonewall.org.uk/about-us/news/stonewall-statement-labours-gender-recognition-act-reform-proposals.
83 See https://d3nkl3psvxxpe9.cloudfront.net/documents/LabourTogether_LabourMembers_231027_Transgender_Rights_W.pdf (fourth question).
84 See www.bailii.org/scot/cases/ScotCS/2023/2023_CSOH_89.html.
85 See www.gov.scot/news/section-35-judicial-review.
86 See www.scottishtrans.org/wp-content/uploads/2022/05/Scottish-Trans-GRR-Bill-EHRCJC-Call-for-views-written-evidence.pdf, p. 2.
87 See www.gov.uk/apply-gender-recognition-certificate/how-to-apply.
88 See www.gov.uk/government/publications/fees-for-citizenship-applications/fees-for-citizenship-applications-and-the-right-of-abode-from-6-april-2018 (fee from 10 April 2024).
89 See www.amnesty.org.uk/have-your-say-gender-recognition-act (emphasis added).
90 See www.amnestyshop.org.uk/products/amnesty-international/amnesty-i-am-who-i-say-i-am-unisex-t-shirt.
91 See www.theguardian.com/commentisfree/2023/jul/25/labour-courage-past-lgbtq-rights-trans-people.
92 See www.theguardian.com/politics/2018/may/23/labour-suspends-activist-challenging-gender-self-identification-policy.
93 See www.cbc.ca/news/canada/calgary/change-gender-identification-insurance-alberta-1.4754416.
94 See www.tdg.ch/il-est-devenu-une-femme-pour-echapper-au-service-militaire-753466576777.
95 See https://documents.un.org/doc/undoc/gen/g21/123/16/pdf/g2112316.pdf, para. 41.
96 See www.oiieurope.org/malta-declaration (emphasis added).
97 See https://yogyakartaprinciples.org/wp-content/uploads/2017/11/A5_yogyakartaWEB-2.pdf.
98 See https://documents.un.org/doc/undoc/gen/g20/071/66/pdf/g2007166.pdf, para. 36(e).
99 See www.ama-assn.org/press-center/press-releases/ama-announced-policies-adopted-final-day-special-meeting (16 June 2021).
100 See https://gtr.ukri.org/projects?ref=ES%2FP008968%2F1.
101 See www.kcl.ac.uk/law/research/future-of-legal-gender-abolishing-legal-sex-status-full-report.pdf (May 2022).
102 Ibid., p. 37.
103 Ibid., p. 16.
104 See www.ethnicity-facts-figures.service.gov.uk/uk-population-by-ethnicity/demographics/male-and-female-populations/latest.
105 Martine Rothblatt, *The Apartheid of Sex: A Manifesto on the Freedom of Gender* (Crown Publishers, 1995).
106 Ibid., p. 1.

204 Notes to pp. 97–106

107 Ibid., p. 62.
108 Ibid., p. 73.
109 Ibid., pp. 79, 92.
110 Ibid., p. 143.
111 Ibid., p. 160.

6 Protecting women-only spaces, categories and capacities

1 See www.loc.gov/item/global-legal-monitor/2024-07-09/germany-new
-self-id-act-for-transgender-intersex-and-nonbinary-individuals-enac
ted (Domiciliary Rights and Access to Protected Premises, citing Article
6(2), which is an exception for access to facilities and rooms and to
participation in events).
2 See https://hudoc.echr.coe.int/?i=001-59608 (24 July 2001), para. 26.
3 Ibid., para. 117 (emphasis added).
4 See https://hudoc.echr.coe.int/?i=001-76999 (26 September 2006),
paras. 11–12, 46–9.
5 See https://hudoc.echr.coe.int/?i=001-203562 (16 July 2020), paras. 123,
133, 135, 142–3.
6 See www.standard.co.uk/comment/freedom-of-speech-trans-gender
-ideology-helen-joyce-b1117409.html (1 November 2023).
7 See https://eu.greenbaypressgazette.com/story/news/education/2023
/12/05/federal-government-launches-investigation-into-sun-prairie-
school-district/71766910007.
8 See https://youtu.be/2d6HGu8RT0k.
9 See www.theguardian.com/us-news/2021/sep/02/person-charged-with
-indecent-exposure-at-la-spa-after-viral-instagram-video.
10 See www.dailymail.co.uk/news/article-13206823/Planet-Fitness-trans
-locker-room-video-alaska-response.html.
11 See https://app.leg.wa.gov/RCW/default.aspx?cite=49.60.215.
12 See https://storage.courtlistener.com/recap/gov.uscourts.wawd.308441
/gov.uscourts.wawd.308441.21.0.pdf (5 June 2023), p. 9.
13 See Equality Act 2010, Schedule 3, para. 27(5)-(7). See also www.
equalityhumanrights.com/sites/default/files/guidance-separate-and-single
-sex-service-providers-equality-act-sex-and-gender-reassignment-
exceptions.pdf (April 2022).
14 Ibid., para. 28.
15 See www.jccf.ca/wp-content/uploads/2019/10/222_Yaniv_v_Various
_Waxing_Salons_No_2_2019_BCHRT_222.pdf (22 October 2019),
paras. 39–40.
16 See https://womansplaceuk.org/2018/06/25/references-to-removal-of
-single-sex-exemptions.

Notes to pp. 107–109

17 See www.theguardian.com/commentisfree/2023/jul/24/labour-will-lead-on-reform-of-transgender-rights-and-we-wont-take-lectures-from-the-divisive-tories.

18 See https://yougov.co.uk/topics/society/trackers/support-for-separate-toilets-for-men-and-women-and-gender-neutral-toilets-in-public-spaces.

19 See https://d3nkl3psvxxpe9.cloudfront.net/documents/LabourTogether_LabourMembers_231027_Transgender_Rights_W.pdf.

20 See https://fairplayforwomen.com/wp-content/uploads/2018/11/gender_recognition_act-1.pdf (table 5, question 5).

21 See www.theguardian.com/commentisfree/2023/jul/25/labour-courage-past-lgbtq-rights-trans-people.

22 See www.england.nhs.uk/statistics/wp-content/uploads/sites/2/2021/05/NEW-Delivering_same_sex_accommodation_sep2019.pdf, p. 12: 'Trans people should be accommodated according to their presentation: the way they dress, and the name and pronouns they currently use. . . . It does not depend on their having a . . . GRC . . . It applies to toilet and bathing facilities (except, for instance, that preoperative trans people should not share open shower facilities).'

23 See Naomi Cunningham, www.legalfeminist.org.uk/tag/fdj.

24 See www.bailii.org/ew/cases/EWHC/Admin/2021/1746.html, para. 88.

25 See https://hudoc.echr.coe.int/eng?i=001-60323 (14 March 2002), para. 64.

26 See www.theguardian.com/society/2018/oct/11/karen-white-how-manipulative-and-controlling-offender-attacked-again-transgender-prison.

27 See www.bbc.com/news/uk-scotland-64438457. See also https://quillette.com/2023/02/06/scotlands-gender-meltdown.

28 See www.theguardian.com/uk-news/2023/feb/09/trans-prisoners-in-scotland-to-be-first-sent-to-jails-matching-their-birth-gender.

29 See www.gov.uk/government/news/new-transgender-prisoner-policy-comes-into-force (27 February 2023).

30 See https://sex-matters.org/posts/prisons/new-moj-transgender-prisoner-policy.

31 See 'Rights and wrongs: how gender self-identification policy places women at risk in prison', https://macdonaldlaurier.ca/rights-and-wrongs-how-gender-self-identification-policy-places-women-at-risk-in-prison.

32 See www.theguardian.com/uk-news/article/2024/may/06/gender-specific-toilets-to-be-required-in-non-residential-buildings-in-england. See also Helen Joyce, *Trans: When Ideology Meets Reality* (Oneworld, 2021), pp. 155–68, 214, 297–8, on women-only spaces.

206 Notes to pp. 110–115

33 Karen Ingala Smith, *Defending Women's Spaces* (Polity, 2023).
34 Ibid., pp. 51–2.
35 Ibid., p. 60.
36 See www.equalityhumanrights.com/sites/default/files/guidance-separ ate-and-single-sex-service-providers-equality-act-sex-and-gender-reassignment-exceptions.pdf, p. 8.
37 See Equality Act 2010, Schedule 9, paras. 1(1), 3(a).
38 See https://rapereliefshelter.bc.ca/wp-content/uploads/2021/03/BC-Court-of-Appeal-Reasons-for-Judgement-2005.pdf, paras. 2, 4, 44, 59 (the Supreme Court of Canada dismissed Nixon's application for leave to appeal on 1 February 2007, https://scc-csc.lexum.com/scc-csc/scc-l-csc-a/en/item/11008/index.do).
39 See https://quillette.com/2024/08/04/gaslighting-scotlands-rape-vic tims-in-the-name-of-trans-inclusion.
40 Equality Act 2010, Schedule 16, para. 1.
41 See https://sex-matters.org/posts/updates/lesbians-without-liberty-2.
42 See https://assets.publishing.service.gov.uk/media/63c68c66e90e074ee cb1c26e/policy-statement-section-35-powers-Gender-Recognition-Reform-_Scotland_-Bill.pdf, para. 31.
43 See *Roxanne Tickle* v. *Giggle for Girls Pty Ltd (No 2)*, [2024] FCA 960, www.judgments.fedcourt.gov.au/judgments/Judgments/fca/single/2024 /2024fca0960 (23 August 2024).
44 See www.legislation.gov.au/C2004A02868/latest/text.
45 See section 159.
46 See section 104(6)–(7).
47 See section 1(1).
48 See www.scotcourts.gov.uk/media/l1imtxvx/court-of-session-judge ment-reclaiming-motion-by-for-women-scotland-limited-against-the-scottish-ministers-01-november-2023.pdf, paras. 3, 65.
49 See www.bbc.co.uk/news/articles/cw59ezd55dpo (17 April 2024); www .equalityhumanrights.com/our-work/advising-parliament-and-govern ments/our-letter-senedd-reform-bill-committee.
50 Section 193(7).
51 See section 23. See also https://sex-matters.org/posts/updates/sex-and -the-law-at-the-end-of-2023.
52 See www.bbc.co.uk/news/articles/c0kkvkkejgno (3 June 2024).
53 See https://publications.parliament.uk/pa/bills/cbill/58-04/0035/2300 35.pdf (clause 3).
54 See Emma Hilton & Tommy Lundberg, 'Transgender women in the female category of sport: perspectives on testosterone suppression

Notes to pp. 115–118 207

and performance advantage', *Sports Medicine* (8 December 2020), part 3.3.

55 See section 19.

56 See section 195(3).

57 See section 195(1).

58 Joyce, *Trans*, p. 6. See also pp. 175–99, 212–13, 257–60, 298–9.

59 Sharron Davies, *Unfair Play: The Battle for Women's Sports* (Forum, 2024).

60 Riley Gaines, *Swimming against the Current: Fighting for Common Sense in a World That's Lost Its Mind* (Center Street, 2024).

61 See https://youtu.be/ydeH-0EstiE; www.letsrun.com/news/2019/05/ what-no-one-is-telling-you-an-athlete-who-ran-ncaa-track-as-a-man-for-3-years-just-won-an-ncaa-womens-title.

62 See https://youtu.be/tukcaqEpGYo. See also https://youtu.be/Twd5cE _-rFQ (Caitlyn Jenner, who won the 1976 Olympic men's decathlon as Bruce Jenner, commenting on the fairness of Lia Thomas's victory); www .swimcloud.com/times (Men: event = 500 free, country = United States, organization = college, date range = 2018–19, 65th = Lia Thomas).

63 See https://fairplayforwomen.com/wp-content/uploads/2018/11/gen der_recognition_act-1.pdf, question 4.

64 See https://resources.fina.org/fina/document/2022/06/19/525de003-51 f4-47d3-8d5a-716dac5f77c7/FINA-INCLUSION-POLICY-AND-APP ENDICES-FINAL-.pdf (Fédération Internationale de Natation, FINA, 19 June 2022).

65 See www.theguardian.com/sport/article/2024/jun/12/transgender -swimmer-lia-thomas-out-of-olympics-after-losing-legal-battle-swim ming; www.tas-cas.org/fileadmin/user_upload/10000_Arbitral_Award __for_publ._.pdf.

66 See https://worldathletics.org/download/download?filename=c50f2178 -3759-4d1c-8fbc-370f6aef4370.pdf&urlslug=C3.5%20%E2%80%93%20 Eligibility%20Regulations%20Transgender%20Athletes%20%E2%80%93 %20effective%2031%20March%202023 (approved on 23 March 2023).

67 See www.bbc.co.uk/sport/articles/cpvymmpyjeko (12 August 2024); www.bbc.co.uk/news/stories-57338207 (4 June 2021; video of Petrillo defeating women in Arezzo in 2020).

68 See https://sex-matters.org/posts/updates/women-in-sport.

69 See www.thetimes.co.uk/article/navratilova-trans-ban-gives-girl-ath letes-a-chance-m6vpzl0f5 (26 March 2023).

70 See www.lgbtmap.org/equality-maps/youth/sports_participation_bans.

208 Notes to pp. 118–124

71 See https://thepostmillennial.com/watch-biological-male-record-holder-in-canadian-womens-powerlifting-complains-about-females-inability-to-lift-more-weight.
72 See www.bbc.com/sport/cricket/66597000.
73 See www.bbc.com/news/uk-53002557.
74 See www.bbc.com/news/uk-politics-58698406.
75 See www.independent.co.uk/voices/margaret-atwood-medical-trans-feminist-b1943534.html.
76 See www.nbcnews.com/nbc-out/out-pop-culture/bette-midler-defends-social-posts-criticized-transphobic-rcna36893.
77 See https://nationalpost.com/opinion/supreme-court-decision-say-word-woman-is-confusing-unfortunate.
78 See section 12.
79 See www.judiciary.uk/wp-content/uploads/2020/04/McConnell-and-YY-judgment-Final.pdf.
80 See *O. H. and G. H.* v. *Germany*, https://hudoc.echr.coe.int/eng?i=001-223924 (4 April 2023).
81 See *A. H. and Others* v. *Germany*, https://hudoc.echr.coe.int/eng?i=001-223932 (4 April 2023).
82 See https://tgeu.org/european-court-of-human-rights-disappoints-trans-families-tgeu-bvt-joint-statement.

7 Protecting children from medical transition
1 See www.unicef.org.uk/wp-content/uploads/2016/08/unicef-convention-rights-child-uncrc.pdf, Article 3(1).
2 See https://hudoc.echr.coe.int/?i=001-58232 (23 September 1998).
3 See https://hudoc.echr.coe.int/?i=001-59455 (10 May 2001), paras. 40, 74.
4 See Hannah Barnes, *Time to Think: The Inside Story of the Collapse of the Tavistock's Gender Service for Children* (Swift Press, 2023), p. 44, citing Richard Green, 'Young transsexuals should be allowed to put puberty on hold', www.theguardian.com/commentisfree/2008/aug/28/sexeducation.gayrights.
5 See www.itv.com/watch/the-clinic/10a3894, at 10:30–11:20.
6 Barnes, *Time to Think*, pp. 73–5, 104–5, 121.
7 Ibid., at pp. 40–1; Sasha Ayad, Lisa Marchiano & Stella O'Malley, *When Kids Say They're Trans: A Guide for Thoughtful Parents* (Swift Press, 2023), pp. 90–1.
8 Barnes, *Time to Think*, pp. 124–6, 341–2; https://people.com/tv/jazz-jennings-talks-sexual-stuff-orgasm-libido-doctor-before-gender-confirmation-surgery.

Notes to pp. 124–127

9 See Abigail Shrier, 'Top trans doctors blow the whistle on "sloppy" care', www.thefp.com/p/top-trans-doctors-blow-the-whistle (4 October 2021).

10 Ibid. See also Lisa Marchiano, 'The ranks of gender detransitioners are growing: we need to understand why', https://quillette.com/2020/01/02/the-ranks-of-gender-detransitioners-are-growing-we-need-to-understand-why.

11 See James M. Cantor, 'Transgender and gender diverse children and adolescents: fact-checking of AAP policy' (2020) 46 *Journal of Sex & Marital Therapy* 307–13, www.tandfonline.com/doi/full/10.1080/0092 623X.2019.1698481; Ayad et al., *When Kids Say They're Trans*, p. 2.

12 See Richard Green, *The Sissy Boy Syndrome: The Development of Homosexuality* (Yale University Press, 1987), www.jstor.org/stable/j. ctt1ww3v4c.

13 See Jiska Ristori & Thomas Steensma, 'Gender dysphoria in childhood' (2016) 28 *International Review of Psychiatry* 13–20, p. 16, www. tandfonline.com/doi/epdf/10.3109/09540261.2015.1115754.

14 See Devita Singh, Susan Bradley & Kenneth Zucker (2021) *Frontiers in Psychiatry*, www.frontiersin.org/journals/psychiatry/articles/10.3389/fpsyt.2021.632784/full.

15 See Barnes, *Time to Think*, pp. 122–3.

16 Abigail Shrier, *Irreversible Damage: Teenage Girls and the Transgender Craze* (Swift Press, 2021).

17 See www.drazhakeem.com/specialist-psychotherapy-for-gender-dysphoria.

18 Az Hakeem, *DETRANS: When Transition Is Not the Solution* (independently published, 2023), p. 68.

19 See www.itv.com/watch/the-clinic/10a3894, at 10:30–11:20.

20 See Barnes, *Time to Think*, pp. 160–2, 174, 176–7.

21 See Debra Soh, 'The unspoken homophobia propelling the transgender movement in children', https://quillette.com/2018/10/23/the-unspoken-homophobia-propelling-the-transgender-movement-in-children; Andrew Doyle, 'The new gay conversion therapy: the ignorance of politicians is putting gay people at risk', https://andrewdoyle.substack.com/p/the-new-gay-conversion-therapy (10 February 2024). See also Ben Appel, 'Homophobia in drag: transgender ideology has breathed new life into a dark, old prejudice', www.spiked-online.com/2023/05/14/the-new-homophobia.

22 See 'Table 5: age-specific suicide rates per 100,000 population by sex and five-year age group, England and Wales, 1981 to 2022 registrations', www.ons.gov.uk/peoplepopulationandcommunity/birthsdeathsandmarriages/deaths/datasets/suicidesintheunitedkingdomreferencetables.

23 See Michael Biggs, 'Suicide by clinic-referred transgender adolescents in the United Kingdom' (2022) 51 *Archives of Sexual Behavior* 685–90,

210 Notes to pp. 127–132

www.ncbi.nlm.nih.gov/pmc/articles/PMC8888486; Barnes, *Time to Think*, p. 131; Ayad et al., *When Kids Say They're Trans*, pp. 154–6.

24 See 'All-cause and suicide mortalities among adolescents and young adults who contacted specialised gender identity services in Finland in 1996–2019' (2024) 27 *BMJ Mental Health* 1–6, https://mentalhealth.bmj.com/content/ebmental/27/1/e300940.full.pdf.

25 See Leor Sapir, 'Pediatric gender medicine and the moral panic over suicide', www.realityslaststand.com/p/pediatric-gender-medicine-and-the (19 July 2022).

26 See Barnes, *Time to Think*, pp. 119–20, 164.

27 See https://quillette.com/2020/01/17/why-i-resigned-from-tavistock-trans-identified-children-need-therapy-not-just-affirmation-and-drugs (emphasis added).

28 See Barnes, *Time to Think*, p. 373 (emphasis added).

29 See William Malone, Colin Wright & Julia Robinson, 'No one is born in "the wrong body"', https://quillette.com/2019/09/24/no-one-is-born-in-the-wrong-body.

30 See 'Female sterilisation', www.rcog.org.uk/media/gcsnxxcu/consent-advice-3-2016.pdf (February 2016).

31 See https://en.wikipedia.org/wiki/Legal_status_of_human_sterilization_by_country#/media/File:Laws_regarding_sterilization_for_contraceptive_purposes_around_the_world.svg.

32 See www.hus.fi/en/patient/treatments-and-examinations/female-sterilizations.

33 See Barnes, *Time to Think*, p. 374.

34 See www.nytimes.com/2024/08/13/opinion/cass-report-trans-kids.html.

35 Ibid., pp. 37–40.

36 See Henriette Delemarre-van de Waal & Peggy Cohen-Kettenis, 'Clinical management of gender identity disorder in adolescents: a protocol on psychological and paediatric endocrinology aspects' (2006) 155 *European Journal of Endocrinology* S131–S137, https://academic.oup.com/ejendo/article-abstract/155/Supplement_1/S131/6695708.

37 See Barnes, *Time to Think*, pp. 96, 123; Michael Biggs, 'The Dutch Protocol for juvenile transsexuals: origins and evidence' (2023) 49 *Journal of Sex & Marital Therapy* 348–68, www.tandfonline.com/doi/full/10.1080/0092623X.2022.2121238.

38 See www.nytimes.com/2018/11/24/opinion/sunday/vaginoplasty-transgender-medicine.html.

39 See https://nymag.com/intelligencer/article/trans-rights-biological-sex-gender-judith-butler.html (11 March 2024).

40 See https://thehill.com/blogs/blog-briefing-room/3991685-majority-of-americans-oppose-gender-affirming-care-for-minors-trans-women-participating-in-sports-poll (6 May 2023).

Notes to pp. 132–138 211

41 See Helen Joyce, *Trans: When Ideology Meets Reality* (Oneworld, 2021), p. 80. See also pp. 75, 82–5, 119.
42 See Barnes, *Time to Think*, pp. 229–30.
43 Ibid., pp. 263–4.
44 See *Bell* v. *Tavistock*, [2020] EWHC 3274 (Admin), www.judiciary.uk/wp-content/uploads/2020/12/Bell-v-Tavistock-Judgment.pdf (1 December 2020), para. 7.
45 Ibid., para. 37.
46 Ibid., para. 47.
47 Ibid., paras. 71, 77.
48 Ibid., para. 81.
49 See *Gillick* v. *West Norfolk and Wisbech Health Authority*, [1986] AC 112 (House of Lords).
50 See *Bell* v. *Tavistock*, para. 138.
51 Ibid., para. 142.
52 Ibid., paras. 151–2.
53 See *AB*, [2021] EWHC 741 (Fam), www.bailii.org/ew/cases/EWHC/Fam/2021/741.html (26 March 2021).
54 Ibid., paras. 9, 69.
55 See *Bell* v. *Tavistock* [2021] EWCA Civ 1363, www.judiciary.uk/wp-content/uploads/2022/07/Bell-v-Tavistock-judgment-170921.pdf, paras. 3, 76.
56 See https://leginfo.legislature.ca.gov/faces/billTextClient.xhtml?bill_id=202320240AB957 (emphasis added).
57 See www.gov.ca.gov/wp-content/uploads/2023/09/AB-957-Veto-Message.pdf (22 September 2023).
58 See www.thepinknews.com/2023/01/20/laverne-cox-anti-trans-bills-us.
59 See https://cass.independent-review.uk/about-the-review/terms-of-reference.
60 See https://cass.independent-review.uk/publications/interim-report, p. 7.
61 See https://cass.independent-review.uk/home/publications/final-report, paras. 82–4.
62 Ibid., paras. 101–2, Recommendation 8 (emphasis added).
63 See www.england.nhs.uk/wp-content/uploads/2024/03/clinical-commissioning-policy-gender-affirming-hormones-v2.pdf.
64 See www.nhsggc.scot/service-update.
65 See https://cavuhb.nhs.wales/our-services/welsh-gender-service.
66 See https://segm.org/Finland_deviates_from_WPATH_prioritizing_psychotherapy_no_surgery_for_minors (2 July 2021).
67 See https://segm.org/Sweden_ends_use_of_Dutch_protocol (8 May 2021).
68 See www.england.nhs.uk/wp-content/uploads/2024/03/clinical-commissioning-policy-prescribing-of-gender-affirming-hormones.pdf.

212 Notes to pp. 138–140

69 See www.england.nhs.uk/wp-content/uploads/2024/08/PRN01451-im plementing-the-cass-review-recommendations.pdf, p. 12.
70 See www.nhsggc.scot/service-update.
71 See www.gendergp.com ('Skip the NHS's 5–10 year wait times. Get gender-altering medications in just 3–5 days.'); www.theguardian.com /society/article/2024/may/03/cross-sex-hormones-available-online-11 -pounds-a-month-young-people-gender-identity.
72 See www.nhs.uk/conditions/consent-to-treatment/children; Family Law Reform Act 1969, section 8(1): 'The consent of a minor who has attained the age of sixteen years to any surgical . . . treatment . . . shall be as effective as it would be if he were of full age [18].'
73 See www.supremecourt.uk/news/permission-to-appeal-april-and-may -2022 (28 April 2022).
74 See Children and Young Persons Act 1933, section 7 (as amended in 2007), for England and Wales; Tobacco and Primary Medical Services (Scotland) Act 2010, section 4; Health and Personal Social Services (Northern Ireland) Order 1978, article 3.
75 See Licensing Act 2003, section 146, for England and Wales; Licensing (Scotland) Act 2005, section 102; Licensing (Northern Ireland) Order 1996, article 60.
76 See Tattooing of Minors Act 1969, section 1, for England, Wales and Scotland; Tattooing of Minors (Northern Ireland) Order 1979, article 3.
77 See Botulinum Toxin and Cosmetic Fillers (Children) Act 2021, section 1, for England. There are no prohibitions as yet in Wales, Scotland and Northern Ireland.
78 See Female Genital Mutilation Act 2003, section 1, for England, Wales and Northern Ireland; Prohibition of Female Genital Mutilation (Scotland) Act 2005, section 1.
79 See https://bills.parliament.uk/bills/3560.
80 See https://publications.parliament.uk/pa/bills/cbill/58-04/0035/2300 35.pdf.
81 See section 4(1)(a).
82 See https://sex-matters.org/wp-content/uploads/2023/10/Banning-modern-conversion-therapy.pdf (October 2023).
83 See www.senat.fr/leg/tas23-138.html.
84 See www.gov.uk/government/news/new-restrictions-on-puberty-blockers; The Medicines (Gonadotrophin-Releasing Hormone Analogues) (Emergency Prohibition) (England, Wales and Scotland) Order 2024, www.legislation.gov.uk/uksi/2024/727/made.
85 See www.judiciary.uk/wp-content/uploads/2024/07/Approved-Judg ment-RTransActual-CIC-and-Anor-v-SSHSC-and-Anor.pdf.
86 See www.gov.uk/government/news/extension-to-temporary-ban-on -puberty-blockers; The Medicines (Gonadotrophin-Releasing Hormone

Notes to pp. 140–145

Analogues) (Emergency Prohibition) (Extension) (no. 2) Order 2024, www.legislation.gov.uk/uksi/2024/1110/introduction/made.
87 See Medicines Act 1968, sections 62, 129(6).
88 See www.cadoganclinic.com/cosmetic-surgery/gender-surgery/ftm-top-surgery.
89 See www.thelondontransgenderclinic.uk/male-to-female-gender-re assignment-surgery-london (view Patient Guide).
90 See www.lgbtmap.org/equality-maps/healthcare_youth_medical_care _bans.
91 See https://protectkidsca.com (Our Causes).
92 See https://protectkidsca.com/wp-content/uploads/2024/01/Protect-Kids-of-California-Act-A2.pdf, section 11.
93 See www.sos.ca.gov/administration/news-releases-and-advisories/ 2023-news-releases-and-advisories/proposed-initiative-enters-circu lation-23-0027.
94 See https://calmatters.org/education/k-12-education/2024/04/trans -youth.
95 See https://protectkidsca.com.
96 See *L. W.* (Tennessee) and *Jane Doe* (Kentucky), www.opn.ca6.uscourts .gov/opinions.pdf/23a0221p-06.pdf (28 September 2023).
97 See *Boe* v. *Marshall* (Alabama), https://adfmedialegalfiles.blob.core.win dows.net/files/11thCircuitDecisionAlabamaGovernor.pdf (21 August 2023).
98 Ibid., pages 23, 40–1.
99 See www.nytimes.com/2024/06/24/us/politics/supreme-court-trans gender-care-tennessee.html.
100 See www.alberta.ca/release.cfm?xID=89690FEFD06CA-AC6A-E4E1 -C9274DADFC0141DC.
101 See Barnes, *Time to Think*, pp. 99–100.
102 See *AB*, [2021] EWHC 741 (Fam), www.bailii.org/ew/cases/EWHC /Fam/2021/741.html (26 March 2021), para. 13.
103 Ibid., para. 20.
104 Ayad et al., *When Kids Say They're Trans*.
105 Ibid., p. 16.
106 Ibid., pp. 8–9.
107 Ibid., pp. 61–2.
108 See https://publications.parliament.uk/pa/bills/cbill/58-04/0035/ 230035.pdf.

8 Why transgender rights are not like LGB rights
1 See https://twitter.com/LittleHardman/status/1587847398356762624 /photo/1 (extracts from her resignation letter quoted in *Private Eye*) (posted 2 November 2022).

214   Notes to pp. 145–149

2   See www.bbc.co.uk/sounds/play/m001fvx6 (16:16–16:30; full interview from 2:56 to 24:30; emphasis added).

3   See www.equality-network.org/wp-content/uploads/2018/02/EfA1.pdf.

4   See *P. v. S. & Cornwall County Council*, Case C-13/94, https://curia.europa.eu/juris/liste.jsf?num=C-13/94 (30 April 1996), para. 24.

5   See R. Wintemute, 'Recognising new kinds of direct sex discrimination: transsexualism, sexual orientation and dress codes' (1997) 60 *Modern Law Review* 334.

6   See www.independent.co.uk/life-style/lisa-a-woman-uncoupled-12497 20.html (8 July 1997).

7   See *Grant* v. *South-West Trains*, Case C-249/96, https://curia.europa.eu/juris/liste.jsf?&num=C-249/96 (17 February 1998), para. 50.

8   See Council Directive 2000/78/EC of 27 November 2000, https://eur-lex.europa.eu/legal-content/EN/TXT/?uri=celex%3A32000L0078.

9   See 'How did the T get in LGBT?', www.salon.com/2007/10/08/lgbt.

10 See www.thetaskforce.org/about/history.

11 See *San Francisco Arts & Athletics, Inc. & Thomas Waddell* v. *United States Olympic Committee*, 483 US 522, www.law.cornell.edu/supreme court/text/483/522 (25 June 1987). I was a spectator at the 1982 Games and began participating in track and field at the 1986 Games (also held in San Francisco). My most recent participation was in swimming and the 5-kilometre road race at the 2023 Games in Hong Kong, the first held in Asia.

12 See www.nyclgbtsites.org/site/national-gay-task-force-headquarters.

13 See https://ilga.org/news/ilga-1978-2007-a-chronology.

14 See www.washingtonblade.com/2017/06/11/history-marching-washing ton.

15 See https://digitalcollections.sdsu.edu/do/c504a3f7-eb87-47aa-89b6-c136f9ae1e7a.

16 See www.glbthistory.org/timeline.

17 See https://arc-international.net/strengthening-capacity/international -dialogues-2.

18 See https://arc-international.net/wp-content/uploads/2017/01/ARC -Dialogue-Policy-Report.pdf.

19 See www.declarationofmontreal.org (26–29 July 2006).

20 See https://yogyakartaprinciples.org/wp-content/uploads/2016/08/prin ciples_en.pdf.

21 See https://ilga.org/news/ilga-history.

22 See https://en.wikipedia.org/wiki/Employment_Non-Discrimination _Act.

Notes to pp. 149–154   215

23 See https://en.wikipedia.org/wiki/Equality_Act_(United_States).
24 See https://quillette.com/2018/12/04/the-new-patriarchy-how-trans-radicalism-hurts-women-children-and-trans-people-themselves.
25 See https://quillette.com/2024/03/11/katie-herzogs-plan-b.
26 Document no longer on Stonewall's website but see www.metroweekly.com/2018/10/alison-moyet-says-she-supports-trans-people-after-inadvertently-signing-anti-transgender-letter.
27 See www.ttalinea.com/news/international-pride-day; www.tmwunlimited.com/project/never-march-alone.
28 See 'As a gay man, I have no pride in Pride month. Radical LGBT bullies have captured it', www.dailymail.co.uk/news/article-12187217/BEN-APPEL-gay-man-no-pride-Pride-month-LGBT-bullies-threatening-fix-us.html (13 June 2023).
29 See 'Police remove lesbians from GAY PRIDE parade in Cardiff . . .', www.dailymail.co.uk/news/article-11153811/Police-remove-LESBIANS-Pride-march-Cardiff-Officer-tells-gender-critical-women-leave.html (28 August 2022).
30 See 'Pride's rainbow flag was a shining beacon of tolerance. But these ugly new versions are divisive, dangerous – and deeply homophobic', www.dailymail.co.uk/news/article-12228733/ANDREW-DOYLE-growing-Prides-rainbow-flag-shining-beacon-tolerance.html (24 June 2023).
31 See www.stonewall.org.uk/list-lgbtq-terms.
32 See www.thepinknews.com/2024/02/08/grindr-issues-today.
33 See 'Grindr users talk about transphobia', www.youtube.com/watch?v=vLrEtSd3ttE.
34 See https://grahamlinehan.substack.com/p/these-are-not-lesbians.
35 See www.theguardian.com/commentisfree/2022/may/29/if-lesbian-prefers-same-sex-dates-thats-not-bigotry-desire-personal-thing.
36 See www.spiked-online.com/2023/08/15/lesbian-speed-dating-is-not-for-men.
37 See www.smh.com.au/national/bid-to-exclude-trans-women-from-lesbian-event-sparks-stand-off-20230913-p5e4cm.html.
38 See www.gaygames.org/gender-inclusion-policy.
39 See www.insidethegames.biz/articles/1124913/fgg-criticises-fina-trans gender-policy.
40 See https://eurogames2024.at/eurogames2024/sports/track-and-field.
41 See https://static1.squarespace.com/static/5311c5ede4b06a95ceb344e3/t/61db68b18503550087ba91fe/1641769138179/Social+Media+Policy+-+Ammended+December+2021.pdf, para. 25.

216 Notes to pp. 154–161

42 See https://teamwear.swimzi.com/brand/out-to-swim.
43 See https://london2023.org.
44 See www.gghk2023.com.
45 See https://bitsofbooksblog.wordpress.com/2017/05/11/iga-confer ence-april-1980-the-fallen-angels-take-pies-fight-to-barcelona (empha- sis added).
46 See Helen Joyce, *Trans: When Ideology Meets Reality* (Oneworld, 2021), pp. 127–9.
47 See https://andrewsullivan.substack.com/p/the-queers-versus-the- homosexuals-cfd.
48 See www.theguardian.com/world/2001/feb/24/jonhenley.
49 See Public Law 103-236, section 102(g), www.congress.gov/103/statute/ STATUTE-108/STATUTE-108-Pg382.pdf.
50 See https://groups.google.com/g/soc.motss/c/ERfDjkhOKTw.
51 See www.nytimes.com/1994/09/18/world/un-suspends-group-in-dis pute-over-pedophilia.html.
52 See https://en.wikipedia.org/wiki/ILGA_consultative_status_contro- versy; https://ilga.org/news/ilga-ecosoc-status-controversy.
53 See R. Wintemute, 'Sexual orientation and gender identity' in C. Harvey (ed.), *Human Rights in the Community* (Hart Publishing, 2005), p. 176.
54 See https://youtu.be/vuqMUO7qno0 ('I Am What I Am' sung by Walter Charles).
55 See Hannah Barnes, *Time to Think: The Inside Story of the Collapse of the Tavistock's Gender Service for Children* (Swift Press, 2023), p. 160: 'He recalls families who remarked, "Thank God my child is trans and not gay or lesbian."'
56 See 'Christine Jorgensen: 60 years of sex change ops', www.bbc.co.uk/ news/magazine-20544095 (30 November 2012) ('In photographs from the time [the late 1940s] Jorgensen looks like a very gay man, which would have been a problem'); Brendan O'Neill, 'The return of gay shame', www.spiked-online.com/2023/02/19/the-return-of-gay-shame ('a memoir by a [male-to-female transgender person] who writes at length about his "internalised shame" over his homosexuality').
57 See 'The gay people pushed to change their gender', www.bbc.co.uk/ news/magazine-29832690 (5 November 2014); 'Sex reassignment sur- gery in Iran, re-birth or human rights violations against transgender people?' www.ncbi.nlm.nih.gov/pmc/articles/PMC9745420 (November 2022) ('eliminating the charge of homosexuality and the risk of execution (punishment for sodomy) is only part of the benefits . . . for transgender people').

58 See the former Stonewall 'Trans Women Are Women' and 'Trans Men Are Men' T-shirts (no longer for sale) at www.thepinknews.com/2018/09/20/stonewall-tshirts-trans-women-are-women-get-over-it.

59 See 'How did the T get in LGBT?', www.salon.com/2007/10/08/lgbt.

60 See www.theatlantic.com/politics/archive/2016/07/l-g-b-t/623604.

61 See https://janeclarejones.com/2018/09/09/gay-rights-and-trans-rights-a-compare-and-contrast.

62 See https://quillette.com/2019/10/26/its-time-for-lgb-and-t-to-go-their-separate-ways.

63 See Stock, *Material Girls: Why Reality Matters for Feminism* (Fleet, 2021), p. 261.

64 See Julie Bindel, https://unherd.com/2023/03/the-lesbian-project-has-begun; www.thelesbianproject.co.uk.

65 See Andrew Doyle, *The New Puritans: How the Religion of Social Justice Captured the Western World* (Constable, 2022), pp. 163–4.

66 See 'The meaningless incoherence of "LGBTQ+"', https://andrewsullivan.substack.com/p/the-meaningless-incoherence-of-lgbtq (2 February 2024). See also 'Gay and Lesbian Independence Day', andrewsullivan.substack.com/p/gay-and-lesbian-independence-day-aef (17 May 2024): 'The only way out of this woke dead-end is to end the conflation of trans and gay identity, and to sever the "LGBTQ" coalition that is sacrificing gay kids.'

67 See https://lgballiance.org.uk.

68 Ryan Anderson, *When Harry Became Sally: Responding to the Transgender Moment* (Encounter Books, 2018).

69 Ibid., p. 9.

70 Ibid., pp. 216–17.

71 See Sherif Girgis, Ryan Anderson & Robert George, *What Is Marriage? Man and Woman: A Defense* (Encounter Books, 2012).

72 Anderson, *When Harry Became Sally*, p. 216.

73 See www.aclu.org/press-releases/appeals-court-declines-to-rule-against-connecticuts-inclusive-policy-for-transgender-athletes.

74 See https://adflegal.org/case/soule-v-connecticut-association-schools.

75 Judith Butler, *Who's Afraid of Gender?* (Allen Lane, 2024).

76 Ibid., p. 16.

77 Ibid., pp. 14–15.

78 Ibid., p. 25.

79 Ibid., p. 15.

80 Ibid., pp. 137, 168.

81 Ibid., p. 149.

218 Notes to pp. 169–177

82 Ibid., p. 96.
83 See Charities Act 2011, section 319(1)–(2) and Schedule 6, column 2.
84 See www.crowdjustice.com/case/save-lgb-alliances-charity-sta (£215,478 pledged for LGB Alliance); www.crowdjustice.com/case/lgba-charity-status (£83,692 pledged for Mermaids).
85 See *Mermaids* v. *Charity Commission & LGB Alliance*, [2023] UKFTT 563 (GRC), www.judiciary.uk/wp-content/uploads/2023/07/Mermaids-v-Charity-Commission-judgment-060723.pdf, paras. 76–7.
86 Ibid., para. 72.

9 From conflicts to co-existence between transgender rights and women's and children's rights

1 See www.pewresearch.org/social-trends/2022/06/28/americans-complex-views-on-gender-identity-and-transgender-issues.
2 See www.bbc.co.uk/news/world-europe-46425774 (3 December 2018).
3 See Helen Joyce, *Trans: When Ideology Meets Reality* (Oneworld, 2021), pp. 139–40.
4 For a list of examples, see https://en.wikipedia.org/wiki/Transracial_ (identity).
5 See www.theguardian.com/world/2023/mar/15/vianne-timmons-canadian-university-president-indigenous-claim (15 March 2023); https://quillette.com/2023/05/15/what-is-elizabeth-hoover-apologizing-for; www.theguardian.com/world/article/2024/jun/28/canadian-woman-sentenced-inuit-benefit-fraud.
6 Compare 'body dysmorphia', www.nhs.uk/mental-health/conditions/body-dysmorphia.
7 See *Ley* (Law) 26.743 of 9 May 2012, www.argentina.gob.ar/normativa/nacional/ley-26743-197860/texto, Article 11 (Right to free personal development), which requires only informed consent.
8 See https://publications.parliament.uk/pa/cm201516/cmselect/cmwomeq/390/390.pdf (14 January 2016), paras. 211–12.
9 See Sasha Ayad, Lisa Marchiano & Stella O'Malley, *When Kids Say They're Trans: A Guide for Thoughtful Parents* (Swift Press, 2023), p. 16.
10 See www.thepinknews.com/2018/09/20/stonewall-tshirts-trans-women-are-women-get-over-it (20 September 2018).
11 See https://whyevolutionistrue.com/2017/09/28/an-excellent-article-on-how-liberals-should-address-transgender-issues.
12 Joyce, *Trans*, p. 4.
13 See, for example, www.psychologytoday.com/gb/blog/addiction-and-recovery/201907/stop-seeking-validation-others.

Notes to pp. 178–184   219

14 See https://slate.com/human-interest/2015/12/gender-critical-trans-women-the-apostates-of-the-trans-rights-movement.html.
15 Ibid.
16 Ibid.
17 Debbie Hayton, *Transsexual Apostate: My Journey Back to Reality* (Forum, 2024).
18 Ibid., p. 90, in ch. 4 on 'Autogynephilia' (pp. 71–92).
19 Ibid., pp. 130–2.
20 See www.telegraph.co.uk/news/2019/12/22/transgender-woman-accused-hate-speech-wearing-t-shirt-stating.
21 See 'Debbie Hayton discusses her book with Andrew Doyle', www.youtube.com/watch?v=9FxQ3txYWSw (4 February 2024).
22 Hayton, *Transsexual Apostate*, p. 214.
23 Ibid., p. 180.
24 R. Wintemute, 'Recognising new kinds of direct sex discrimination: transsexualism, sexual orientation and dress codes' (1997) 60 *Modern Law Review* 334, https://onlinelibrary.wiley.com/doi/10.1111/1468-2230.00084.
25 See www.gov.uk/change-name-deed-poll.
26 See 'Disaggregating gender from sex and sexual orientation: the effeminate man in the law and feminist jurisprudence' (1995) 105 *Yale Law Journal* 1, p. 7, https://chicagounbound.uchicago.edu/journal_articles/1100.
27 See *E. B. v. Bar Lucky 7*, www.canlii.org/fr/qc/qctdp/doc/2024/2024qctdp9/2024qctdp9.html.
28 See *Laskey, Jaggard & Brown v. UK*, https://hudoc.echr.coe.int/eng?i=001-58021 (19 February 1997).
29 See https://lawcom.gov.uk/document/criminal-law-consent-in-the-criminal-law (1995), proposal 5 (p. 198), proposal 31 (p. 206) (emphasis added).
30 See, e.g., www.ncbi.nlm.nih.gov/pmc/articles/PMC8907681 (3 March 2022): 'transgender women taking [hormone therapy] have increased risks of myocardial infarction [heart attack], ischemic stroke and VTE [blood clots in veins]'.
31 See www.dailymail.co.uk/femail/article-3303645/Transgender-British-Army-officer-undergoes-final-stage-gender-reassignment-tweets-post-op-snap-hospital-bed.html (4 November 2015).
32 See https://quillette.com/2022/11/25/gay-not-queer.
33 Karen Ingala Smith, *Defending Women's Spaces* (Polity, 2023), p. 167.
34 Joyce, *Trans*, p. 135.
35 Miquel Missé, *The Myth of the Wrong Body* (Polity, 2022), p. 56.

220 Notes to pp. 184–185

36 Ibid., pp. 82–3, 89, 93. See also pp. 98–9.
37 Ibid., pp. 118–19.
38 Ibid., p. 121.
39 Ibid., p. 123.
40 Ibid., p. 127.
41 See www.washingtonpost.com/opinions/2022/04/11/i-was-too-young-to-decide-about-transgender-surgery-at-nineteen.
42 See https://sober.com/aa-serenity-prayer.